# 41 Shots . . . and Counting

Syracuse Studies on Peace and Conflict Resolution

Louis Kriesberg, *Series Editor*

Other titles from Syracuse Studies on Peace and Conflict Resolution

*The American Nuclear Disarmament Dilemma, 1945–1963*
    David Tal

*The Broken Olive Branch: Nationalism, Ethnic Conflict,*
*and the Quest for Peace in Cyprus, 2 vols.*
    Harry Anastasiou

*Conflict and Cooperation: Christian-Muslim Relations in Contemporary Egypt*
    Peter E. Makari

*Global Liberalism, Local Populism: Peace and Conflict*
*in Israel/Palestine and Northern Ireland*
    Guy Pen-Porat

*Interactive Conflict Resolution*
    Ronald J. Fisher

*Preparing for Peace: Conflict Transformation Across Cultures*
    John Paul Lederach

*Re-Centering Culture and Knowledge in Conflict Resolution Practice*
    Mary Adams Trujillo, S.Y. Bowland, Linda James Myers,
    Phillip M. Richards, and Beth Roy, eds.

*Taming Ethnic Hatred: Ethnic Cooperation and Transnational*
*Networks in Eastern Europe*
    Patrice C. McMahon

*Thinking Peaceful Change: Baltic Security Policies and Security Community Building*
    Frank Möller

# 41 Shots . . . and Counting

## What Amadou Diallo's Story Teaches Us about Policing, Race, and Justice

### BETH ROY

SYRACUSE UNIVERSITY PRESS

All Rights Reserved
First Edition 2009
09  10  11  12  13  14        6  5  4  3  2  1

The paper used in this publication meets the minimum requirements
of American National Standard for Information Sciences—Permanence
of Paper for Printed Library Materials, ANSI Z39.48–1984.∞™

*Credits:*

COVER: *Amadou Diallo, 2002.* Copyright © Malcah Zeldis. Courtesy of the
Andrew Edlin Gallery. Malcah Zeldis is a renowned Jewish-American folk artist.
Her work is widely exhibited, with collections at the Smithsonian American Art
Museum, the American Folk Art Museum, the Jewish Museum, the Milwaukee
Museum of Art, and the International Folk Art Museum. Her work has been
published in numerous books, including *Moments of Jewish Life: The Folk Art
of Malcah Zeldis.*

EPIGRAPH (p. vii): "American Skin (41 Shots)" by Bruce Springsteen.
Copyright © 2001 Bruce Springsteen (ASCAP). Reprinted by permission.
International copyright secured. All rights reserved.

For a listing of books published and distributed by Syracuse University Press,
visit our Web site at SyracuseUniversityPress.syr.edu.

ISBN-13: 978–08156–0940–7 (cloth)
ISBN-10: 0–8156–0940-X (cloth)

**Library of Congress Cataloging-in-Publication Data**
Roy, Beth.
41 shots—and counting : what Amadou Diallo's story teaches us about policing,
race, and justice / Beth Roy. — 1st ed.
p. cm.—(Syracuse studies on peace and conflict resolution)
Includes bibliographical references and index.
ISBN 978-0-8156-0940-7 (hardcover : alk. paper)
1. Police—New York (State)—New York.   2. Racial profiling in law enforcement—
New York (State)—New York.   3. Law enforcement—New York (State)—New York.
4. Diallo, Amadou, 1975–1999.   5. Immigrants—New York (State)—New York.
6. Racism—New York (State)—New York.   7. New York (N.Y.)—Race relations.
I. Title.   II. Title: Forty one shots—and counting.
HV8148.N5R69 2009
364.1'32—dc22
2009007635

*To S.Y., and all the other mothers who, like her,*
*work with love and dedication for social justice*

BETH ROY is a long-time mediator in the San Francisco Bay Area. She writes books on social conflict, including *Some Trouble with Cows: Making Sense of Social Conflict* (an oral history of Hindu-Muslim clashes in South Asia) and *Bitters in the Honey: Tales of Hope and Disappointment Across Divides of Race and Time* (an exploration of race relations today, based on stories by ordinary people involved in the desegregation of Central High School in Little Rock in the 1950s). Her book *Parents' Lives, Children's Needs* is a practical guide to addressing all the many conflicts and stresses in modern family life. She holds a Ph.D. in sociology from the University of California, Berkeley, where she teaches in the Peace and Conflict Studies program. She is a founder of the Practitioners Research and Scholarship Institute (PRASI), and an editor of the PRASI volume *Re-Centering Culture and Knowledge in Conflict Resolution Practice,* also published by Syracuse University Press.

No secret my friend
You can get killed just for living
In your American skin
41 shots
      —Bruce Springsteen
        "American Skin (41 Shots)"

# Contents

# Illustrations

# Preface

## *Heroes and Terrorists*

I BEGAN EXPLORING the many meanings attached to Amadou Diallo's death in winter of 2000. A year before, the young Guinean immigrant had been killed by four officers of the New York Police Department. I was moved to begin my project the day the news was announced that the police officers responsible had been acquitted of murder charges.

Writing histories of current events is a chancy enterprise. History, by definition, is an ongoing narrative, and sometimes the speed at which it goes on is disorienting. Much of what I was investigating was how ordinary Americans perceived and interpreted the actions of the four officers who fired the forty-one shots that killed Diallo. To some people, those officers were simply human guys doing a thankless job. Maybe they made mistakes, maybe they were set up to make mistakes by the politics of their city and times. To others, however, especially to many people of color who daily encounter demeaning and frightening confrontations with members of the New York police force, the "men in blue" were dangerous predators. "As an African American living in this neighborhood," said one lifelong resident of the Bronx, "I feel like the law, law-enforcement officers are the greatest threat to my life."

But on September 11, 2001, the meanings attached to the NYPD changed decisively. It became virtually impossible to regard those same men and women as anything but heroes. Early that morning an airliner crashed into the first of two towers of the World Trade Center. Thousands of people worked in the building, and the NYPD responded quickly to rescue as many as possible. So prompt was their response that they were present when a second plane hit the second tower, and they were still on the scene a couple of hours later when first one, then the other, tower collapsed. Twenty-three members of the police force died, along with an even larger number of firefighters and other rescue personnel.

There is no question that the group of individuals employed by the city of New York to police the streets acted heroically, and paid an unfathomable price. The families of those killed mourned deeply, and they were joined by colleagues of their lost ones, and by people all over the world who did not know them but regarded their human drama with empathy and sorrow. The New York Police Department was valorized again and again as memorials followed one another with harrowing frequency. Newspapers were filled with advertisements expressing sympathy and gratitude.

Not only did New York cops become the very definition of "hero," but the act of which they stood accused when they shot Diallo, racial profiling, was also transformed. From a concern involving African American and Hispanic peoples, racial profiling became a tool for finding Middle Eastern and South Asian terrorists. The image of a profiler changed from a man clothed in blue to a man wrapped in red, white, and blue. Yet it did not take long for Diallo's drama to reoccur, as more and more young men of color (and an occasional woman) were shot in New York and elsewhere around the country. Among the most noted by media were Patrick Dorismund, Sean Bell, and Timothy Stansbury in New York; Kathryn Johnston, an elderly black woman in Atlanta; and Juan Herrera in Los Angeles.

Before September 11, debates about policing and race too often took the form of accusing or excusing officers of the law. Are the NYPD good cops or rogues? Are the members of the Street Crime Unit (to which the Diallo officers belonged) terrorists or heroes? Do police serve or oppress people—or do they protect some people by terrorizing others? Such polarizations are as thankless as they are endless.

As time has passed since Diallo's death, as other shootings have taken place and more acts of terrorism, more and more urgency has grown around an awareness that dualistic, either-or thinking about these issues distracts from more useful inquiry. Police departments are both autonomous organizations and also creations of the governments they serve,

An unsung young man from the West African country of Guinea, Amadou Diallo left behind few photographs when he was shot and killed by New York City police officers on February 4, 1999. Diallo had been returning to his home in the Bronx after working late at night in Manhattan as a street vendor when he was challenged by four white officers from the Street Crimes Unit. His shooting is now widely viewed as a symbol of brutal police policy that unjustly targeted an innocent young man of color. *AP/ Wide World Photos.*

and, more broadly, of the societies within which they operate. In this latter regard, policing and terrorism strike parallel themes. What they do is a function of how power works, of the contradictory attitudes we have toward very fundamental things, such as violence and masculinity and music, race and religion and community life, and more. If we do not address the nature of our world on those many levels, we can only hope to accomplish temporary reforms of enduring problems, knowing that there will be new instances of tragedy, new waves of controversy, again and again in the future.

Just before this book went to press, history overtook text one more time: Barack Obama was elected president. Meanings of power, of politics, of race and more shifted dramatically. To have a black man in the White House marks significant social progress on so many different levels. Some Americans (mostly white) believe it means that there is no racism in America any more. Others (mostly people of color) fear it means the end to confronting racism. Once again, a shared moment in history is experienced very differently. In unison, however, many people all over the world celebrate the ascendance of this talented leader to a position of power with all the more élan because he symbolizes the possibility of overcoming racial oppression. Despite racist attempts during the election campaign to associate Obama with terrorism, in a multitude of eyes, he is instead a hero.

To ask, then, whether the particular four young officers who shot and killed Amadou Diallo were heroes or terrorists is a meaningful question only if the very starkness of the characterizations serves to open a portal into a very different universe of discussion. It is in that spirit that I offer the conversations, the cries of anger and pain, the defenses and thoughtful reflections of the many people who contributed to this book.

# Part One

# Foreground

# Introduction

## *The Tragedy of Amadou Diallo*

> Louima and Diallo were probably the two most high profile cases in
> the New York City Police Department's history. And they both came
> the same year, and I got involved in both of them. There was no sense
> of race in my thinking in [either] case.
>                           —John Patten, a white attorney

> The slaughter of Diallo was a classical case of racism. . . . As an Afri-
> can American living in this neighborhood, I feel like the law, law-
> enforcement officers are the greatest threat to my life.
>                           —David Grant, a black resident of the Bronx

FORTY-ONE SHOTS ended Amadou Diallo's life and began his legacy.
No longer the living man, Diallo, he became a case, *Diallo,* a symbol, a
cause, a chapter in a troubled history of police-community relations.

"Case," "symbol": cold words, dry and abstract, jarringly incongru-
ous with the deep emotion evoked by Diallo's story. Amadou Diallo, a
young immigrant from West Africa, was killed inside the foyer of his
own apartment building by four white officers of the New York Police
Department's Street Crime Unit. Diallo, a hard-working twenty-two year
old making his way into the good life in the land of promise, was the
very model of the innocent. In a bygone era, his sort were mythologized.
Immigrants on the road from rags to riches exemplified everything the
new world stood for: the land of opportunity, peopled by sturdy folk
unafraid of the perils of a new start. But in the world in which he died,
Diallo represented another myth. To many Americans, he was the feared

dark-skinned interloper, one of the mass of ex-colonial subjects importing new levels of racial division, new intensities of racial animosity.

The police officers, too, were symbols. To some, they were clean-
cut young men, like Diallo also upwardly mobile, guardians of a just
and productive social order, standing between obedient citizens and the
criminals who prey on them. To others, the four officers represented
a very different reality, armed perpetrators of a discriminatory society,
dangerous men to be feared and avoided. After massive street protests,
the four police officers were indicted for murder. In a trial moved to
Albany to escape the charged and emotional atmosphere of New York
City, all four were acquitted. Feeling ran deep and wide in New York and
across the country.

▼  ▼  ▼

To write about the case of Amadou Diallo is to wrestle with at least two
hard American problems: race and policing. Both have been subjected
to reams of expository paper, hours of vituperative discourse. Issues so
emotional, so urgent, compel controversy; it is hard to turn away. But it is
also hard to look beyond immediate questions of wrongs and reform, to
move through the problems that explode when a young man of color is
killed by police officers, to come to a point beyond anguish where we can
confront the very fundamental matters of national concern that surround
the storm and lie behind it.

I do not believe we can understand what happens on dark nights in
the hearts of our cities without speaking out loud the imbedded values
and assumptions out of which lethal confrontations arise. Crime, violence, and the security measures that accompany them are expressive acts.
They arise from tensions between the principles we wish to believe our
country embodies and the realities of life for too many of its citizens,
those inhabiting both sides of the law. They challenge us to face truths
about who we are as a society, what compromises with dissatisfaction we
have accepted, what powers to act and to count we have ceded to deper-
sonalized processes we barely understand.

This book is an examination of the issues surrounding one act of killing on one street in America. There have been many other such killings,
before and after Amadou Diallo died. I write about Diallo, not because his

story is unique, but because it exemplifies so many of the themes underlying matters of race and criminal justice in our society. It was an event of enormous drama, evoking strong emotion for people of every racial identity. Yet people's responses also varied, and in doing so gave expression to a racial divide that is dangerously endemic to American society.

I write as a white woman, intent on contributing to social change. Diallo's story begs for attention out of concerns for justice in the widest possible sense of that term: not only criminal justice but also economic, environmental, health care, and every other kind of justice. In different aspects of my life I am, or have been, a journalist, a sociologist, a mediator, a therapist, a teacher—and the mother of a young man of color. Each of those perspectives motivates and informs my writing; none dominates.

In truth, this book is only tangentially about Amadou Diallo's killing. I draw on that particular story to focus attention on the broader problems manifested as police killings of innocent black men. If we blame either the officers involved or the victims, we collude in an obfuscation of urgent and prevalent wrongs in our society. Blame may be emotionally satisfying, but it is not analytically useful; above all, it does not contribute to change. To look beyond the individuals is to turn our minds to core contradictions in American society. In particular, it allows us to grapple with institutional racism, that complex and obscure reality of injustice lying in a tangle of interactive social dynamics that lead so regularly to tragedy.

Above all, this book is a plea for belief in an alternative future, for the vision to engage, concretely, practically, in unity and with effectiveness, in a project to correct course toward that idealistic and discredited objective: a just society.

▼ ▼ ▼

We in America talk often about talking about race. We convene commissions and hold dialogues. We gather in community forums and listen to addresses by experts. We watch Oprah Winfrey and through the medium of an interview or a book selection, we searchingly declare our opinions and air our feelings. But somehow we come away from all that effort feeling something on a range from vaguely frustrated to passionately enraged. The trouble is that race divides not only people of different races but also the ways in which those people talk about race.

Americans who are white may talk about violence in schools, crime, affirmative action, neighborhood decay. They may puzzle over statistics that demonstrate discomfiting social features—how many black babies die relative to how many white babies; how many teenagers of color bear children out of wedlock; how many people of such and such heritage live how many percentiles below the poverty line. White Americans talk about race in terms of crack epidemics, teen motherhood, welfare abuse, and illegal immigrants, and they rue these phenomena without ever mentioning the word "race."

For people of color, the conversation about race is parallel but very, very different. It is about neglected schools, police brutality, job discrimination, gentrification. For them, there is nothing mysterious about statistics measuring inequities. A large percentage of their life experience is filtered through racial realities, and among themselves they speak frequently and emotionally about what they perceive as endemic, searing injustices. At a gathering in Washington, D.C., a few days after an armed intruder had been stopped by guards on the White House grounds, an African American woman commented dryly, "When I heard he'd been shot in the leg, the one thing I knew for sure was that he wasn't black."

Black Americans tell me the subject of race almost always figures into their conversations with friends. In contrast, white people often disclaim their ability to say anything of interest about race. "I don't have a problem," they tend to say, in one way or another. "Color doesn't count for me." But in so dismissing the subject they speak eloquently about the central racial divide in the United States. Way beyond perception, many steps even beyond interpretation, the difference between white people and people of color lies in the most basic realities of everyday life. It is these fundamental differences that stand in the way of conversations across racial lines; people talk from within frameworks so discordant as to allow little mutual understanding of one another's simple sentences. To discuss race is therefore to engage in conflict, and it is a conflict about which people of all races feel bleak, resentful, and above all powerless.

People of color are angry about having to fight for the validity of their viewpoint. White people are defensive about accusations that they are oblivious or, worse yet, racist in their incomprehension. Again and again, white people approach me after I talk to diverse groups of people about questions of race, and they complain that they, too, feel discounted. "I know a lot about diversity," many say. "I grew up in a diverse neighborhood. Race didn't signify; we were all poor, all struggling, all the same. I'm not racist.

"Besides, I have my problems, too. Life is not so easy for me, either."

Most often when I speak in public about these subjects, white audience members who have chosen to attend do so from a good-hearted concern and interest. But that in itself can be offensive to others. Generosity connotes power; we can only give that which we possess. It is very hard for whites to find ways to join shared projects of racial healing with humility and no guilt, with eagerness and no condescension. People of color, attuned to the subtleties of the subject, are quick to pick up demeaning nuances and greet expressions of sympathy with less than gratitude. White people are, again, hurt and puzzled: What is the problem? they ask plaintively. And behind that question lurks more dangerous ones: Why do we try? and, Why should we care?

Indeed, whether apparent or not, there *are* vital ways that race matters to white Americans, reasons more self-interested than an admirable but fragile yearning toward justice for all. How people of color are afflicted by racial inequities is clear and measurable. How white people are injured is not obvious. Many perceive themselves to be victims of a reversal of fortunes; said a white woman I interviewed a few years ago, "They're getting more and more, you see it on TV, they're getting, they're getting, they're being given, given, given, and that makes us bitter." Imbedded in this woman's sense of injury was a deeply ingrained assumption: that she herself was deprived of something others were getting. She was mistaken about that; in fact, there are much data showing that white people still enjoy greater access to college admission, jobs, financial credit, and many other resources. But the woman's statement did also contain a certain truth: that she herself *was* deprived of many things about which we, as a nation, rarely talk.

Many of us who are white live the American dream, residing in comfortable suburban homes, holding down well-paid jobs, carefully planning our investments to accommodate both college for the kids and retirement for the parents. But then something dramatic happens that exposes a harsher reality. Suddenly it is clear something is amiss, something we cannot in normal times quite catch hold of, a vague dis-ease with what is labeled a good life, something left out. Sometimes that event is economic in nature: a wave of layoffs in what everyone thought to be a secure sector; a collapse of the housing market. Sometimes, though, the one who shatters the surface of comfortable living is a teenager. Commonly, the challenge to the family story that everything is just fine is a well-kept secret: a child hooked on bad drugs, a daughter pregnant, a son dropping out of school. But sometimes the transaction is far more cataclysmic. Bad news spews from the barrel of a gun on a high school campus. The myth of American opportunity suggests that school should be a happy route to a promised future of abundance. With what particular horror we therefore regard the deafening demise of that future for a white youngster with a gun and the classmates he kills.

For black and Hispanic Americans the moment when tongues can no longer be stilled comes in mirror-image form. It, too, stems from violence involving young men, but often the crisis here is about the shooting of a youth on a city street by a white policeman. That is an event likely to put questions of race on the front pages of newspapers: another death at the hands of the law, another trial acquitting the shooters, another occasion for rage and denial and painfully unmediated disagreements across racial lines about whether justice has been done.

Because different communities are so disparate in talking about race, when something happens so traumatic that it demands conversation, the dialogue that ensues is badly frustrating, adding to a sense of futility about trying to solve anything. People of color see these incidents, frequent and tragic, as yet one more proof of the inevitability of racism, while white people tend to believe police killings are not about race but about rogue cops, or about criminals who may not deserve to die but who nonetheless contributed to their ill fortune by their suspicious actions.

One such moment when the nation, citizens of all races and origins, collectively gasped and turned toward each other in genuine dismay and need, only to fall once again into familiar disagreement, happened when the media reported that Amadou Diallo had fallen under a hail of police bullets in New York City.

▼  ▼  ▼

David Grant, an African American man nearing retirement age, lived his adult life in the Bronx, very near where Diallo died. I stopped by his home late one evening with my friend, his sister-in-law, who had a brief piece of business to do there. But when he heard that I was researching the Diallo case, David grabbed me. "Interview me!" he insisted. It was late at night; I was tired; he was both humorous and ardent, his intensity finally overcoming my reluctance.

We settled in the rec room of his tidy Bronx home, washing machine humming cozily in the corner. Hard-working, sensible in every way, a homeowner and parent of successful grown children, David burst forth: "The slaughter of Diallo was a classical case of racism!" The feeling propelling that statement contrasted with the formality of the language and the sweetness of the setting. I asked him what it meant to him, personally, and he said, "Well, as an African American living in this neighborhood, I feel like the law, law-enforcement officers are the greatest threat to my life."

Out tumbled stories of police harassment, many, many stories, echoing complaints I heard from every man of color I interviewed, every mother of sons raised in African American or Latino neighborhoods. Those experiences fueled the pain with which people talked about the Diallo killing. Michael Wright, a member of a men's fellowship in a Harlem church, exclaimed in a breaking voice:

> It's been going on for a long time. So we can't hide these things any more. Because for a man to get shot that many times, when you go hunting, you only shoot a deer once, you only shoot it one time, and the deer is going down. When you shoot a lion, you can shoot it with one shot and it's going down. But here a man gets shot forty-one times. . . .

Lorraine Cortés Vázquez was the president of the Hispanic Federation in New York and a member of the Citizen Complaint Review Board that exercises oversight of the police department. Despite her involvement with city affairs, or perhaps because of it, she had felt no optimism about the outcome of the trial:

There was no way that the Diallo family could have gotten justice, and I believe in this justice system, I believe in this judicial system. But there's no way that a panel of twelve jurors in Albany could ever feel the same outrage, terror that people either in the Bronx, Brooklyn, or Queens could have felt.

Chris Cooper is currently a sociologist and a lawyer, but for many years he was a police officer. Nonetheless, his view of law enforcement was primarily formed by his experiences growing up in a black neighborhood in New York:

I was socialized to realize, it's not *believe* but to *realize,* that many white police officers are not my friend. There are white parents, I've been told, that tell their white children that the police officer's their friend, go to him in a time of need. My mother was a good mother in warning me to be careful, in warning me to watch out, in warning me not to necessarily see them—I don't know how to say this—on the one hand I wasn't to see them as the enemy but to be cautious. But on the other hand I was to see them as the enemy.

It was into this troubled atmosphere of racially based tension with police officers that Diallo fell when he immigrated to the United States.

▼  ▼  ▼

Twenty-two years old when he died in the Bronx, Diallo had lived in the United States barely three years. His people came from a place called Hollande Bouru, a village in the West African country of Guinea. Today, he is buried there, under a fig tree.

The child of educated and respected parents, Amadou had followed a well-trodden path of emigration to the United States in pursuit of the good life. He landed in a part of the Bronx called the Soundview section because that was where his uncle and cousins lived. Like many an immigrant before him, Amadou discovered that life in America had its hardships. He supported himself by selling cheap goods on the sidewalk in front of a shop in Manhattan, often working twelve-hour days and arriving home in the Bronx at midnight.

Nonetheless, when it came time for his visa to expire in April 1999, he tried by whatever means possible to extend his stay. He filed a false application for asylum with the Immigration and Naturalization Service, claiming he was from Mauritania and his parents and other kin had been killed in the course of racially based persecution.

Ironically, tragically, when Amadou Diallo died shortly afterward, many people believed his killing was an example of racially based persecution by agents of a white-dominated state.

Edward McMellon was one of four white police officers who killed Amadou Diallo on February 4, 1999. Late in 1998, three months before Diallo died, McMellon joined a unit of the New York Police Department called the Street Crime Unit. Formed in 1971 at the height of a law enforcement buildup nationwide, this group, considered elite within police culture, was charged with the task of spearheading the New York authorities' battle against crime, specifically with getting guns off the streets. Accused by police critics of concentrating their aggressive efforts in communities-of-color, the SCU was, at the time of Diallo's killing, 90 percent white. Their motto was "We own the night," and they had t-shirts printed with a quote from Ernest Hemingway: "Certainly there is no hunting like the hunting of man and those who have hunted armed men long enough and like it, never really care for anything else thereafter."

According to their own testimony later, Ed McMellon and his partner, Sean Carroll, spotted Amadou Diallo after midnight the night of February 4, 1999, as they slowly drove the streets in an unmarked car. Together with Kenneth Boss and Richard Murphy, McMellon and Carroll were in plain-clothes and patrolling the Soundview section in search of a reported rapist and, more routinely, any other suspicious activity. The officers claimed that they spotted Diallo on the stoop of an apartment building that later turned out to be where he lived. At the time, of course, they had no way of knowing that. What they perceived was a man looking up and down the street. It was the middle of a winter night. As they approached, he turned back into the vestibule of the building. The officers later testified that they held their weapons at their sides and displayed their shields, or badges. They therefore interpreted Diallo's movement as suspiciously evasive.

There ensued a scene of lethal confusion. The police officers say they called to Diallo to come out and speak to them. By now, they had climbed the few steps to the vestibule doorway, and from that position, they later testified, they observed Diallo, who had moved to the rear of the small enclosure, reach into his back pocket and, as he turned sharply toward them, extract a small black object.

Carroll claimed he yelled, "Gun! He's got a gun!" McMellon and Carroll simultaneously fired and retreated. As he backed down the steps, Carroll a few paces behind him, McMellon stumbled and fell backward, flinging his arms over his head. Seeing him fall, officers Boss and Murphy joined the fray. The vestibule was by now a scene from hell. Light flashes reflected off the high-gloss walls, bullets ricocheted, Diallo fell or crouched against the rear wall.

It took only a few seconds—by some estimates no more than eight— for the four men to fire forty-one shots. Semiautomatic firearms require the user to pull the trigger for each bullet but allow that operation to happen very quickly. Nineteen bullets struck Diallo. After the lead storm was over, Carroll and Boss approached the bloodied, collapsed figure and discovered—to their intense dismay, they later reported—that he had no gun. He'd pulled a wallet from his pocket instead. McMellon, who by now had righted himself, "threw his hat to the ground and kicked it in frustration," claimed *The New American*.[1] Carroll, according to the same report, frantically administered CPR, weeping all the while.

News of the killing spread quickly, and protesters took to the streets. African American community leaders were joined in acts of civil disobedience by celebrities and a mass of citizens of all races, demanding that justice be done. The four officers were indicted and tried on six counts each. A year later, on February 25, 2000, they were acquitted of all charges. Protest gatherings, largely peaceful, continued outside Diallo's building for many days.

▼  ▼  ▼

The story of Diallo's death echoes dozens of other tragedies in as many American cities. Two notorious (although nonlethal) cases especially seized national consciousness in the nineties: the videotaped beating of Rodney King in Los Angeles and the torture in police custody of Abner Louima in New York.

Rodney King's notoriety began with a routine police stop in 1992 in the course of which a sizeable group of police officers repeatedly struck him while he lay grounded on the pavement. By chance, an onlooker videotaped the scene—a black man felled and battered by four white officers—and provided the tape to news media. Demands that the officers be prosecuted led to a trial that ended with their acquittal. Riots broke out and lasted for four days; by the end, fifty-five deaths and a billion dollars worth of damage had resulted.

In 1997, Abner Louima, a Haitian immigrant, was arrested by New York officers in the course of a fracas outside a nightclub. In transit to the station, Louima was beaten by several different cops, including a white man named Justin Volpe. Once at the police station, Volpe and another officer took Louima into a bathroom, and Volpe sodomized him with a plunger handle. So extensive were Louima's injuries that medical attendants reported the torture to authorities. Some five thousand New Yorkers took to the streets, demonstrating against police brutality. Two months before Diallo's killer was acquitted, Louima's torturer received a thirty-year sentence. Some other officers involved in the incident received far lighter sentences or were acquitted.

Meanwhile, many less well-known incidents were also happening throughout the country. The white officer who in 1999 shot and killed Gary Albert Hopkins Jr., a nineteen-year-old college student, in Prince George County outside Washington, D.C., was acquitted of murder charges a little over a year later. In 1997, Jonny Gammage, a black man, was shot to death by white police officers near Pittsburgh. Gammage seemed suspicious to them because he was driving an expensive car in a wealthy neighborhood. It turned out the car belonged to his cousin, a famous athlete, whom he was visiting in the neighborhood. In 1995 Aaron Williams, a black man, died after being pepper-sprayed by white arresting police officers in San Francisco. On Martin Luther King Day 1989, two black men died in Miami when a Hispanic police officer fired on them. Two white Louisville police officers shot and killed Desmond Rudolph, an eighteen-year-old black man, on May 13, 1999. The officers were later awarded medals of valor by the police chief, who in turn was fired by the mayor. While the media were still filled with stories about the Diallo trial acquittals, Malcolm Ferguson, a twenty-three-year-old black man, was killed by police officers, this time a racially diverse group, a few blocks from where the earlier killing occurred. Within the month, another incident hit the headlines; Patrick Dorismund, a young man from a prominent Haitian family, was shot and killed in the course of a New York undercover operation. Having just left a nightclub, Dorismund was standing, unarmed, on a Manhattan street, waiting with a friend for a taxi when he was approached by an officer pretending to seek a drug buy. When Dorismund resisted the transaction and a scuffle ensued, the officer's partner intervened with lethal force.

Like most informed Americans, I noticed these news stories, and I shuddered. When the police officers who beat Rodney King were acquitted, I was shocked. While the Louima case ran its course, I was horrified. The morning after the officers who shot Diallo were acquitted, I sat at my breakfast table, deeply troubled, reflecting morosely on the inadequacy of the courts to address all the many issues raised by a case like this one. I read interviews with members of the jury explaining how they had come to decide on acquittal.

"Everybody [on the jury] had reservations about whether the police acted properly," said Helen Harder, a seventy-two-year-old white juror, "but given the parameters, we decided they did.

"Two or three days earlier," she continued, "I would never have expected the verdict. . . . It surprised me. We were charged by the judge and told that the prosecution has to prove its case or there is no case. Well, that made it different."[2]

I did not believe Harder's opinion revealed deficiencies in the men and women who sat in the jury box. Nor did it seem to be to be a problem adequately explained by a flawed prosecution. Courts are designed to decide very specific questions in highly formalized ways. The issues raised by *Diallo*, I believe, are far too complex, cut far too close to the bone of American society, to be so narrowly defined and determined. Yet the kind of dialogue that might get at the truly relevant questions too readily falls into a space that is racially polarized, and here, also, the issues are flattened under the weight of emotion and of politics, until genuine inquiry becomes impossible.

Part of the power of a writer lies in the slowness of the process of writing. As a sociologist who deals in people's life stories, I realized I had access to a forum that bypasses some of the problems frequently besetting attempts to talk about race. I have the enormous good luck to be able to talk with many different kinds of people, to engage them in thoughtful exploration of their particular angle on the issues raised by Amadou Diallo's death and the deaths of so many other young men of color. This book is the result of my decision to take on what I knew to be a huge project, a disturbing engagement with painful things, questions of violence and racial profiling and crime and state coercion, the many urgent topics lying tangled at the heart of *Diallo*, the case. My project took me to the Bronx, but it also led me to courtrooms in Maryland, attorneys' offices in San Francisco, churches in Harlem, suburbs of Boston, and more.

Each interview approaches the subject from a particular vantage point. Framed together, they sketch a landscape of police and community relations. It is a picture distorted by frustration, lacking perspective; in one and the same breath people offer tired solutions and sigh their pessimism about the prospects for even those changes. Behind the practical discussions in the foreground, the perceptive viewer can glimpse a dimly realized background, a hazily sketched distance consisting of undelineated themes, such as the reasons why men continue to be socialized for violence, why women fall effectively silent in the face of human tragedy. Beyond these strata are even more shadowed realities. Like a wash covering the canvas and underlying it all, there is a reality of coercion so rarely glimpsed by white adults beneath the prettier surface tones of our multihued American democracy. To bring into view these and other compelling dynamics that contribute to lethal confrontations like Diallo's, I use the many conversations contained in this book as a brush, painting a picture of a single event in full spectrum colors, in order to explore more vivid ground for change.

# Defining the Question

## *In the Courtroom*

It's really funny, because I thought [Judge Teresi] was a balanced judge until that moment. [*Laughs*] It's very interesting the way he handled that case.

—Lorraine Cortés Vázquez

The basic issue you have to determine, the only issue for your determination, is whether the People have proved any defendant guilty beyond a reasonable doubt. No other issue, no other institution, no other persons are on trial here.

—Judge Joseph Teresi

THUS JUDGE JOSEPH TERESI began his charge to the jury. In fairness to the four men who sat at the defendants' tables, the judge instructed the seven men and five women of the jury (four of the latter black) to rule out of their reckoning anything but the explicit questions framed by the law as he presented it.

But for the nonlegal public, for the average person seeing sound-bites from the trial on the evening news or reading digested stories in the morning paper, the questions under consideration were wider and deeper than the judge would have it; they were precisely about other issues—race, violence, immigration, youth, the inner city—and other institutions, especially the police. Just as Diallo was transformed from a flesh-and-blood man into a national symbol at the moment the forty-one shots were fired, so too were the four police officers now both more and less than human individuals.

At the trial of the four New York City police officers accused of murder in the shooting death of Amadou Diallo, Judge Joseph Teresi instructed the jury on how they were to consider evidence in their deliberations. He was accused later of defining the questions so narrowly as to exclude the relevant context of race. *AP/Wide World Photos.*

In many respects, the court of law in which Sean Carroll, Ed McMellon, Kenny Boss, and Rich Murphy were tried was the one place least equipped to deal with the profound pain and tragic contradictions manifested in the shooting. Ill-suited as it was to grapple with the issues, the court proceedings nonetheless, in very subtle ways, acted out those very issues. The particular means by which it abstracted justice from discrimination and separated judgment of lethal acts from the troubled social institutions mandating those acts expressed vividly the very dynamics that were, by law, excluded from the jury room—and most urgently relevant.

Indeed, the trial of the four officers who shot Amadou Diallo offers a rare opportunity to focus light on normally obscure details of how injustice works in our society. Judge, jury, and prosecutors have all been criticized for what many onlookers saw as a miscarriage of justice. But seen through the lens of Judge Teresi's charge to the jury, a more profound set of realities emerges. It is as if a parallel universe lies behind the concrete behaviors of the courtroom, a universe rarely glimpsed, poorly described, unbelievable therefore to most of the populace. But magnified by the trial, and especially delineated with stark boldness by the jury charge, the dimensions of that universe take on line and shape and contour.

## On the Way to Court

If the courtroom was an inadequate venue in which to address what most everyone agreed was, at best, a deadly error, how did the trial nonetheless become the spot where hopes for resolution were placed? When a lethal-force incident happens and a community is traumatically impacted, people cast about for a way to deal with the tragedy. Funerals become public events, places where people can grieve, in both senses of that word: "to mourn" and "to protest." Reactions range from raw anger to a thoughtful search for remedies.

All these outpourings reflect a need for emotional expression as well as political action, for passionate speech and the empathic connections that happen in consequence among human beings. Janice Tudy-Jackson, a lawyer-mediator in New York, described a time when she led such a process in an atypically effective way:

> A few years back a police shooting took place involving a youth, a teenager, in a community where the relationship between the police and that community has been lethal. I mean, people getting hurt on both sides. And when this death occurred, I was asked to come in to work with the community leaders, who needed to respond to this and were having difficulty. I mean, this was so highly charged! . . .
>
> It's rare that community leaders have a forum to express how *they* feel. They're always speaking for their constituents.
>
> But in this forum I really gave them an opportunity to express how they personally felt, because until they had an opportunity to articulate it, put it out there, have it heard, experience some empathy, they couldn't get past that to some of the real serious stuff that they needed to deal with. So that was quite remarkable.

It is precisely such personalized discourse that is ruled out of admissibility in a court of law. The drama of a trial lies in its very understatement as narratives of pain and mayhem unfold in formal and stylized language.

But most public forums for responding to use-of-force tragedies are little better suited to a human-level engagement of the issues. Police departments launch their own investigations. Effective or compromised as these processes may be in a given locality, rarely are they equipped to deal either with the reactions of the community or with meaningful reform. Police internal affairs investigations are secretive; the public is not invited into the process, ostensibly because they are judging personnel matters, but also because they are so often highly political. The aggrieved community is likely to be largely alienated from law enforcement as an organization, so people greet even a degree of disclosure of internal affairs processes with skepticism.

Meanwhile, other civil organizations may conduct their own investigations. Human rights groups issue excellent reports on the problem of police force nationally. Community advocacy organizations such as New York's Hispanic Federation poll their constituents on the subject. The NAACP holds hearings in cities across the country. But all these processes are slow and ill-publicized. Though they reflect various views of the problem, they tend to end up proposing solutions that are already being talked about, perhaps in some places implemented, but that are somehow drained of the drama and impact that might get at the essential problems.

So it was that when Amadou Diallo died, the place concerned New Yorkers turned to deal with the aftermath was the criminal court. Demands quickly arose that the four officers be prosecuted. It was not obvious that the police officers *would* be indicted. That decision was made in a climate of political contention. For weeks, demonstrations took place. The Rev. Al Sharpton, an outspoken critic of racism in policing, took the leadership, daily calling for indictments of the four officers involved. Civil disobedience took place; one celebrity after another was handcuffed to unknown citizens and trotted off to jail.

At length, an indictment was handed down and the officers were tried on six counts: intentional murder, depraved indifference murder, first- and second-degree manslaughter, criminally negligent homicide, and reckless endangerment.

Rev. Al Sharpton quickly became a spokesperson for continuing protests against police brutality and the mayor's policies. Widespread press attention recorded the arrests of celebrities, as massive numbers of demonstrators performed civil disobedience, demanding that the officers be indicted. Here, Rev. Sharpton rallies the crowd on March 31, 1999, outside the Bronx courthouse where the officers are being indicted. Amadou's parents accompany Sharpton, father Saikou Diallo on the right and mother Kadiadou Diallo on the left. *AP/Wide World Photos.*

## In the Courtroom

"The Crucial Defense Element: The Judge's Instructions" headlined a story in the *New York Times* on the case the day after the police officers were acquitted.[1] The judge's parameters were constructed within a narrow framework of legal considerations. In his instructions to the jury, he charged them to stay focused on whether the officers were justified in using deadly force in the course of apprehending someone they judged to be a suspect:

> You must accept the law as I give it to you and apply it when examining the evidence in order to arrive at a just and proper verdict.

You, and you alone, are the sole and exclusive judges of the facts. You are to confine yourselves in your deliberations to the evidence only in this case. You are to determine this case upon the evidence alone, which consists of the testimony of the various witnesses who have testified here, both on direct and cross-examination, and the exhibits received in evidence.[2]

The jury accepted the judge's legal frame for considering the verdict, agreeing that good citizenship dictated "put[ting] aside their personal feelings."

"In a court of law, it doesn't matter what you feel," an anonymous juror is quoted in the *New York Times* as saying. "I can live with the decision I made on a legal standpoint. . . . You have to go with the evidence presented before you."[3]

"Judges can always define the issues," Stuart Hanlon, a defense attorney in San Francisco, told me. "Even before you get to jury instruction, to define the evidence is in the judge's hands. When you have a judge with a bias, it's really devastating."

"It's really funny," said Lorraine Cortés Vázquez, president of the Hispanic Federation in New York, "because I thought [Judge Teresi] was a balanced judge until that moment. [*Laughs*] It's very interesting the way he handled that case."

Throughout the trial of the Diallo officers Judge Teresi's rulings had sometimes favored the prosecution, sometimes the defense. Did he depart from that practice when he charged the jury, as Lorraine perceived? He was precise, indeed pedantic, in his rendering of the law. But did that legal precision constitute balance, or did his dry exposition bias the jury toward the defense?

A judge's charge to the jury always comes at the very end of a trial. It is the moment when the law is officially articulated and defined. With formality, the judge instructs the jury on the legal framework within which to consider their decision and coaches them in how to think about the standards they are charged with applying. Among other things, it is intended to teach them how to apply legal criteria to their deliberations while explicitly excluding the broader social questions that might otherwise occupy their minds. The judge's instruction is a ritualized moment of transition, preparing the jurors to turn from the passivity of listening to the action of decision making. For the Diallo jurors, that moment came after four weeks of testimony from medical experts, criminologists, neighbors, and, most emotional of all, the defendants themselves.

Judge Teresi metamorphosed from kindly elder to stern legal authority as he lectured the jury for three hours on how they were to consider their verdict:

> Since it would be improper for the Court to invade your province as to the facts, so it would be improper for you to invade the Court's province in determining what the law in this case is. You must accept the law from this Court without question, without reservation, and with strict obedience.[4]

Judges draw on a variety of printed resources to construct their jury charges. From some official, some commercial volumes, they pick excerpts to adapt to the particular case before them. How they construct their charge is subject to negotiation with the attorneys involved. "I took it straight out of the book," said Teresi at one point in response to a complaint by a defense lawyer about how he had phrased something. Piece by meticulous piece, he recited the first count of the indictment, murder in the second degree, or murder by intent, and the lesser charge they might consider if they acquitted on the major one, manslaughter in the first degree. What followed was a straightforward discussion of what those charges mean and how to think about assessing them. To prove murder in the second degree, the prosecution must show, beyond a reasonable doubt, that the defendants shot Diallo, that they intended to cause his death, and that they did cause his death. After parsing each of those aspects in legal idiom, which is to say, stating the obvious from many different angles and in the process making problematic that which initially seemed beyond question, Judge Teresi turned to the heart of the matter—justification:

> If you have determined that the People have established all of the elements of the crime of Murder in the Second Degree in the first count, then you must turn to consider the defense known in law as justification

but which is commonly referred to as self-defense. In doing so here you must consider each justification defense I am about to charge you separately as to each defendant. Even if a defendant is otherwise guilty, if you should determine that he acted in self-defense; that is, with justification, then he must nevertheless be found not guilty. . . .

There are three separate self-defense charges that I will give you:

1. Defensive use of deadly physical force.

2. Defensive use of deadly physical force against robbery.

3. Use of deadly physical force by a police officer to effect an arrest. . . .

In respect to the first; that is, defensive use of deadly physical force, I charge you self-defense is a defense recognized in law. When a defendant raises such a defense and offers some evidence that he was acting in self-defense, it becomes the burden of the People to convince you beyond a reasonable doubt that he was not acting in self-defense. . . .

According to the law, a person may lawfully use deadly physical force against another person when (1) he reasonably believes that such use of deadly physical force is necessary to defend himself or a third person from (2) what he reasonably believes to be the imminent use of deadly force against himself or a third person by such other person.[5]

First, notice that the task of the prosecutor is difficult in the extreme, in this very common application of the law. The prosecutor must prove that the officers did *not* believe themselves to be in mortal danger and that they *did* believe there was an alternative to firing the shots that killed Diallo. Police officers are very rarely convicted in use-of-force cases, both because of this logical structure and because judges and juries tend to believe, through a thick bundle of cultural assumptions, the word of men-in-blue. In the Diallo-killing case, evidence on which to contest a self-defense interpretation was especially sparse. There was evidence given about the lighting in the foyer: how clearly could the police officers see what Diallo was doing? Testimony about the trajectory of the shots might argue that Diallo was already down and helpless when the fatal bullets were shot. But that testimony was inferential and the inferences suggested by the prosecution were disputed by other experts. Did the officers shoot more often than needed, as evidenced by where Diallo's body was hit by bullets, when he fell, what posture he took in either self-defense or death spasms? Was a pause in the firing reportedly heard by a neighbor timed such that it suggested a choice by the officers to resume a barrage once stopped? Overall, the question rested on whether it was believable that the police officers might mistake a wallet for a gun, and whether that mistake was a reasonable one for them to have made, under the circumstances.

Beyond the material evidence, though, the jury had to judge whether Diallo's demeanor and gestures created a context in which the officers might reasonably form a perception that he was armed.

Each defendant contends that he reasonably believed two things: (1) that the use of deadly physical force was necessary to defend himself or a third person, and (2) that Ahmed Diallo was committing or attempting to commit the crime of robbery.

In deciding what the defendant reasonably believed, the law imposes upon you two tests.

The first test is a subjective test—what defendant, not some other person, reasonably believed. To apply that test, you should figuratively put yourself in the shoes of defendant and consider how the situation which confronted him appeared to him. You should consider, for example, what Ahmed Diallo did before and during the encounter, any indicia of a robbery, such as any actions of Mr. Diallo that defendant may have observed, those observations, the circumstances of each defendant's observations and the conditions existing at the time of those observations, any prior experiences defendant may have had with robbery.

All such factors must be taken into consideration by you in determining whether defendant, in fact, believed that deadly physical force was necessary to defend from a robbery.

The second test is an objective test—was the defendant's belief reasonable under all the circumstances? The second test requires you to consider and determine whether the average reasonable person confronted with the situation in which defendant found himself would also reasonably believe that deadly physical force was necessary to defend himself or a third person from what he believed to be the commission or attempted commission of a robbery.

On the basis of both such tests, you must determine what a defendant reasonably believed.

> I instruct you, on the basis of the law I have given you, if you find
> the defendant reasonably believed that his use of deadly physical force
> was necessary in order to defend himself or a third person against what
> he reasonably believed to be the commission or attempted commission of
> the crime of robbery, then you must find that he acted in self-defense.[6]

The notion of an "average reasonable person" occurs frequently in legal canon. It is a natural corollary to the idea of a jury of peers. Criminality is most often defined as that which departs from the norms of a society as those norms are embodied in law. The definition of those norms and the perception of deviation lie in a process that involves decisions about what is normal. But what is normal to one group of people may well be exceptional to another. The more diverse a society is—and most known societies are diverse, even when racially homogenous, by virtue of differences in occupation, wealth, gender, age, and so on—the more likely it is that norms will vary. The concept of law suggests a unitary society, one in which definitions and values coincide for all segments of the community. In fact, all societies embody a good deal more contention. If a body of law is to be established, one group's values must come to dominate. "Average" becomes defined not necessarily numerically but by virtue of who is in a position to prevail in a legislative process that is actually a contest of norms.

Judging how an "average reasonable person" would perceive the transaction that led four police officers to fire forty-one times at an unarmed man is, therefore, a very dicey task involving several levels of inquiry. First, was it reasonable for the police officers to believe they were in mortal danger? Second, would it be reasonable for you, the average citizen as represented on the jury, under those same conditions to believe yourself in danger? Neither subjective nor objective viewpoint allows the jury to consider a third question: Would your perception of danger be, was the officers' perception of danger in fact, distorted by a set of beliefs and assumptions about dark-skinned men on the street late at night?

That any human being's perceptions of another may be influenced by social conditioning and unexamined assumptions is well demonstrated both anecdotally and by social science. There is ample evidence that very subtle stereotypes significantly influence perceptions of jeopardy. An African American fighter pilot explained why so few student pilots of color succeeded in qualifying for the job by describing nuances of the training regimen. The pilot in training sits in an aircraft in flight, controls in hand, in front of an instructor, who has in *his* hand an instrument that allows him to override the trainee's control instantaneously if he judges them to be in danger. It needs only a hairs-breadth extra nervousness on the part of the instructor, inevitably in this speaker's experience a white man (a consequence, no doubt, of the fact that so few flyers of color qualify), to take over from a black student, whose body language may seem just a little less familiar to him, with whom he may have a sliver less rapport, to whose success he is a half-measure less devoted. Added together, a host of subtle dynamics can lead to the disqualification of pilot-trainees of color in significantly greater numbers than their white counterparts.

One of those dynamics in a street policing context is the readiness of police officers to presume guilt in a suspect of color. The four men who shot Diallo claimed they were hunting a rapist in the neighborhood. Stereotypes of the black rapist are very common. Moreover, the disproportionate frequency with which men of color are stopped and searched for weapons both derives from and reinforces the belief that these men are more likely to be armed than an average white man, an assumption that has been seriously challenged by scholars (I will say more on this topic later on). That the Albany jury concluded the officers were reasonable to believe themselves in danger thus begged the question of whether a confrontation with a white man in similar circumstances would, first, have happened and, second, terminated in the same lethal conclusion.

Assuming the officers felt vulnerable, were they dutiful in their response to that feeling? Police departments write elaborate use-of-force policies precisely because the nuances of such actions are many and the stakes so high. The Diallo jury had to judge whether the four police officers had indeed followed those procedures. Middle-of-the-night confrontations in streets deemed dangerous by the men and women who patrol them are dramas of great rapidity and tension. Policy requires that certain warnings be given and that force if required be graduated from disarming to lethal. But in reality those acts collapse one into the other with great rapidity in a real moment of fearful decision. Facing a man with a gun is the very definition of vulnerability. Yet law enforcement people debate the premise that the presence of a weapon automatically justifies the use of lethal force by officers.

When Chris Cooper worked for the Washington, D.C., police force, he was assigned to a tough area called Anacostia. While there, Chris was earning his doctorate in sociology specializing in policing issues, and, later, a law degree as well. An African American who grew up in New York City, where we met to talk about the Diallo case, Chris disputed the idea that the officers' belief Diallo had a gun sufficiently explained the shooting:

> If you're working in a big city in a community with a great deal of crime, there are many situations when deadly force policy, when the law allows you to shoot. But if you have respect for human life, if you are a person with integrity, if you are a professional, and most important if you have respect for human life, you look for ways to avoid shooting another human being. Good cops, good cops who have respect for human life and good solid police officers have courage. . . . Yes, physical might is very important in police work. You must have courage, that doesn't mean you shouldn't feel [fear]. In some cases, courage means that you have to use that physical might that you should have as a police officer to try to avoid shooting another human being.

The jury were not charged with judging the efficacy of the NYPD use-of-force policies, but simply determining if the four officers followed them. But all around that question buzz a dense swarm of other considerations: what implicit instructions are communicated to officers along with the explicit ones? How do such policies reflect politics of the department and the city? What assumptions are imbedded in determinations of the appropriateness of potentially lethal force in the enforcement of law? In my interviews, I heard a number of critiques of the Diallo officers' implementation of use-of-force policy as well as compelling discussions of the influence of mayoral politics on the incident. I will return to these discussions later, when I turn to the subject of policing and larger power dynamics. For the moment, I want to note that here again, the very nature of the law ruled out of discussion these very relevant matters.

**Testimony and Other Stories**

The process of adjudication in American courts is based on rationalist premises that truth can be constructed from evidence. Much of the evidence in the trial of the four officers was detailed and physical. But ultimately all that testimony was used to prove or disprove the stories told by four living, breathing men. The drama of their stories outweighed the physical evidence, especially since the testimony of the fifth person involved could not be introduced in evidence, for he was dead. Diallo's story was most vividly told by the coroner, constructed out of elements like the trajectory of bullets (a wound to his toe, said the coroner, could only have been inflicted after he was down; therefore, the shooting must have continued after Diallo had fallen), the lighting in the foyer, the tracing of bullet holes in the walls. That construction of events from Diallo's perspective was later disputed by another forensic expert testifying for the defense in support of the officers' contention that Diallo had not been supine while they shot but had assumed a combat-like crouch in the vestibule corner. The story from Diallo's perspective was secondhand, arguable, theoretical.

The officers' testimony, however, was easily readable by the jury in very human terms. The men were emotional, sincere, ardent, in short, believable. From "four officers who shot Diallo" they became four young distraught guys as they described *their* ordeal the night of February 4.

"When I looked into the vestibule there was not a doubt in my mind that he had a gun. I had a sick feeling in the pit of my stomach that I was going to be shot." Richard Murphy was twenty-seven years old, a fresh-faced fellow who had joined the NYPD five years before the shooting. For much of that time he had participated in a community-policing program in Queens, the borough where he lived with his wife and a young son. Only months before he had celebrated his promotion to the Street Crimes Unit. Of the four officers involved, he was the only one who had never faced a complaint before the Civilian Complaint Review Board. That critical night, he fired four shots into the vestibule.

When most of us tell a story, we organize it according to a particular time sequence. We start at the beginning and end at the end. Occasionally, we interject asides or get ahead of ourselves. Often, there is a point to

John Patten, defense attorney for New York City police officer Sean Carroll, holds up a starter's pistol during closing arguments Tuesday, Feb. 22, 2000, in the Albany County Courthouse in Albany, New York, in the trial of Carroll and his three co-defendants. Patten dramatized the moment when the officers mistook Diallo's wallet for a gun, arguing that the error was understandable. *AP/Wide World Photos.*

a story, an argument being pursued or a subtext lurking in the margins. But the ordinary storyteller works within a chronological framework because the convention is so strongly imbedded in our understanding of narrative. Stories told in testimony, however, are orchestrated by attorneys explicitly seeking to advance a particular understanding of events, and so they are consciously organized strategically.

Nowhere was the constructed nature of courtroom narrative more evident than during the closing statement of Sean Carroll's attorney,

John Patten. To the public, both white and black, the power of Diallo's case lies in his innocence. With the exception of stories that circulated for awhile about his false application for amnesty, nothing was ever reported to suggest that he was in any way criminal. Nonetheless, as John Patten built the argument for his client's acquittal, with or without intention he also suggested a picture of the victim as somehow furtive, his gestures unlikely, warranting suspicion. The attorney acted out the critical moment when Diallo pulled a wallet from his pocket and Sean Carroll mistook it for a gun. The dry representation that is a court reporter's record could not do justice to what John considered the decisive moment in his summation. As we talked in his office, he articulated the critical question:

> It was wrong for the officers to fire the gun. When I say wrong, I mean, it was really not justified in a layman's kind of thinking. All right? But was it reasonable for him to believe—my client who yelled out, "He's got a gun!"—was it reasonable for him to believe that the black wallet in [Diallo's] hand was suggestive of a gun and that they misread the scene?

Like a play within the drama he was describing, John jumped up from his desk chair and as he spoke repeated for me the courtroom performance he believed most swayed the jury. He took several steps toward the window. "And when he went to the door and then turned"—crouching and holding his wallet close to his side, he turned suddenly, startlingly toward me—"that turn, you know, was the devastating thing for him and those officers, because that turn with the black object in the hand they mistook to be a gun and they fired. Okay? And as I said in the case, bam bam bam bam, it's over. Okay?"

To be sure, it was John Patten's job to defend his client eloquently and effectively. But in arguing that Sean Carroll's confusion of a wallet for a gun was believable and unavoidable, by mimicking a gesture he had not himself seen, John introduced into the courtroom a portrayal of Diallo that contrasted dramatically with the wholesomeness and emotional frailty expressed by the officers. Their misunderstanding became understandable; something "suggestive" became a reality in the minds and trigger fingers of the police officers. Diallo's "devastation," in John Patten's account, was not the victim's alone; it was shared by the officers.

It was in this emotional and discursive context that the jury listened attentively to Judge Teresi's direction . . . not once but many times. For each of the three charges, and for each of the three lesser-included charges, the Judge delineated the terms for decision, and each time he listed the three grounds for considering whether the defendants' actions were justified. Again and again and again, the formal, somber words lapped against the consciousness of the jurors. Emotional as the young officers' testimony had been, dramatic as John Patten's enactment of Diallo's behavior at the critical moment, so also the repetitive recitation of carefully parsed ground on which the jury might decide innocence had, I imagine, rhetorical impact, rendering what might have been a debatable rendition of law indisputable.

When his instruction was done, the jury was escorted from the courtroom and the attorneys were invited to quarrel with the charge. And quarrel they did. The defense attorneys raised several points they wished Teresi to revise. Asked to repeat some charge he had given in one context so the jury might be clear it applied to another charge, the judge protested, "If I gave it once, I gave it ten times."

"I know that you said it a million times," said one of the attorneys, then arguing for a further clarification. In the end, the judge denied all their requests, save two.

The jury returned and Judge Teresi said, "I have a couple of clarifications." He had told the jury that each defendant was liable for the actions of the others, that is, if they found one officer to be guilty of a particular charge then the others were as well. Now he emphasized that the point applied "to each and every count and each and every lesser-included offense." To the onlooker, the clarification seemed minor.

But the next one was clearly more important. To his charge on the three different possible justification defenses they could consider, he now added another:

> I further charge you that a person who reasonably, though mistakenly, believes that he is about to be attacked and/or who reasonably, though

mistakenly, believes that another is about to commit certain defined felonies, in this case I did charge you on robbery, and a police officer who reasonably, though mistakenly, believes that a person has committed or is about to commit a crime, and you recall I charged you on robbery and criminal possession of a weapon, may use physical force against another and in some circumstances deadly physical force.[7]

Here was a crucial point indeed, for it warned the jurors that knowledge *after* Diallo's death of his innocence had no relevance to the four officers' belief at the time that they were justified in shooting him. Short of interviewing the jurors, and they have declined that activity, we cannot know how they digested all they heard, but it is tempting to believe that the late addition of this particular instruction caused it to stand out of the repetitive mass and gave it particular importance. To the citizen in the street a substantial part of the powerful significance of the Diallo shooting lay in the young man's innocence. This instruction placed his death in the same category as the many other killings at the hands of police officers of young men of color on the streets, where innocence may have been subject to more doubt. It fell against a background of common assumptions about young black men's probably guilt.

And so the jury retired to consider John's question and no other: Was it reasonable to believe that the black object in the hand of a black youth was a gun threatening the officers with imminent death?

But the questions disallowed in the courtroom reverberated outside its doors:

• Were the officers justified in being where they were, on that Bronx street searching for miscreants?

• Was their suspicion of Diallo reasonable and justified?

• In using lethal force were they within the boundaries not only of police procedure but of human morality?

Even as the jury parsed the evidence in obedience to the judge's instructions and decided the officers were innocent, people outside the courthouse, struggling with a different set of questions, were coming up with very different answers.

# Defining the Question

## *In the Street*

"I see Mr. Diallo, he's crouched, I see a gun," Boss said. "I think, 'Oh my god, I'm going to die.' I start firing."
—Officer Kenneth Boss's testimony

"I held his hand and said, 'Don't die, keep breathing, don't die.'"
—Officer Sean Carroll's testimony

"THE BOOK ON THIS CASE IS NOW CLOSED," declared Teresi after the verdict, while dismissing the jurors. But in fact the book is wide open. Issues left hanging by the trial compel attention, both by the law enforcement sector and by the citizenry. They are particularly intense, of course, for communities of color where a disproportionate number of police shootings occur. Every police shooting, justified or not, brings into alignment legal, ethical, social, and political matters. Together, they form an ideological matrix on which our social structure rests.

Social structure is an elusively abstract concept. It is nothing one can touch, smell, or feel. Yet such a thing exists, with vast impact on the life of every individual. Social structure describes a network of relationships and possibilities: what one must do, for instance, to obtain those resources needed for survival: housing, food, companionship, dignity. Does the typical citizen till her own plot of land, or does he work in a corporate office? Is he unemployed, is she underpaid? Can they retire comfortably on stock holdings? The term "social structure" employs a metaphor that is misleading; true, there is an edifice built of institutions within which life goes on, but it is not static like a brick and steel building. Its architecture more resembles that of an organism, something forever changing through time. Some years ago, from one week to the next the economy of my city underwent traumatic transformation as the "dot-com" industry suffered a gigantic reversal. Housing for several years before had been largely unaffordable for those working in less highly paid jobs; vacancy rates fell almost to zero. But after the dot-com bust, for-rent signs suddenly appeared in windows. Prices tottered at towering levels briefly, then began to fall. Peace Corps recruiters found their job abruptly easier as young people corrected course, choosing the pathways they had bypassed only a few years before when they had emerged into the Internet economy as technologically desirable new graduates.

In 2008, the multiple interdependency of economic, political, and personal structures was proved indisputably. Within a few weeks, people found themselves reconsidering the most private of decisions—wedding dates, plans to conceive a baby or to retire, Thanksgiving dinner invitations, and so on—as the impact of collapsing financial markets raced like wildfire through society. Barack Obama might have been elected even in the absence of economic disaster, but his ascent was ensured, and along with it another significant blow against racism, as more white Americans overcame remaining hesitations about race in order to vote their economic interests.

It is these arrangements of social relations, distribution of power and resources, of rights and protections, that are the crucial elements of which the Diallo tragedy is made. These building blocks are precisely the same ones that constitute the problem of race in America, or, more accurately, that transform racial differences into racism. To delve more deeply into the matter of the needless use of deadly force on men of color, it is essential to see the social structural background against which vividly illustrative acts of violence occur. Those acts tell us there is a problem, but they do not in and of themselves testify to its essential nature. The very glare of the foreground, the horror of tragedy, can obscure the background, the daily facts of social life that give rise to such bloody confrontations to begin with. Judge Teresi ordered the lawyers and the jury to focus on the image in the center without distraction from the background. My task is to move back and forth, from foreground to background, to manipulate light and shadow in a way that illuminates less visible depths of social reality.

John Patten, the attorney who represented Sean Carroll at trial, gave me a stunning example of how awareness of the one can emerge suddenly out of the other. John came to the Diallo case via Louima. In the latter, attention focused on a police officer who seriously injured a black man by sodomizing him in a police headquarters bathroom with the handle of a plunger. Other officers stood by and then later covered up the event; they too were in the docket. John successfully defended a more secondary figure, the sergeant on duty at the time of the attack. As he began to tell me about the Diallo trial, John declared:

There was no sense of race in my thinking in the case.

*Beth: In Diallo or in Louima?*

John: Both. In Louima you had a police officer who went berserk, went out of control. It was really sad in one way, because for a few minutes or a few seconds' craziness he will now do thirty years in jail. And also Louima's scarred for life, the trauma of having whatever happened to him happen. Okay?

But Nickerson, the judge, said to the jury panel that was seated in the room, and it was amazing how once he said it, it seemed to end, he said, "This is not a case about race. This is a case about what happened in the bathroom. This is an assault case. It's not a case about race." That was Louima.

In Albany, Judge Teresi treated the case as a straight homicide murder case. And while there were certain questions in the *voir dire*— you know, you didn't want absolute haters on either side to take the jury box—the case was also treated as not about race. So although Diallo was an African, a black man, to my mind it was just, was the shooting justified? That's how I approached it.

The only time it became an issue in my mind about race was when you turned about, you looked back and the courtroom was divided in half. . . .

It was not a good scene. I mean, one half of the courtroom was black American, supporters of the Diallo family. Except for a few politicians who were Hispanic out of the Bronx. And the attorneys were white. They were sitting with Mr. and Mrs. Diallo throughout. But that side of the courtroom was black, and this side of the courtroom were supporters of the police department and the families, and they were white.

The immutable fact ruled out of discussion in the courtroom emerged clearly in the disposition of the audience; background emerged. The social reality arrayed there was for many the central fact of the lethal confrontation under scrutiny. In the dark of night five living men came face to face in the Bronx; four white, one black. In the details of their meeting, in the subtleties of their gestures, in the nuances of their perceptions of each other and their interpretations of each other's intentions lay tragedy, but also clues to the underlying dynamics that set up the confrontation to be what it was.

If social structure is abstract and hard to see, gestures, as John Patten wisely understood, tell concrete and eloquent stories. I turn now to a different reconstruction of the drama of Diallo's killing, one no more true or false than that built during the trial. Stories, as I have said, are malleable things. My story of the Diallo shooting is pieced together from various sources: published text; testimony at trial by the four officers; testimony by the coroner and the few witnesses that constitute a circumstantial version of Amadou Diallo's account; commentary by people associated with the police officers and Diallo, friends, acquaintances, relatives; defense attorneys; reconstructions by other cops; the reported gestures and actions themselves.

In chapter 1 I put together a version of "what happened" that drew primarily on published accounts, burnished by interviews with the defense attorneys and excerpts from the trial transcript. It is a straightforward narrative over chronological time: he did this, they did that, this consequence resulted. It draws primarily from statements by the police officers, and we have little way to know if their account is accurate. As I have commented, the four officers who are the primary narrators were speaking for their lives. Because of the forty-eight-hour rule, a period after a shooting when police officers cannot be compelled to submit to investigation, they had ample time to coordinate their accounts, smoothing out any internal inconsistencies that might suggest fabrication. Under the expert tutelage of attorneys and advocates, they were coached to construct a version that best promised their own exoneration. Even if there were no legal motivations at work, their memories might be expected to contain distortions and revisions. That is normal; we all do it. I once witnessed a car accident and two years later was asked to testify to what I had seen. I was certain about who had been at fault. The event was crystal clear in my memory. But when I was deposed, it turned out I had every detail wrong—who was where in the intersection, where I myself was, which vehicle had hit which, where they had come to rest. What I had right, however, was who was at fault, who had run the stop light.

Emotion and time alter recollection as much as purposefulness. In the end I take the stories of the four officers with a grain of salt, even giving them the benefit of the doubt that they meant to tell the truth, because I think they could not help but shape their accounts in all these ways. Need we then dismiss their testimony as useless? I do not think so. I believe the very distortions tell a story, but it is a more complex one, more difficult to obtain. I start with close attention to the details of the interaction between the four officers and Diallo and draw back in the chapters that follow to look at the background, the context in which they occurred and the larger story they tell.

The five individuals who occupied the moment of interest came there from very different places. But they also brought into the confrontation some stark similarities. Who were they, and how did they come to occupy that particular moment in time?

## Diallo

We know relatively little about Amadou Diallo. Our sources are the media and a book written by his mother, Kadiatou Diallo.[1] Two pictures of him appeared in the press: the first profiles him as an earnest and hardworking young immigrant, the other focuses on the one illegal act he seems to have committed. By his mother's account, he was an unusual young man, quiet and simple, relatively privileged in his homeland, but willing to make sacrifices to follow his star.

Diallo came from a small West African country struggling with post-colonial troubles. Rich in mineral reserves (over 30 percent of the world's bauxite, for instance), Guinea remains beset by poverty. Eighty percent of the workforce is agricultural; 40 percent of the population lives in poverty, as defined by the *World Factbook*, a publication of the CIA. Guinea pays interest on a foreign debt of about $3.4 billion. Wars and dynamics of globalization inhibit progress. In every respect Guinea is a poster child of stalemated development.[2]

In this land of hardship, the Diallo family was distinctly upper class. Building on his grandfather's fortunes gained from cattle trading, Amadou's father Saikou, in his twenties at the time, set up shop in Liberia, a country more kindly inclined toward capitalist dealing than socialist-leaning Guinea. By the time Kadi, his second wife and Amadou's mother, joined Saikou on the Atlantic coast of Liberia, the Diallo empire included three gas stations, five markets and drugstores, and a lumber mill with a work force of fifty.

Despite the father's affluence, life was filled with contradictions for the family. Kadi was sixteen when she gave birth to Amadou, three years after her marriage. She went on to birth five more children. Amadou was, by her description, a silent boy, unusually beautiful and sensitive. He stuttered; he called out for her in his nightmare-inhabited sleep. She held him close to her heart, her eldest. As Amadou grew to manhood, the family moved many times, pursuing safer environments, more promising business climates. Eventually, the parents divorced and Kadi established her own business as a gem dealer. The family lived for a time in Thailand. Saiko settled in Singapore. In 1993, Kadi visited New York on business. By that time Amadou, who with his siblings attended an elite French school in Bangkok, had developed a taste for "all things American. He began wearing Tommy Hilfiger shirts and Nike sneakers, and rooting for the Chicago Bulls." Bruce Springsteen's "Born in the U.S.A." was a favorite.[3] At twenty, Amadou left for the United States.

A different portrait of Diallo was briefly suggested by the press after his death. It told the story of a false application he filed for amnesty, a strategy for getting an extension on his U.S. visa. The document itself was available on the Web. In what was presumably Diallo's handwriting, it told a detailed story of a young man fleeing racially motivated violence in Mauritania, a country near Guinea where ethnic conflict was rampant. He claimed his parents had been killed, that he was being sheltered by his uncle in the United States, and that his life would be in jeopardy if he were to return home.

There is something of a mystery about why the story failed to remain in the public eye. One wonders what the story of the story might be. Was it a mistake on the part of some journalist who confused one Amadou Diallo with another? (Diallo is a common surname.) Or was the implication that Diallo was not the innocent he at first appeared to be so offensive to those who advocated for him after his death that the media was persuaded to take another tact?

We cannot know the answers (or at least I do not know them). But at worst the story suggests something with a probable ring of truth to it, that Amadou Diallo badly wanted to stay in the United States. Such an assumption leads us in the direction of an identity for Diallo as an individual: the determined immigrant seeking a better life. That figure populates the history of the United States. Diallo's aspirations were little different, in this version, from those of my own grandparents and from millions of other residents and citizens of this country.

Newly liberated ex-colonial countries hold limited prospects for young educated men and women. It takes several generations before a modern middle class takes hold, before that group's youths see genuine life choices before them. Television, music, and movies come well before material access to modernity. The impetus to migrate to more industrialized lands is strong. Diallo may also have been motivated by idealism, by a story of America that put equal opportunity in the context of democracy and freedom. Here again, I am speculating. But the mixture of personal goals and idealistic ones commonly populate the imaginations of young immigrants to this country.

The reality he found was not quite that rosy picture. He lived a marginal life in the Bronx, traveling daily to Manhattan to sell wares on the sidewalks. New York City's streets are thick with bargains offered at makeshift sites by young men. It is a way of making a living with minimal dependence on a labor market that is unfriendly to young dark-skinned immigrants. Diallo's working visa had expired (or, in some accounts, was soon to expire), his legal status was insecure. Working as a vendor offers a certain amount of control over the conditions of employment, but it is also quite literally unrooted in the structure of American society. Vendors move as necessary from one place to another. They are licensed by a special city agency, but otherwise in the course of the day have only fleeting interactions with customers, perhaps more consistent interaction with each other.

Residing in the Bronx, commuting to the City, returning home late at night to a shabby apartment shared with two other young men from his homeland, his immigration status in question, Diallo's life was a hard one, even aside from the problems of racism described by African American men like David. According to his mother, that winter night Amadou came home tired and hungry. He visited briefly with roommates, fell asleep on the sofa, woke and realized there was little to eat in the apartment. He set out to find some food, but he hesitated at the front door to the building. It was dark and cold; was he more tired than hungry? As he hesitated, four white men approached him.

**The Officers**

Like Diallo, the officers themselves remain only superficially known to me and to the public. We have slight profiles of each, but none of the four has consented to be interviewed, nor spoken beyond his story of events as told in the witness chair, about his own version of himself. There may be various reasons for that relative silence, the most obvious being their legal entanglements. What I know of the four men is hearsay. I have encountered people who are acquainted with them. I have spoken to two of their defense attorneys. I have read a great deal of what has been published about them. I give you here a hypothetical portrait, built of many elements, but clearly fictional, a product of my imagination.

Facts beyond dispute are these: all four officers are white and, at the time of the shooting, in their twenties or thirties. None had belonged to the NYPD for longer than seven years, nor to the Street Crime Unit for longer than two years. Sean Carroll, the oldest of the quartet at thirty-six, joined the SCU two years before, although he had entered

Listening intently to testimony, Officer Kenneth Boss holds in his right hand what his
lawyer called "Greek worry beads." *AP/Wide
World Photos.*

the Police Academy about the same time as the others. Both Ed McMellon and Richard Murphy started working with the SCU within four
months of the shooting, Kenneth Boss sometime the year before. Boss
was involved in another fatal shooting; he was cleared of wrongdoing
and prevailed in a civil suit brought against him by the victim's family.
Of the four, Murphy alone had never had a complaint brought against
him and had never before discharged his gun; the other three had
among them a total of eleven complaints, none upheld by the Civilian
Complaint Review Board. McMellon and Murphy also earned several
commendations for excellence.

A prototypic profile of New York police officers drawn from my
interviews is of a young man (or increasingly but still less often a young
woman) drawn to the job as a career step. Many people see themselves

as passing through the department, and then get hooked on the work out of a combination of idealism, excitement, and socialization. I elaborate these themes in chapter 5, when I introduce interview material from police officers. In their quest for decent and meaningful working lives, young people in law enforcement may well share motivations with young immigrants like Amadou Diallo, a common vision of social status and economic security.

I have been told that all four cops were New York boys. "There is a level of sophistication in these kids who become policemen," John Patten claimed, "that goes with coming from the New York City area here. Not to malign any other state, but they're not like guys from West Texas, or somewhere down South." Patten went on to say that he had no doubt they had their share of prejudices, but he argued that they were unlikely to be overtly racist.

But racism comes in many forms, organizational and systemic as well as individual. As a teenager, one of the four ran in a multicultural social group focused on rap music. The African American rappers in the circle were the heroes, the preferred boyfriends of girls of all races. It came as a huge surprise to his friends when one of their circle joined the force, and an even greater surprise when he began to speak in critical generalities about people of color. New York cops may be no more intrinsically prone to stereotypes than other people, but that statement leaves a good deal of room to imagine they exist. Moreover, there are dynamics of policing that lend themselves to stereotyping, especially a practice officers call "reading the street."

**The Encounter**

I visited the vestibule where Diallo died. Wheeler Avenue is a narrow thoroughfare lined on both sides by parked cars in front of small brick apartment buildings. The houses are diminutive, three or four stories tall, very narrow, each one the mirror of its neighbors. The street was said to be quite dark, the vestibule darker still. Three or four steps lead up from sidewalk to entrance. Inside the front door is a room, barely wider than my arms' reach, only a dozen steps deep. It seemed to me to be more closet than lobby. A row of mailboxes is imbedded in the left-hand wall.

When I saw the room, it was still wildly pocked with bullet holes that clustered most thickly around the far right corner.

As Diallo wavered at the doorway, the four officers saw him. Did they speak to each other? We do not know. But in the cops' perception, as they later reported it, Diallo was standing at the top of the stairs, peering up and down the street, and "looking suspicious." Unpacking the nature of their suspicion is key to the story. How much was it influenced by Diallo's race? Would they have seen a white man in the same way? Were they, in other words, performing the hotly debated practice of racial profiling?

That was a controversial topic in New York and the nation at the time and one I return to in detail. Other police officers told me that profiling is really a form of "reading the street." Gerry,[4] a New York officer we meet in greater detail later, described the process:

> I can walk down the street and I'm alert to, not just anyone else walking up and down the street, I'm alert to someone else who's also scanning the street. That guy in the doorway, why is he scanning the street? Is he waiting for his date, looking for her in the crowd, or is he looking for someone to rob? What's [happening] on this block now? I start looking around the block. Does this store have ATM machines and he's looking to see who uses the ATM machines?
>
> When we go out at night, when they turn us out at night, they give us robbery pattern descriptions. All right. We have two male blacks who are doing robberies in this sector, and we think they're following people from the subway station. So logically, who else am I going to be concentrating at, especially when I'm in that sector, especially around the subway station? It's profiling on one level, and it's good police work on another level. Profiling has a dirty, has a bad name to it right now. But it's been a useful police tool.

Gerry worked a beat in New York, cruising the same streets day after day for years; he knew his streets intimately, claimed he could recognize somebody or some action out of the ordinary right away. McMellon and his colleagues were unfamiliar with Wheeler Ave. McMellon himself had worked in Brooklyn, not the Bronx, before joining the SCU a scant three months before the encounter with Diallo. "Suspicious," therefore, was very much something read against an unfamiliar frame. Guineans cluster in the Soundview neighborhood of the Bronx, but they are rare in Brooklyn. Were there some particular mannerisms McMellon might have recognized had he been familiar with the community? Might he have known that Diallo stuttered and therefore, in a tense moment, might not be able to find the words to respond to the officer's challenge?

McMellon and Carroll approached the man they viewed as suspicious, McMellon in the lead, mounting the steps to within five feet of where Diallo stood and, according to their testimony, clearly announced their identities. Murphy remained standing on the sidewalk, and Boss crouched behind a parked car.

What did the police officers see? A small-framed black man with a mustache, he matched the description they say they had of a rapist. But then so did thousands of other young black mustached men in New York that night. Diallo's gestures are the pivotal element in the four officers' story. He retreated into the vestibule and turned his back, say the officers, while pulling a dark object from his pocket—the gesture John Patten acted out for the jury.

What did Diallo see? Four white men dressed in civilian clothes with guns visibly in their hands. The officers insist they identified themselves as police very clearly. If Diallo heard and understood that identification, perhaps he feared that they were connected with the Immigration and Naturalization Service, the most vulnerable spot in his life. In that case, he saw them as authorities who threatened him with danger. Even if he made no such association, recognizing them as cops may have caused him fear, simply because they represented authority. What encounters had he had here in New York with cops? Had he been treated disrespectfully, either as he sold his wares or, as David and so many others reported, simply walking in his neighborhood? Again, we do not know for sure, but we can speculate that he did not welcome four white cops bearing down on him in the middle of the night as an event holding promise of anything good. Like Chris Cooper, Diallo may well not have viewed the police as his friends.

There is an alternative story we might construct. What if Diallo failed to recognize the four as police officers? There has been some speculation that his English skills might have been inadequate to the encounter.

I tend to think he was a competent English speaker, given his family, education, and time in America. On the other hand, English was not his first language, nor even his second; accessing comprehension in a tongue not your own in a moment of extreme stress is difficult. On a dark and abandoned street, four white men accosting him may well have raised enough alarm that Diallo's cognitive assessment of the situation became distorted, a process to which we are all subject, in any language. Strong emotion dramatically affects what we see and hear. I have wondered if Diallo might not have believed he was being robbed—he was said to have been carrying $169—if he might have offered his wallet to obviate violence he feared impending.

Did Diallo see the four as authorities or as criminals? We have no real evidence for one interpretation or the other. What becomes of his story in the absence of evidence is the important point for my inquiry. The four officers who testified about the details of the encounter knew less about Diallo's identity, perceptions, intentions than you or I now do. To them, the man they confronted was represented solely by externals—his appearance and gestures—and by the circumstances of their meeting. Diallo may or may not have misread them, but we know for sure that they misread Diallo.

From the moment of meeting, the actions that followed were apparently rapid, leaving little time for thought or analysis: McMellon called out for Diallo to freeze; Diallo retreated, McMellon advanced; Diallo turned, wallet in hand, McMellon fired and retreated; McMellon fell backward down the stairs, Carroll began firing into the vestibule and fell, too; Boss and Murphy advanced, firing repeatedly.

This choreography of advance and retreat embodied one common factor: fear. I think it safe to surmise that whatever Diallo thought, he was scared. The officers reported themselves after the fact to have been frightened, too: they testified in court that they believed McMellon had been shot, and they thought they themselves to be in danger. How much they registered fear in the moment we cannot know. How much their reconstruction of the events on the stand consisted of memories, how much strategic representations we can only guess. I imagine a mixture of the two. Other cops I have interviewed have described what pounding adrenaline at such moments is like. Some described the need for a primacy of will, for withstanding the impulse to act in those crucial few seconds until the situation clarifies itself. Adrenaline focuses the senses on that which is immediate and central. Acting without thought is an animal instinct that police training seeks to moderate. But the four officers were new to each other, new to the particular streets, new to the unit, all conditions that we can expect would heighten their temptation to think the worst and act without restraint.

The key representation of how much they were in a mode of purely physical response was, of course, the number of bullets fired. Surely any cognitive consideration would have told them that Diallo represented no further danger after only a few shots. The cops insisted that he remained upright, standing against the corner of the vestibule, such that they could not be sure a threat to them was over. But that was a point of considerable contention. The coroner's story, our only source of information from the victim's perspective, was very different. Autopsy showed entry wounds in the bottom of Diallo's foot, an event that could only have occurred if he had been shot while on the ground. Even more decisively, one bullet entered his calf just above the right ankle and lodged in the back of his knee, a trajectory only explained by a horizontal path, since if he had been standing the bullet would have traveled from shin to the back of his leg but not upward. That the hail of bullets was so prolific has been interpreted by various people in different ways. To some it represented the police officers' terror, to others a racist dehumanization of their target.

Based on the public record about each of the four men, I imagine differences among them. They were not, after all, any more carbon copies of each other than are occupiers of any other formal identity. McMellon and Boss had both been involved in shootings before, both had been accused of using excessive force. Neither record is, of course, anywhere near conclusive, but they leave open that possible interpretation. It was Murphy, the only one who had never before fired his gun, the only one with no record of complaints against him, who expressed his fear: "I had a sick feeling in the pit of my stomach that I was going to be shot." He came upon the scene last of the four, fired least times, only four. He was also the only officer to be in an impeccable position for the confrontation, shielded by a parked automobile. It was Carroll who administered CPR afterward, weeping as he did.

Nor, I imagine, were the four officers exclusively fastened on their perceptions of Diallo. Their awareness of each other probably mattered, too. They testified that they believed McMillan had been shot, and, despite fears for their personal safety, they felt compelled to come to his aid. If that story is true, moving forward rather than away at such a moment called for some very compelling motivation. Care for a colleague, someone with whom they could empathize because they themselves might easily be in his situation, likely figured in an important way. But also I would wonder if care for their own reputations and self-images did not motivate them as well to advance and fire. To be seen as cowardly, to see himself being seen doing something judged cowardly, is not something most men care to experience. I write in part two more about the influence of masculine ideas about courage, as well as some police views on the subject.

I am imagining some fairly generic dynamics; only the individual men involved in the shooting can say what does and does not apply to them. Every individual is a complex mixture of forces. Just as the motivations and reactions of the four officers were undoubtedly not identical, nor, I would expect, were they consistent for any one individual among them. A mixture of fear and anger, of recognition that Diallo was flesh and blood like themselves and a denial of his sameness, an image of him as a human and as a black man, a sense of panic and a sense of duty, may all have muddled together in the split second of decision.

But that must have been very similar for Diallo, the quick succession of feelings, beliefs, strategic thoughts, actions. Until McMellon's finger closed on the trigger of his semiautomatic weapon, these five men, with their very different identities, roles, degrees of vulnerability and agency, may nonetheless have shared a paradoxical emotional similarity.

Once the firing began, however, their likeness was severed forever. Afterward, Diallo lay dead, his story as an individual ended. But the stories of the four officers were dramatically launched in very new directions.

I do not know who intervened next. Who did they call? Which superiors, medical personnel, other colleagues, neighbors arrived on the scene? We next know the officers' stories through the process of their consultations, with each other and with their union and legal advisors. We know about the inquiry and the pressure of political action to bring about indictments, about the trial and their acquittal and the subsequent civil suit. We know the officers were reassigned to desk jobs and that ultimately at least two of them left the department for other jobs.

It is here that my questions depart from these five particular men to look more deeply at the groups and dynamics they represent. We cannot know how the scene appeared to Amadou Diallo himself, but the community around him had a great deal to say for themselves on the subject of his death.

# Defining the Question

## *In the Community*

Shooting him is murder. Shooting him 41 times is discrimination.
—Saikou Diallo, Amadou's father

Your people to my people, it's like *I* have reason to be afraid of *you,*
not for you to be afraid of me.
—Kevin Davenport, Convent Avenue
Baptist Church Men's Fellowship

DETERMINED THOUGH JUDGE TERESI might have been to rule race
out of his courtroom, he could not succeed, and in the world beyond, race
stood at the very center of the clamor raised by Diallo's death. What was
only tangentially discernable in the court seemed boldly clear to people
of color in New York City. From where they stood, the most glaring light
illuminating the tragedy shone on the color of Diallo's skin. The scenario
described in the courtroom focused on the fears and perceptions of the
police officers, but the drama playing in minds and conversations in the
community was starkly shaded by a different set of fears engendered in
their neighborhoods through daily interactions with law enforcement.

Forty-one bullets reverberated shockingly against the background
of Diallo's innocence to spark passionate outcries against the practices
of racial profiling that, to many people, seemed to lay at the heart of
the tragedy. Yet even as many voices demanded an end to those practices, the very drama of the tragedy also served to overwhelm attention
to more quiet strands of racism, the day-to-day context within which discriminatory police practices take place. Racial profiling happens against

a background that is intangible, subtle, persistent, and it is that ongoing context we need to describe if we are to change the circumstances that give rise to unacceptable tragedies like Diallo's.

On a Sunday afternoon, I interviewed a group of African American men at Convent Avenue Baptist Church in Harlem. They had just completed a meeting of the Men's Fellowship, and six of them stayed on to talk with me about the Diallo case. We got to the point of discussing the trial, and Kevin Davenport, the group's leader, asked the others if they had been surprised when the officers were acquitted. Cecil Johnson, a dapper man in his seventies neatly dressed in a mustard-colored blazer, had been listening to the conversation silently for awhile. Now the room quieted when he announced matter-of-factly, "I was shocked they weren't convicted, yes."

There was a pause. "You thought they were going to be convicted?" asked Kevin, his eyebrows raised in disbelief.

"Of course," said Mr. Johnson (as he was consistently addressed by the younger men in the room.) "They should have."

Kevin quickly countered, "I'm not saying they shouldn't have. Don't get me wrong, I'm just saying that I was not surprised when they were found innocent."

Michael Wright interrupted, "But you were up there."

"Yeah," assented Mr. Johnson, "I was up there."

"Were you there for the trial?" I asked, surprised.

"Yeah," replied Mr. Johnson, adding, "I'm a 32nd degree Mason. I've been all over the world. I was a Boy Scout. I was a scoutmaster. I do a lot."

I thought attending the trial was a more complex form of good citizenry or sightseeing, however, and so I pressed the point, asking him to tell us exactly why he'd gone. "Well, Convent had a bus going up. Al Sharpton was there, also. I was up there for a whole day.

"And then the next day to find that all those policemen were getting free, I cried. Right in my kitchen. What else?"

"I cried, too," I said, "but I wasn't surprised."

Mr. Johnson considered for a moment. "Well, I wasn't surprised, and I was. It wasn't fair." There was a long, reflective silence in the room. At last, Mr. Johnson repeated sadly, "It wasn't fair."

Mr. Johnson's sadness was echoed in many a conversation, but often it was accompanied by a lot of anger. "When you shoot a lion, you can shoot it with one shot," Michael said. "But here a man gets shot forty-one times." Michael then ran out a mixture of pain, rage, proposals, and pessimism:

> Forty-one shots, that went down. We have to really look at this. It's been going on, this is just coming out, it's been going on in the black community for some time. But no one seems to like hearing us. . . . Seems like something drastic has to happen.
>
> And I believe something drastic's probably going to happen sooner or later. You know, blacks are going to get tired. Everybody's going to come together and probably retaliate. Because the generation's coming up now, they're not going to stand for this anymore. It's like a holy war, I believe. It's going to be a terrible thing when we do retaliate. Even a dog gets tired of being hit. It takes a long time, and then we just get up and say, "No, this is not going on anymore." I guess everybody's close to that point.
>
> But I think it's a shame for someone to be shot like that. There wasn't no cause for it. Like I stated before, you can shoot a deer and a deer is huge!—you can shoot a deer with one bullet and it goes down. It doesn't take forty-one shots.

I thought Michael's heartfelt statement expressed more pain than anger, and indeed he continued in a different tone, proposing alternatives to violent reaction:

> Talking is cheap. Something has to be done, we have to go inside the police department. [There are] blacks that already are in the police department, which we have very few in there, acting for us in there. But the black community has to have a majority of black officers.
>
> I think commonly that, because a white comes inside of [a black] community, you already have someone who is undercover prejudiced. . . . You know, some things haven't changed. They've just been modified. That's all it's been, dressed up. But it's still basically the same.

I asked how he saw such a critical change coming about, and he said sadly:

Well, that'll be centuries before that happens. Because white society isn't going to let that happen. They want to keep the dominant control over us in our neighborhood.

Michael's perception that the core issue is dominance was very widely shared by people of color I interviewed, and very widely denied by many white interviewees. This difference is a key one in the gap between views of race matters in the two groups. Michael looked beyond the behaviors of individual officers, even if he criticized them for particular acts and attitudes, seeing instead a system of power and control of an entire community, not just of young men or even of miscreants.

Our conversation was taking place in a church that clearly housed a community, not in the abstract sense in which the word has come to be used, but very literally. I could hear children playing somewhere in the building, could sense the multiplicity of activities going on as I spoke with the Men's Fellowship. The conversation turned to the role of the church in protecting the children as Michael went on:

A Christian community is safer, because our kids are always in church. There's something going on all summer long. Some communities have gotten so devastated, the kids are suffering from this here, they won't let them go outside to play. A lot of sisters, she won't even let her son go outside after he leave out of church. And that's a shame. A lot of mothers are like this here.

Can you imagine how Amadou Diallo's momma must feel, you know, her son was shot like this here? Her *son,* not her brother, but her son. It wasn't my kid, but I can imagine the breakdown . . .

I think officers should live in these neighborhoods. You know, they should live in Manhattan, not in Suffolk County. If they live in Suffolk County, work in Suffolk County. If they live in New York City, work in New York City. If you live in Manhattan, work in Manhattan. If you live in Queens, work in Queens. In your own community. Because when I was coming up, police officers knew all of our families' names in the neighborhood. You know, everybody's name. They used to walk up and down the street.

But today a kid see a cop, and this is for real, my little nephew, he runs in the house! I'm serious. When I was going with him crossing the street, he took off and ran in the house when he saw the cop. And he's only eight years old. Can you imagine what is going to happen when he sees [news of a shooting like Diallo's] on TV?

Life on the streets contrasts with life in the church. Children, protected by mothers who fear the devastation visited on Diallo and his mother, suffer confinement within safe walls. When they learn the reality outside those walls, however, what Michael imagines them feeling is shock and rage, and beyond the fear of a child an eventual grown-up will to retaliate in kind.

Indeed, the contrast between the subject we were discussing and the setting around us could not have been more stark. Convent Avenue Baptist Church is a huge structure set in a charming, tree-lined section of Harlem. I was there through the invitation of a friend who had grown up in Harlem and whose sister was one of the first women deacons recently installed at Convent. Unlike most born-and-bred New Yorkers, my friend is an enthusiastic driver. I had followed her in my rental car to the church, and she had led me a thrilling inadvertent tour through Harlem, twisting and turning along her favorite routes, backtracking now and then when a street was unexpectedly closed off by construction crews or other traffic devils. It was a sunny July day, and many, many people were out and about. Along the way, I saw only two white people, one a policeman sitting in a patrol car with a black partner, the other a young dad pushing his baby in a stroller. No one seemed to be taking much note of the former. The father, I suspected, reflected the neighborhood gentrification I had been reading about. Harlem has become a popular place for up-and-coming young families of all races to buy affordable housing, renovate, and settle. This dad had stopped for a friendly chat with an African American man I thought probably a neighbor.

We arrived at the church some time after Sunday worship was over. The Men's Fellowship meeting was just ending, and while we waited in the corridor people walked by carrying books and pans of food, hollering at kids and greeting each other. It was the prototypic scene of a Sunday-gathered community, busy and inviting, very much consistent with Michael's comments about a safe environment for children.

It was hard to believe that outside at night the climate might be something very different from what I was seeing. I began to see the scene as a painting: idyllic fellowship the focal point, bathed in sweetness and safety, but hidden in the background a very different reality, one in which youngsters ran and hid at the sight of a policeman like the one I had seen sitting in his car.

As the members of the Men's Fellowship went on to describe their experience of race, I reflected on the way their story was a nuanced description of a lived reality, in contrast with the abstraction of the courtroom process.

Kevin Davenport is a large man, soft and unassuming. He had been relatively quiet as he listened to Michael and Mr. Johnson speak. Another member, a man from the Caribbean named James Manning Jr., had been explaining how he avoided racism and lived his life as if it did not exist. Now Kevin interjected wryly, "Racism to me happens even in the most inopportune moments in which I don't want it or don't need for it to happen." He went on to give an example:

> When I initially changed jobs, I think about four or five years ago, I got on the elevator and this lady, presumably white, she looked at me. First she looked me up and down, and she decided she won't get on the elevator. This is the first day. So, I don't see her the second day, but three or four days later she kept on seeing me, so she got comfortable getting on an elevator with me, and it was okay.
>
> One day, there was another [black] guy who came on the elevator. She looked at him, she didn't want to get on the elevator. But when I got on the elevator, she came in behind me.
>
> So that was to me just racism, because she doesn't know who that was, I mean he was black and she was white, I was black. At first, there are some people reacting to you just because of who you are. Maybe because I'm big, I don't know, big or black. Or maybe both. People will just react to me in a different way. I wasn't even paying any attention to her.
>
> I'm getting better than I was in college. Your people to my people, it's like *I* have reason to be afraid of *you*, not for you to be afraid of me. But I didn't say anything, I just said, Okay, let me just go and do my job.

So it's the little things. I can be quiet and be calm, but this kind of stuff will occur. It's not that you're looking for it or wanting it or whatever, it just happens. And that's just one example. That's not so bad.

Later, Matt Meachem joined the conversation. A tidy middle-aged man wearing a t-shirt sporting the slogan "Save the whales, save the rainforest, save up to 75% on designer clothes," Matt spoke with quiet intensity as he brought us back to my reason for being there:

But on the Amadou Diallo case, I mean, I think it was a true reflection of the paranoia that police officers have on the black community. And it's framed, like he's saying on the elevator, when that lady sees him, she has already framed you as big, black. Whoever you are, she'll see something else.

Diallo, he was a working man, he was a vendor, making an honest living. And whether he was a recent immigrant, they didn't have knowledge of that information. All they saw was a young black male. It couldn't have been much of an intimidating situation. It's just their own paranoia and fear of the black image. . . .

We've had a high-ranking black police officer come here. . . . He was the highest ranking black on the police force. And he talked about some of the things he had seen in that organization, some of the people that he had mentored. Very seldom do you see a career police officer, and now you have the Young Black Police Association and they're more of an advocacy group against the police department. Because a while ago a black cop on the subway was shot down by his peers because, again, he fit that frame.

That's what [people] see. Matt Meachem, when I come in [the door], they don't see that I'm an accountant or all these other things in me. What [they] see as you is that first impression of what mold you fit.

As opposed to being so aggressive, in time I've changed. Because a lot of things are new, I'm more formally educated, I expect more. I expect you to respect me if I don't disrespect you. . . . And by the same token I'm *going* to respect you. I'm not going to disrespect you because you're a person of the law.

But I don't know, New York Police Department, they have a lot of acronyms, they have a slogan now, "Professionalism, Courtesy, and

Respect." At some point, you have to stop and ask, What exactly does that mean? Outside of coming out of a class, you don't have that imbedded into you. They don't reflect that. To be courteous when you curse at my women and not respect my kids, because the eight-year-old you mentioned, an eight-year-old has a fear of cops!? That's not right. You know, when you're eight years old, you want to go up to that cop and say, "Can I see your badge?" You know, they look just so dapper in uniform and things of that nature.

Judge Teresi asked the jury to consider whether the police officers' reactions were based on beliefs that would be shared by "the average reasonable person." Reasonable though they clearly were, Kevin, Matt, and the other fellowship members apparently were not those persons. For one thing, their view of the matter was not narrowed by legal blinders. So often had they personally experienced stereotyping that it was difficult for them to imagine that the cops could have seen Diallo as an innocent individual, no matter what his behavior. To them, racial profiling was not simply a matter of police strategy, not even of police injustice; it was a daily, detailed occurrence in their lives.

This question of how a given group of people is framed, in Matt's phrase, and thereby prejudged to be certain ways is relevant not simply to determining whether the four officers were justified in believing themselves to be in jeopardy. It goes to the more systemic question of why they were patrolling that street in the Bronx at midnight to begin with.

During the time I was interviewing people in New York for this book, racial profiling was a very hot topic. Most people of color found it hard to believe Diallo's killing was anything but racial profiling, while many white people fell somewhere on a range from uncertain to sympathetic to the police. These contrasting views nestled inside a dense set of beliefs about criminality. Where African Americans and Hispanics assumed bias in the very fact that a special police force roamed a largely black and immigrant neighborhood late at night on the look-out for suspicious behavior, many white interviewees, attuned as they might be to the injustices contained in the Diallo story, nonetheless tended to accept the premise that the Bronx was a high-crime area and therefore the appropriate place for a police presence. Moreover, they leaned toward believing that the lethal mistakes made by the four SCU officers who shot Diallo, though tragic, were nonetheless understandable, given the high-risk nature of the work the men were doing. People of color, on the other hand, were sure that the policemen reacted out of a web of stereotypes and misapprehensions that were systemically racist in nature.

The Diallo case joined with a series of other events to shine a spotlight on accusations of racial profiling by police departments around the country. To some observers, the language itself was deeply flawed. "One thing that's difficult to swallow," said John Patten, the defense attorney, after I mentioned racial profiling, "you have to have another word for it." He went on to elaborate his point:

> There's a reaction. That's a very charged thing in the law enforcement field, for both sides. . . . The one statistic I think the cops would be very likely to advocate is, if we stopped a hundred people who were actually charged with possessing guns on the street, how many of those hundred would be minority, black, Hispanic, and how many would be white?
>
> And I think the police argue there would be 80 percent or more black or Hispanic. So if you had 80 percent of those guns actually taken off blacks, then the cop thinks that this guy is going to be more dangerous to me than that guy.

Going from Harlem uptown to John's offices downtown was for me like plummeting through the rabbit hole into a wholly different reality. By pure coincidence, John's office building was right across the street from the World Trade Center, which, by the time of my second visit to him, had become Ground Zero.

"Let it be clear," John wrote me at a later time, "that racial profiling is totally unacceptable and has never been condoned by me." Indeed, he has worked closely with police officers and is convinced that New York City officers do not practice racial profiling. The city's police personnel are recruited from street-savvy young people who are no more or less discriminatory than the average American citizen, John attests.

But that statement is hardly reassuring. The average white American citizen participates in discriminatory actions often without awareness of the subtleties and complexities of the process. Systemic racism is a process that takes place beyond the intentions of individual white people. Gerry, the New York cop who spoke in an earlier chapter about reading the street, talked about good and bad profiling practices. He gave an example of his attentiveness to someone scanning the street, and he also offered an example drawn from the post-9/11 atmosphere prevailing at the moment we talked:

> Who's the most likely person to blow up a plane? An Arab Muslim male. I mean, out of fairness you have to search all of the passengers. And out of thoroughness you have to search all of the passengers. But who am I going to be looking closest at? And that's profiling whether I'm going to admit it consciously or unconsciously. Even unconsciously I'm going to be, if I'm one of these airport security people, I'm going to be screening an Arab male who's sweating, you know, and he might be sweating because he's not used to the climate. He's used to a dry heat, we have a more humid heat.

"Or he might be sweating because he knows he's being profiled," I said.

"Right. Yeah," Gerry responded.

Doug Muzzio is a professor at State University of New York. He was part of a team of academics who were creating new training tools on multiculturalism for the New York Police Department. He described a conversation among some of the department's advanced trainers as "informatively nuanced," and I asked him to tell me in some detail what they'd said:

> Well, that there needs to be profiling, that profiling helps the police, that you need to know generalized stereotypes if you don't buy into it totally, but they give you cues and put you on alert, that they are very valuable. There was a consensus there.
>
> But that it's not a matter of policy, certainly that, you know, a racial element comes into it. So you're looking at a black kid with his hat on backwards with baggy pants, he's a perp, and he may not be a high school kid who has to dress that way to survive to get to school. So there's an immediate stereotyping of people into certain classes, particularly to the detriment of black and Hispanic kids. And it happens all the time. . . .

So you've got this knee jerk [*snaps his fingers repeatedly*] identification that happens all the time. And it's difficult not to do, the cops
argued. But you got to get beyond that. But at the same time, there are
cues that dress give you and, you know, other colors, and where they
wear the key rings and where they wear their earrings and all that stuff,
that do make a difference. So the cops are saying it's a very fine line.

*Beth: What's the difference that it makes?*

Doug: Well, I mean, it makes a difference for the cops, number
one, in terms of their physical safety to understand these cues. It also
makes it better for the citizenry that, you know, if they're reading the
cues correctly, then they're protecting the citizenry, and also they're
not busting the chops of the people who ought not to be busted. That's
if you're reading it right. If you're reading it incorrectly, it's the negative
of all those things.

So, the more I listened to it, I mean, my knee jerk reaction is, lock
all the cops up, and racial profiling is inherently a dangerous tool. But
then you hear the nuances of it. Clearly, racial profiling is anathema.
But profiling makes sense as a police tool.

That such split-second assumptions are seen as cues necessary to the
safety of the officers and to the proper execution of their duty, the justi-
fications Doug and Gerry offered, is precisely the problem. Each officer
comes to that moment of judgment in a context that goes well beyond
policy, well beyond individual prejudice. The moment when the Diallo
officers fired forty-one times was made of up very many layers.

John Patten's statistical argument suggests the intersection of individual dynamics and policy ones. By the time an officer, those involved
in the Diallo shooting or any other anywhere in the country, comes to
a confrontation with a man in the street who is possibly armed, that
officer's sense of danger has already been shaped by a series of steps I
believe to contain significant racial bias. We have ample evidence that
men of color are stopped more often (a reasonable thing if indeed officers think them more likely to be armed and dangerous.) We know that,
once stopped, men of color are more often than white men searched. We
know that once found armed, men of color are more likely to be charged
and, once charged, convicted than are white men. But the statistic the

police cite is based on convictions involving weapons. The idea that more men of color carry weapons is thus based on circular reasoning. It reads back from the end of a multiple series of acts involving a multiple series of biases to a statistic at the beginning that is highly speculative.[1]

We do have some good data about dynamics like these. A sociologist named John Lamberth studied accusations that officers were disproportionately stopping and searching black and Hispanic drivers on the New Jersey Turnpike. The matter was highly charged; two troopers fired eleven shots into a van carrying black and Latino men in April 1998. In their defense, the officers admitted they had been trained to focus on drivers of color on the theory that they were more likely to be drug traffickers.[2] Yet Lamberth's data showed that contraband, mostly drugs, were found on 25 percent of whites stopped in New Jersey, 13 percent of blacks, and 5 percent of Latinos. Lamberth actually counted drivers of different ethnicities along turnpikes and highways and used these numbers as benchmarks against which to measure huge disproportions in stops. He repeated his investigations in many different states and situations over a decade, finding similar patterns extensively demonstrated. In Maryland, for instance, 73 percent of those stopped and searched on a section of I-95 were black, but the percentages of those found with drugs were equal for blacks and whites. He studied U.S. custom's searches as well:

> While 43 percent of those searched at airports by the Customs Service in 1998 were black or Latino, illegal materials were found on 6.7 percent of whites, 6.3 percent of blacks and 2.8 percent of Latinos.[3]

Lamberth's study of Customs Service searches resulted in radical changes in those practices, resulting in a far higher degree of effectiveness. Admittedly, drugs and guns are different things. But there are associations made between the two, and the police practices involved are interconnected.

In the early 1990s the NYPD instituted a set of linked policies. Fighting "quality of life" crimes directed police attention to low-level activities like graffiti, "aggressive" panhandling, public drunkenness, and other nuisance crimes. The theory was that restoring a sense of public order and discipline would help encourage law-abiding community members to retake their streets and promote a higher level of intolerance for more serious crime:

> The link between the campaign against low-level disorder and the effort to reduce gun violence was explicit Departmental policy: "By working systematically and assertively to reduce the level of disorder in the city, the NYPD will act to undercut the ground on which more serious crimes seem possible and even permissible." The practical impact was intended and equally clear: "Stopping people on minor infractions made it riskier for criminals to carry guns in public." If criminals, fearful of arrest for minor violations, stopped carrying guns (the argument went), fewer violent crimes, and fewer violent deaths, would occur. In this sense, the Department's "quality of life" and "getting guns off the streets" strategies were and remain closely interrelated.[4]

One tool for implementing this approach was a policy called "stop-and-frisk." Authorized to stop people for very minor infractions, officers could proceed to frisk them for probable cause, usually suspicion that they were carrying drugs or guns:

> Order maintenance theory encourages officers to intervene in instances of low-level disorder, whether observed or suspected, with approaches which fall short of arrest. A "stop" intervention provides an occasion for the police to have contact with persons presumably involved in low-level criminality—without having to effect a formal arrest, and under a lower constitutional standard (i.e., "reasonable suspicion"). Indeed, because low-level "quality of life" and misdemeanor offenses are more likely to be committed in the open, as a theoretical matter, the "reasonable suspicion" standard may be more readily satisfied as to those sorts of crimes. To the extent that "stop" encounters create points of contact between police and low-level offenders, such contacts can lead to the apprehension of persons already wanted for more serious crimes, or who might be prepared to commit them in the near future.[5]

Who was most likely to be stopped and frisked? Lamberth studied the question in 1998 and 1999 and "found that while police disproportionately stopped young black men, the hit rates were actually marginally higher for whites than for blacks or Latinos." People of color, in other words, were stopped disproportionately but were found to be carrying contraband less often than whites.

Even while I doubt John Patten's implied conclusion about racial profiling, that the disproportion to which it refers is a deserved one, there is a sense in which I do have reservations about the term. It is too simple, too obliterating of the complex interactions that give the phenomenon dangerous life. A profile is a line on a two-dimensional surface. By definition, it is the point beyond which the eye cannot see. To profile is (according to the *Merriam-Webster Dictionary*) "to shape the outline of by passing a cutter around." Within the outline, detail disappears. Beyond the outline, reality is cut away. It is a flat and flattened description of a probable suspect, but it says little or nothing about the actual human being with whom a given police officer comes face to face.

Here are three descriptions of the experience of being profiled by people of color. David Grant is retired now, but for years he worked as a quality-control inspector for an automobile manufacturer. David is distinguished looking, a solid burgher who owns the home in which he and his wife raised three law-abiding children. Said David:

> I remember going to work 3 o'clock in the morning, and so many times I was stopped. In those days I had a new Cadillac, and they just assumed it was stolen. They wanted to see every piece of information I had, every piece of identification. They'd raise up the hood and check the number. They'd say, "This is not a stolen Cadillac." And I'd say, "But this one here, I bought this one."
>
> "Where do you work?"
>
> "For General Motors."
>
> "Well, no wonder you can drive a new Cadillac!" They'd just assume I was a car thief. Coming from work, on my way to work, it was the same thing.

Kevin Davenport, too, was stopped while driving and had an experience similar to David's, in that the officer was in the end convinced of his innocence. Kevin is a large African American man in his late thirties, a college graduate employed in a white-collar job in New York:

I was on my way to church this past week. I had rushed in [to my home], I'd changed my clothes. [But] I left my wallet, I left everything [at home], and I got stopped. What I did, I got out of the car, I had to get out of the car because I couldn't get to my pocket. So I said, "Officer, I have to get out of the car." So he said, "Okay." He let me out of the car. So I said, "Well you know, I really left my wallet at home with my license and everything else." And you know what he told me? "I believe you." I believe you!

Well, that's just me. You know what I'm saying? [*Laughter*] I mean, they won't let you get out of the car, you know what I'm saying! It struck me because, I'm not special. He should treat everybody like that. When he said, "I believe you," he made it clear to me that it was only *me* that he was believing, not everybody. If it would have been somebody else, he would have said, "Stay in the car." I pulled out my cell phone, I could pull out something which was a cell phone, just because he felt comfortable with me. And I think that's the way it should be. Officers have to feel comfortable with the next black person.

A third example of racial profiling came out of my conversation with Lorraine Cortés Vázquez, the president of the Hispanic Federation, about the results of her group's survey of attitudes toward law enforcement in her community. They reported that police were feared by people of all sorts, no matter what their class status or age. Lorraine illustrated the point with a story from her own recent experience:

There is no difference in terms of class or color in the Latino community. There was one officer not too long ago, whom I felt the need to inform that I was a member of the Civilian Complaint Review Board, because of his derogatory smirks and facial expressions. I was double-parked and he requested that I move my car. I replied, "Fine." At the time, I was waiting for my husband who was in the bakery I was parked in front of. But then I obviously didn't move fast enough. I don't know what I was supposed to do: gun the motor? His tone was so abusive. I informed him, "Sir, I heard you. I am moving. If you get out of my way, I could probably move faster. There's no reason for you to speak to me in that manner." A small interaction like that, totally discourteous and disrespectful. Here I am, good car, relatively clean looking person, it doesn't matter. There's just a tone and an abrasiveness that is uncalled for and really needs to be managed by the NYPD.

What each of these people describes is not that he or she was suspected of carrying concealed weapons, of being a threat to life in the community. They speak quite simply of demeaning behavior on the part of police personnel who have no particular reason to suspect them of anything at all. That behavior might or might not be racial profiling, but so ingrained is their expectation of bad treatment from police that they cannot help but read it that way. Kevin saw his own courteous interaction as being noteworthy precisely because it was so exceptional. In turn, an individual treated discourteously might perhaps respond in a similar way, further fueling negative expectations by officers. Round and round it goes, grounded systemically, ending tragically.

We might think of these experiences as falling into a category of "racial backgrounding," that area of subtle, persistent, systemic dynamics involving race that is vividly present to the consciousness of people of color but that vanishes into an invisible negative space for most white people. Think of that experiment in perception, the outline drawing of an hourglass that turns into the profiles of two faces when you squint in a particular way. Foreground becomes background, and the picture is a wholly different one.

So, too, the lived experience of race in America is the foreground, the profile if you will, for people who are not white. But police officers are trained and operate within a frame where the foreground is crime and in the intensity of its representation, the background of race pales to invisibility.

# Policing the Boundaries

## *In the Precinct House*

The problem is police officers are out there with this badge and gun. When the good police officers cover for the bad ones, it's really a dangerous situation.

—Stuart Hanlon, criminal defense attorney

You know, trusting cops is not so bad. I mean, I have two children, and when you're raising children and there's trouble, you call the police.

—Stuart Hanlon, father of young sons

"THERE'S THREE SIDES TO EVERY STORY," a police officer named Sid O'Conner said to me. "There's my side, there's your side, and there's the truth." Kevin, David, and Lorraine told one story, full of pain and anger. The four individual police officers involved in Diallo's shooting no doubt would have a very different tale to tell.

The cop on the beat, who today may appear either pedaling a bicycle or driving an armored vehicle, who may be clothed in dungarees or shielded in full riot gear, is the visible human manifestation of state control. Those who sit in halls of governance to make the laws rely on those who literally face the populace to enforce them. Whether as servant of the people or tamer of the dangerous miscreant, the police employee generally perceives him or herself as the ultimate enforcer of a social order, as McMellon and his colleagues were indeed sent out to Wheeler Avenue to be. In several respects, the individual officer is often very similar to the criminal he confronts. I have commented on some of those similarities between the young officers who shot Diallo and their victim, especially that they all had jobs that set them on the street in the middle of the night and brought them to collision point, and that for all of them ambition was at least one motivating factor for being there. In general, both criminal and law enforcer constitute the rank and file of a massive criminal justice system. Both populate institutions that are complex and critical to definitions of modern society.

## Blue Lines, Thick and Thin

Gerry McCarren is a New Yorker born and bred, Irish in name and identity. The nephew of NYPD cops, he joined the force right out of college. I asked him why:

> Just financial reasons. The economy wasn't doing too well in New York in the early eighties. Finished college, and I didn't have enough money to go to graduate school. I was looking for work that might be able to pay for that.
>
> When I started looking for jobs, entry level positions, they were offering me only $14,500. And at the time, the police department was paying well. They had increased salaries back then to prevent corruption.
>
> So I saw the ad in the *Times,* starting salary with NYPD was $27,500, almost double what they were offering me in the private sector. So I took the test. And I figured with that, I could go to school part-time and get an advanced degree.

This story of joining the police force as a step up in the world resonated with many others I heard. For Chris Cooper, too, the financial support to pursue higher studies was one of several incentives for becoming a cop.

But Chris became quickly disenchanted with racial conditions in the department. Gerry, on the other hand, found himself becoming more and more enamored—up to a point:

> I became less and less interested in graduate work. I was getting more and more interested in police work. . . . The first seven years of the job I loved it. I thought it was a great job. And I was very gung ho out there. . . .

> The first seven years I loved it so much I had trouble even turning it off. I would be on vacation, we were in Paris, and we see the gendarmes cruising by real slow. . . .

Gerry went on to tell me a long story about noticing that the French police were searching for a suspect, spotting a man duck into an alley, chasing and capturing him. He told the story with great élan, finishing with a chuckle. "I needed that little adrenaline rush to grab a collar," he said, "because I'd been on vacation, and I felt like I was going through withdrawal."

Organizations have distinct characters of their own. That is true of every group from mom and pop on up. Like families, all organizations signify boundaries, dividing lines between those inside and those outside. How a given group presents itself to those not included says something about the nature and purposes of the entity. For police organizations, famous for turning a sharp blue shoulder to an inquiring world, the most defining characteristic of the job is adrenaline: the daily experience of dealing with danger. It is the belief that they and they alone know about the perils they confront that police officers most often cite as the dividing line between themselves and the rest of the world.

"What was it that I heard a young officer once say to me?" Lorraine Cortés Vázquez reflected quizzically:

> I had asked him about this blue wall of silence, and he had said something like, "All blood runs blue in the department." It's like, Jesus Christ! That's a little dramatic, don't you think?! I said, "Don't you want to have a little independence? Isn't your mother's pride in you worth something?" [*Laughs*] He was a little embarrassed. I was a little taken aback by his silliness, you know. One thing is to think that, another thing is to mouth that. [*Laughs*]

Silence is powerfully expressive. What goes unsaid preserves options available to those in the know and denied to others. The spirit of solidarity that Lorraine's officer suggested, absurd in his exaggeration, defines a code of behavior by police that is deeply ingrained and also severely enforced. Maintained by a thick bundle of official policies and unwritten traditions, by legal action and by social interaction, it is a dynamic central to the Diallo case.

Stuart Hanlon, a white man and a highly regarded San Francisco defense attorney, elaborated on Lorraine's perception. Well known for having defended Geronimo Pratt and other political figures, Stuart is, paradoxically, also close friends with cops. From that vantage point, he described the most personal of elements constituting the blue wall.

I met Stuart Hanlon in the Victorian residence converted to offices where he conducts his law practice. The setting bespoke Stuart's principles. Unassuming, a bit dowdy, the building is an old San Francisco beauty, a rundown piece of the prized texture of the city. Stuart kept me waiting. I sat on a bench in a corridor, listening to a young man act receptionist from a desk tucked under a grand staircase. Several people hurried in and out of Stuart's office in the front of the building, consulting him about this or that. At length he approached me, inviting me to join him.

In shirt sleeves and rumpled trousers, Stuart clearly communicated that he was taking time out of a busy day. The phone rang repeatedly. One of those calls involved a very respectful conversation with a police officer. Stuart called him by his given name as he negotiated the surrender of a client. Later he talked with the client and, like a nurturing parent soothing a frightened child, reassured him that the officer was trustworthy, would treat him well and respect the arrangement they had made.

Sometime during our conversation, Stuart had made a passing reference to a police war on society. Now, I asked him what he had meant, and, in a nice contrast to his tone on the telephone, he explained:

> The war on society is more an attitude by the police, which is that they are separate from the rest of society. They realize that a lot of people don't like them. They realize that they're wanted to do the dirty work. So it's Us against Them, Us being law enforcement and Them being the rest of society. They don't interact socially. . . .
>
> The last several years, I've become friends with cops and I've gone to social functions. Normally, except for a couple of lawyers who are ex-cops, I'm the only non-cop there. My wife would be the only non-cop-related woman. It's really an in-grown group. I know in my life I try to *not* hang out with lawyers because I'd get a jaded view of the

world, in my social life and personal life. And police don't have that; most police people hang out with other police officers, in family and social [settings], picnics and vacations.

It has an effect. You know, "Society's the problem." Because the "Them" are the people the "Us" are supposed to protect and serve. A lot of Us don't have respect for Them. It goes around and around, you know, there's not an easy answer.

Among the police themselves there is an explicit recognition of the problem Stuart delineated. "The job says we're supposed to avoid this mentality, Us against Them," Gerry said, and went on to add layers to Stuart's conception of the matter:

Us against Them means [*pause*] it means largely blue, police officers versus the public. But it could be police officers versus the press. Police officers versus the brass. Police officers versus detectives. Police officers versus the FBI.

But it's not an all bad thing, it also binds us together. And so I have no problem working with black or Hispanic officers, you know, as long as they're wearing the same blue outfit I'm wearing.

Cops of color tend to have a very different view of solidarity. I talked with officers about the perils of working out of uniform, for instance, when they were subject to the same racial hazards as the ordinary citizen. Chris Cooper described the hostility of his seniors to his higher educational activities and saw that attitude as explicitly discriminatory. Black officers' organizations responded to the Diallo shooting and others of its kind critically, intentionally crossing the blue line. I say more about this distinct contrast between Gerry's view and Chris's later. It is not unusual; it commonly characterizes perceptions across power lines. Those in privileged positions assume a greater degree of harmony and camaraderie than do those experiencing discrimination. To share identity with a marginalized group at the same time one is occupationally associated with a dominant one is a severe example of the sort of double consciousness W. E. B. DuBois described, very evident on one side, wholly invisible on the other.[1]

"Police solidarity" is therefore a qualified notion, very true but not in the same way for everyone. Stuart attributed the tendency to become

Aggrieved by Mayor Rudolph Giuliani's lack of support for their salary demands, several thousand off-duty police officers and their supporters rallied to demand higher pay at New York's Battery Park in June 2000. By coincidence, Bruce Springsteen's song "41 Shots" protesting Diallo's shooting was released the day before, adding to the disaffection of the police. *AP/Wide World Photos.*

socially ingrown to the function police are required to serve, doing society's "dirty work," and to the public's resulting dislike for them. Gerry agreed. He talked at some length about the tedious parts of the work—writing parking tickets and handling neighborhood noise complaints, for instance—and about the heat they took from the public, which brought him back to the subject of danger:

> A new street nickname for cops replaced agents, after an officer was assassinated on the street. He was assassinated sitting in a car, guarding a witness. They started calling us "targets."

At length, after a pause in the conversation, Gerry sighed and said, "I joined for salary reasons. And then I got into the mission of the job, you know, trying to make a dent in crime or something. And then I got soured on it, and I thought it was all the joke. I became much more cynical."

Gerry was a slight man, short and thin but obviously strong. It turned out he was a long-distance bicyclist and an avid sailor. The day we first met he had a bad cold. He told me he thought he had gotten run down because he was working a second job, moonlighting in an effort to save money for early retirement. In fact, all he could think about, he said, was counting the days until he could get out.

So in the end the police force was a limited vehicle for Gerry, a white man, just as it had been for Chris Cooper, although for different reasons. Gerry had told me that he did not care what color skin lay under the blue, that they all were bound together by their status as targets. But in fact there were ways race did matter to him:

> With the early sergeant's exams, there was also some quota sergeants that were made. They got extra points for being [*pause*] ethnically diverse. Some of them, someone should have screened some of these guys. Some of them, uhh [*pause*], like guys who legitimately passed the test had a tougher time because of these quota sergeants.

Those pauses in Gerry's statement were silences speaking loudly of his negative judgment of these newly promoted sergeants-of-color. In those spaces, he both questioned their competency and registered protest against the perceived injustice done those who "legitimately passed the test." Added points violated Gerry's sense of fairness, but they also interrogated his sense of entitlement. The whole business of what I guessed had been an affirmative action program offended his concept of legitimacy. What lay beneath the blue in this rendition was trouble not unity, resentment that belied theories of police solidarity. Suddenly, Gerry's story of race in the department moved a whole lot closer to Chris Cooper's version.

Stuart had talked about the cultural aspects of police society from the other side of the coin. "Predominantly, major cities pick police from white working class groups of men," Stuart said, "and now from women. San Francisco cops are Irish Catholic, you know, Italian: this is where the police come from." Ethnic traditions still mark police departments, even as the nation's population becomes increasingly diverse and departments consciously seek to reflect that evolution, either by choice or by political and legal pressure. But the roots go deep; children follow their fathers into the work and extended family histories intertwine with the departments they serve. To a belief in entitlement to jobs and promotions prevalent among white Americans generally is added this particular culture based on a sort of ethnically inherited organizational territoriality. These hard-to-break dynamics of community dominance and familial hegemony exist in other fields as well. But the unique feature of police work, the experience of danger, compounds their consequence.

Few among us are prepared to say that the muzzle of a gun is not reason enough to react dramatically. But the very fact that firearms are so intimidating buttresses the isolation of law enforcement people from scrutiny and criticism. Cops do get killed in the line of duty. Policing is a more hazardous occupation than writing books. Nonetheless, Chris Cooper, the ex-cop from D.C., claimed a certain authority to contradict the officers involved, if not to question the basis on which they invoked immunity from guilt:

> As a police officer, I chased after many people who had guns, who *really* had guns. I stopped countless, countless, countless numbers of people. I have stood in the shoes of those officers. When you stop so many people, when you approach so many people, you can, you *can* Monday-morning quarterback.
>
> You see, in police work there's a saying: If you weren't there, you can't talk about it. You always hear police officers say, when they talk about shooting situations, "I wasn't there." As a police officer criticizing other police officers, when anyone criticizes a police action, he or she will always have to contend with that other side saying, "You weren't there. You weren't there. You weren't there."
>
> But you know, YES that argument works really well when you're criticizing a civilian. But it does not work as well when you're criticizing another police officer. I don't need to be there. Thousands of black police officers who were not there on February 4th, 1999, did not need to be there. It's because of our experiences on the street, those experiences from approaching hundreds and hundreds and hundreds and hundreds of people, that they (black police) can have an almost accurate sense of what happened. They do this night after night after night after night after night. I did not have to be there!

"Not being there" forms a dividing line both cognitive and emotional. There is a force to the claim of privileged knowledge that comes from fear. I can claim that nobody knows what it is to write a book except other authors, but few people care deeply about what I experience at my computer terminal. My travail is neither severe enough nor significant enough to give my statement much importance. Police work, however, evokes fear that many people do feel in daily life. The specter of "the criminal" is very present in modern-day life, and few people have escaped moments in which, rightly or wrongly (remember Kevin's story of the white woman avoiding the elevator), they have perceived themselves to be endangered. Public culture is rife with dramas of street danger, either from the perspective of the victim or of the protector. Not only does the ordinary citizen identify with the experience of endangerment, but he or she also shares in a collective fantasy of protection. The hero figure in popular culture is as prevalent as the perpetrator. Whether *Batman* or *Law and Order,* it is no accident that films and television programs depicting these battles command the public attention.

When a police officer says, "You weren't there. You don't know," most of us are ready to believe him. Officer Kenneth Boss described how he came upon the scene to find Ed McMellon on the ground and Sean Carroll firing his gun. "My God, I'm going to die," he testified he thought. His partner, Richard Murphy, told the jury, "When I looked into the vestibule there was not a doubt in my mind that he had a gun. I had a sick feeling in the pit of my stomach that I was going to be shot."[2] Few jurors could fail to conjure up vivid scenes—the danger, the terror, the heroism—suggested by the words.

If you combine an ethnically ingrown group of people who see themselves as thanklessly defending a society that inadequately appreciates them, with the belief that facing danger is an experience unique to them, it is easy to see the human elements out of which that blue wall of silence is built. Personal experience builds into an organizational dynamic. To dwell in a world of violence, to be comrades engaged in battling an enemy, to share similar community roots, all combine to create organizations hidden from scrutiny, buttressed against criticism and redress. And in that environment, violence flourishes. The danger anticipated becomes

Officer Richard Murphy listens to testimony as it is reread to the jury deciding Murphy's fate and that of three other white police officers. *AP/Wide World Photos.*

a reality visited on certain segments of the public in an escalating contest of deadly force.

When an incident like Diallo's death hits the airwaves, all these dynamics come up for question. Suddenly, the other side of the blue wall is bathed in the light of public scrutiny. What citizens in the protected mainstream may have seen before as a righteous phalanx of honest protectors is suddenly depicted as a barrel of bad apples, scary guys who are armed to the hilt, racist, and apt to use their lethal powers impulsively. From the perspective of the police, especially those not immediately involved, the injustice of that view encourages an even greater alienation from society, a heightened sense of Us and Them. And as the police close ranks, the ability of outsiders to distinguish good cops from troubled ones reduces to zero.

## Bad Apples or Toxic Trees?

Stuart Hanlon, the fighting defense attorney, told a story of a recent client:

> I work with a young man [Michael] who was driving with his friend and with a seventeen-year-old girl. They didn't know that the friend had a warrant out for him here in San Francisco. And the police were waiting to arrest the friend on a warrant.
>
> The police came up in plainclothes and cut off Michael's car [as it was] leaving the driveway, and he tried to maneuver away from the police car, and they shot into the car and killed the girl. They charged my client, the driver, with murder of the girl, saying that he forced the police to shoot by his driving at the police officers.
>
> Which was total bullshit. That was clearly police misconduct, police murder.
>
> *Beth: Where did it occur?*
>
> Stuart: In San Francisco, out near the ocean. In a middle-class housing development out near the ocean.
>
> *Beth: What were the races of the people involved?*
>
> Stuart: He was Hispanic. The perp they were looking for was black. The passenger, the girl was white. And the cop was a psychopath. Officer Breslin.
>
> *Beth: What race was he?*
>
> Stuart: White. White Irish. The police developed this theory that was called "provocative acts," meaning Michael's driving provoked the shooting. The police lied, as they do in all these cases, saying they'd identified themselves, saying they were showing badges, saying Michael drove at the officer at 40 mph. And all the witnesses said he drove at 2, 3, 4, 5 miles per hour, trying to evade this lunatic with a gun, and he didn't know they were cops.
>
> I think it's not typical for cops to be psychopaths, but for the police to cause confrontations and overreact, and to lie, is typical. Those things are typical. It's sad, because it's not typical that people die all the time.

I started to challenge Stuart's characterization of the officer as pathological. "You referred to the cop as a psychopath, a lunatic," I said. But Stuart, a step ahead of me, interrupted and said:

This particular officer was. He's a career officer with serious problems, emotionally and mentally. I think other police officers who I can't name agree with that.

I think generally you do have mostly good police officers. But the bad ones they're not willing to deal with, because they're all brothers and sisters in this war on crime and war on society, and they're not willing to deal with the bad police officers. Just like lawyers don't deal with bad lawyers, and doctors don't deal with bad doctors. We kind of protect our group, sort of thing.

The problem is police officers are out there with this badge and gun. When the good police officers cover for the bad ones, it's really a dangerous situation. And I think everybody in law enforcement who knew this cop knew that he was dangerous, had a history of incidents, but they couldn't stop the situation, and then they covered up.

I mean, this is an extreme situation, Michael's case. But it happens in smaller ways all the time. I can't tell you how many times this scenario [is claimed]: drug dealers supposedly drop drugs at their [the policemen's] feet as they pretend to search their cars. These are mostly African American and Spanish men: they'll never drop drugs [where they can be easily found], they'll never present the cops with anything. But the cops lie about it all the time, it's a standard lie. You can predict what the police will say after awhile. There are so many lies they use all the time.

In the course of my interviews, I often heard the sorts of characterization that Stuart made. People referred to psychopathic officers, to bad cops, to the worm in the barrel of apples. While I was researching this chapter, the *New York Times Magazine* published a compelling story about a scandal within the Rampart district station of the Los Angeles Police Department. A series of flukes led to revelation of grave wrongdoing by officers of a special gang-fighting unit, with the eventual dramatic result that the LAPD was brought under federal control. The *Times* story's author, Lou Cannon, traced in some detail the interweaving of the particular police officers' malfeasance with systemic problems in the department as a whole. "While Rampart started as a police scandal," wrote Cannon, "it has rapidly exposed deep flaws in the entire Los Angeles County legal system." Yet the story was entitled, "One Bad Cop."[3]

Clearly, neither Rampart nor the Diallo tragedy can be attributed simply to one bad cop. "When the good police officers cover for the bad ones," Stuart had said, "it's really a dangerous situation." How distinct is the contrast between good and bad cops? How do they fit together in a systemic dynamic enforced on other levels of reality?

When something like the Diallo killing takes place and becomes public, the police involved are protected by official mechanisms that abet the culture of solidarity. The blue wall takes legal form, as policy, and in doing so moves the story of police relations with the citizenry to a different level. Lorraine commented incredulously on this aspect of the problem:

> When an incident happens and you have a forty-eight-hour rule that says that you can be silent, to regroup, re-collect your thoughts, there's something wrong with that.

The forty-eight-hour rule states that police officers can remain silent for two days after a use-of-force incident, during which time they can consult their union, their attorneys, and each other. By the time they speak to the public, they have been able to recover from emotion and craft a consistent story.

> That's a luxury afforded to only one segment of the population, in a crisis situation. If you are a bus driver and you have a car accident, you immediately have to go for a drug test, you're immediately subject to investigation. Any other public servant does not have that luxury. Any other citizen does not have that luxury. So we have policies in place that are just allowing certain behavior, things that would be abhorrent to us under normal circumstances, to fester.
>
> And what does that do? That young officer, who is unsure and maybe did something rashly or out of fear, or just had a bad impulse, it might make them cross the line and no longer be a principled, ethical officer.

Lorraine Cortés Vázquez is in a position to know. She is a member of the New York Citizens Complaint Review Board. Many cities have such bodies. Usually comprised of political appointees, their assignment is to provide oversight of police behavior. Rules like the one Lorraine cited buttress the tendency of officers to turn their backs to the world, making the work of civilian oversight agencies near impossible.

I interviewed Lorraine at her offices on the fifteenth floor of a financial-district high-rise. She had not arrived when I got there; as at Stuart's office, I sat for some time in the waiting room. Soon, she arrived at a trot, rolling her eyes and complaining in a good-natured way about New York traffic snarls. Lorraine Cortés Vázquez bristled energy. She hurried to her expansive desk, briskly organized several stacks of paper, gave instructions to her assistant that ranged from coffee request to business-at-hand, and settled in to give me the majority of her attention. She fiddled with objects on her desktop, silver bangles jingling, and told me about the CCRB:

> The Civilian Complaint Review Board, although it is the only mechanism we have, it is not a mechanism that has a lot of power. It can and I think it should be empowered to do more. But as it stands, we have findings and we share those findings and make recommendations to the police department. The police department is the one that makes the final decision.
>
> *Beth: Do you have your own investigative apparatus?*
>
> Lorraine: There's an incredible operation. An incredible operation! It's a major financial investment on the part of the city.
>
> *Beth: What do you make of the contradiction between the elaborateness of that apparatus and the lack of power that the board has to do something about the problems it finds?*
>
> Lorraine: Well, I think it's just indicative of this whole notion of a Civilian Complaint Review Board. There has been a long-standing battle whether there should be an independent agency or should it continue to be an arm of the police department. I think that in response to the public [demand] there is this investigatory body, but it just can do findings and recommendations. And then the board reviews them and substantiates them, and supports those findings, and then refers them over to the police department.
>
> But I think that it's just indicative of a city that has been very conflicted about a civilian police review process. This is not new, this has been going on for years, for decades, about whether it should be independent or not. . . .

The saga of New York's CCRB began in 1966, when then Mayor John Lindsey established it by executive order. Lindsay was newly elected and determined to intervene in police affairs in a way previous mayors had not. Two incidents made his position politically wise: riots in Harlem in 1965 during a time when the civil rights movement was awakening protest in communities-of-color around the nation; and the Kitty Genovese incident. The outburst in Harlem had involved an off-duty New York cop who shot and killed a young black man in the victim's own community. A very different tragedy had happened the year before. Kitty Genovese had been assaulted by a man with a knife and murdered in her sedate Queens neighborhood. Her screams for help were heard by many residents. But nobody responded. Interviewed later, people expressed a range of reasons from unconcern to fear of involvement. The two events together galvanized New York, raising questions of a profound nature about citizen involvement, danger, crime, unrest, and more.

On the heels of these dramas Lindsay came to office, promising a new relationship between citizenry and police. But no sooner had he created the CCRB than the Patrolmen's Benevolent Association (the police union) mounted a campaign aimed at its defeat. In the end, Lindsay compromised and placed police representatives on the board, effectively creating a hybrid institution with tied hands.[4]

So the CCRB remained for almost three decades, until David Dinkins was elected mayor. An African American figure of considerable stature on the New York political scene, Dinkins quickly reorganized the CCRB. In July 1993, it was reborn as an independent body. Nonetheless, battles for control continued.

### Breaks in the Blue Line

Contention over public oversight of law enforcement is an element in the construction of police departments as Stuart and Lorraine described them: homogenous groups of loyalists who resist incursions from outsiders. In fact, as Gerry suggested, there is another reality at work, within the NYPD and elsewhere, as the police, like many institutions in American life, have become increasingly subject to pressures, legal, political, and social, to become more diverse. As the number of recruits from other ethnic, racial, and social groups has expanded, so also has conflict and criticism from within the ranks grown. Typically, that conflict is implicitly articulated by white cops, through the kinds of public silences that occurred in my talk with Gerry, and I do not doubt more explicitly in private among themselves. For police personnel of color, however, the issue is clear and public:

> What you have now, unlike in the past, is you have a breakdown in police solidarity in departments throughout the country. And you have a breakdown in solidarity because you don't have the cohesiveness that was once there. Because as police ranks have changed, we see a breakdown. As women come into police work, as blacks come into police work, as gays come into police work, as Latinos come into police work, that homogenous character of policing, of all white males from specific ethnic groups is no longer there. All these new types of people are coming in and the traditional police subculture is not welcoming of these people, so we suddenly have a breakdown in police solidarity. Which is great. For the most part, the norms of the police subculture are detrimental to black and Latino people.

Chris Cooper's description echoed that of other officers-of-color I interviewed, and other white officers as well. Ruth Nestor is an African American mother of two New York City police officers. Ruth Nestor lives in a section of the Bronx not far from where the Diallo shooting took place. But her neighborhood consists of neatly coifed small homes owned by the people who live in them. A semiretired nurse, Ruth Nestor is the widow of a highly regarded social worker who headed a community agency for many years. I asked her why she thought her sons had become policemen, and, echoing Gerry, she replied, "Well, what happened is job opportunities." She went on to tell me something of her sons' histories:

> Jason, the older one, wasn't highly motivated as a student. He was the one who told my husband, "I don't want to go. I don't think I want to go to college." And my husband said, "Well, everybody doesn't have to go to college. You have options: you can go to college, or to technical school, or to work." Jason opted for college and graduated from

Oberlin College. Afterward, he taught, in daycare. He was excellent. But eventually he didn't want to continue in that field.

Meanwhile, Jason's younger brother acquired a law degree:

Samuel graduated from law school and took a whole battery of exams. Every exam that came around—I don't think that he went in for the fireman, but he took the police, and he encouraged this one [Jason], to take the exams, too. You don't lose anything. And the interesting thing was when they both were to go in at the same time.

Both Samuel and Jason became officers, but their mother entertained some mistrust:

And another thing with the police department, I don't feel that it has been white by chance. I feel that it's been white because that's what they wanted it to be. Jobs were passed down from generation to generation, within families.

When I went to Jason and Samuel's graduation, I could see that was still true, people of color were really very limited in number, far fewer than in the general population.

Now, Samuel went in because he passed. And he's waiting . . . using this as a stepping stone. You know, a lot of police are lawyers. So he's in for that reason. . . . That's how they happened to be policemen.

The Nestor brothers' stance toward the police department both resonates with that traditionally drawing white officers, and also dramatically differs. For them, it is a good job, but it is not a way of life. A stepping stone to other things, a job in law enforcement is something to do while deciding on a life's work, a place to be that will do no harm to a career but is not the career itself.

For Chris Cooper, service in the police may not have harmed him vocationally, but it was certainly not free from injury. Chris came away from his time there with deep resentment over what he identified as racial discrimination:

I knew that I had a scholarly interest in policing. I knew that I wanted at some point in my life to engage in policy research, to improve and/ or ameliorate conditions in police work. But I realized how important it was that I have practical experience. . . . You have to be there to know where someone is coming from.

*Beth: How did your fellow officers regard your graduate studies?*

Chris: For a lot of them, but not all, in a very negative fashion. In my department there was always a sense on the part of black officers that the department was very enthusiastic about white officers who pursued higher education and that black officers were discouraged from pursuing higher education.

I remember a captain calling me into his office one night, I say "one night" because I pretty much worked the midnight shift, and prior to the beginning of a tour of duty he called me into his office, and he says, "I hear you're taking more classes than allowed by the police department." And he told me that if he ever found out that I was doing more coursework than allowed, that's a time issue, that he would bring me before a police trial board, basically he would try to have me terminated. This was a white captain.

I always felt, and my fellow black officers who noticed, and some liberal white officers noticed, that those whites who were in school were always given an opportunity to study when they had exams. They were given what we call the hospital detail, because in the hospital detail you can study. You can sit with a prisoner and study. Or you're given a station assignment. In other words, white officers were always encouraged to pursue academics, whereas I always felt, I always had the fear that the department would find out that I was taking more than the allowed amount of coursework.

[There were] white officers who we used to refer to as the Great White Hope. . . . This is a police department that had a large number of black officers and a large number of blacks in the ranks and at the time a black police chief. This is a police department that for years refused to integrate. It was under the Barry administration that the department hired a large number of blacks. In other words, Marion Barry, a black mayor, made it a point, and it was proper for him to do that, to hire black police officers.

So the Great White Hopes were those white officers of the old school who, we as black officers [believed], hoped that these white officers would once again regain control of the police department. That's why we called them the Great White Hopes.

I want to make it very clear that there were many, many white police officers in the Metropolitan Police Department who were friends of black people. So I'm not trying to criticize all white officers. But there were still some white officers who wanted to maintain political control of the police department.

And then I had to deal with those white officers who harbored very racist stereotypical views, and they thought it was very odd and unusual that a black male would pursue an education, and that appears deep. I mean, many of the close-minded white officers I ran into never believed it. They were convinced that I was lying, that there was no way that I could be pursuing a Ph.D. They did not believe that any black person had the intellectual wherewithal to pursue such a high academic degree.

The Diallo officers do indeed reflect the old policing order. The NYPD has become a little more diverse over the years, but by 1999, significant disproportions still existed:

> In New York City, 25 percent of the general population is black, but only 13 percent of the NYPD is black; 27 percent of New Yorkers are Hispanic, but only 18 percent of the NYPD is; and 9 percent of the City's population is Asian, while Asians comprise only 1.5 percent of the NYPD. By contrast, only 39 percent of the City's population is white, but 67.5 percent of NYPD officers are white. In short, in a City where minorities account for 61 percent of the general population, they comprise only 32.5 percent of the police force. Moreover, according to the 1990 census, women comprise approximately 53 percent of New York's total population. However, they account for only 13.8 percent of the NYPD.[5]

Worse still are the figures for leadership. By 2008 only 3.7 percent of leadership positions were held by black men and women.[6] At the time Amadou Diallo was killed, black police officers comprised only 3 percent of the elite Street Crime Unit to which the officers belonged.[7] The SCU was 90 percent white.

Still reacting to how cops insist anyone not there cannot comment on what happened, Chris dramatized one of the many contradictions obvious to him:

It's interesting, when we look at how police officers will piece together that crime involving that black man who they're saying killed that person—I mean, trying to show that Joe murdered Sally. And the police and the prosecutors say that they are so sure about what happened. They weren't there, but they always say that they are absolutely sure they got the right man. Yet, look at all the black and non-white Latino guys who spend years in prison for something they didn't do. "This is what this guy did and this is why he committed that heinous crime, and we're so sure of it." And, "Here you go, Prosecutor." And, "You have a prime facie case, and you can make this case, we're so sure of it."

But notice when it comes to police officers, specifically white police officers gunning down black and Latino people, gunning down people of color, you always have to put up with this *crap*, the you-weren't-there arguments.

## Rooted in Policy

Divisions and power struggles inside police departments are rarely witnessed by the average citizen. As with many organizations that present a public face to the public, law enforcement groups have an interest in maintaining an appearance of solidarity. They operate as political units in a highly contentious world of policy making and funding. Here again are where the dynamics Stuart Hanlon described play a role. The tendency to see themselves as warriors in a battle, whether with society as a whole or with a segment of society, feeds the desire to privatize inner dissension.

They are able to do so because of policies like the forty-eight-hour rule. Lorraine went on to talk about such police policies:

> Those are the kind of things you have to question: what is it in our policies, in our methodologies, in our strategies, that are encouraging, fostering behavior that we would find abhorrent?
>
> *Beth: I want to ask the question that lies behind that one. If there are policies that protect wrong-doers in the department, what does that say about the political system? Why are the mayor, the commissioner continuing those policies?*
>
> Lorraine: You know, it's funny, because I've asked that question; I've never gotten a straight answer. I don't know why that policy's in place. No one can ever really explain that. I'd be very curious if you ever

interview the commissioner, that would be something very important
to ask. If you answer that question, your book will be a hit. I think the
civil rights commission asked that question. I don't believe that that
question has ever been accurately or appropriately answered. Because it
defies logic. And that's only one of the rules. I think that's a significant
one, but it just defies logic, absolutely defies logic.

"Those institutionalized things are like a conspiracy," said Stuart
Hanlon, dramatizing Lorraine's words and also contradicting her analy-
sis, "because they give people the opportunity to cover up their stories."
Lorraine talks about an absence of logic, Stuart about its presence. Where
Lorraine sees irrationality, Stuart suggests a hidden logic. I do not think
Stuart meant "conspiracy" in a literal sense, but his metaphor is meaning-
ful. Conspiracies are purposive covert acts intended to further a particu-
lar agenda of some people at the expense of others.

At the overt level, the forty-eight-hour rule is not without a certain
coherency. According to the American Civil Liberties Union, the rule
was created to balance the legal requirement that government employees respond to inquiries about events connected with their public duties.
That law supersedes the right of an individual against self-incrimination,
where civil matters are concerned. The forty-eight-hour rule, which eventually became a matter of contract for New York police personnel, offered
officers a chance to sort out their obligation to report from their need
for self-protection. The ACLU argues, however, that such a rule is not
needed, because where criminal charges are in the offing the requirement to report is superseded by Fifth Amendment protection against self-
incrimination. In the event, the rule has become a strategic advantage for
law enforcement employees, privileging their ability to construct a self-
interested story. Clearly, their interests are served. But if those interests
conflict with the public good, why do the police commissioner, mayor,
and other officials concur?

The question of political collusion in departmental dynamics chips
away pieces of the over-painting to reveal the wash beneath. To get elected,
candidates cater to an electorate filled with people who fear crime. "The
last twenty, thirty years," said Stuart Hanlon, "every politician has run
on a war on crime, the evil of criminals. Really, there are so many evils

in our society that crime is just one aspect of, housing, education, food shortages, you can go on and on. And yet we talk about crime, and the police are given [a mandate to make war against it]."

One version of how those dynamics may have played out in the Diallo case was offered me by Sid O'Conner, a New York police officer with sixteen years experience on the force. He himself was once indicted on a brutality charge, accused of "dropping" a hand-cuffed suspect to the sidewalk and rendering him unconscious. Sid was acquitted, but the experience left him embittered toward the department he had served so long. From that perspective, he created an imagined narrative of the Diallo shooting very different from the story acted out by John Patten in the courtroom. Sid had no reticence about Monday-morning quarterbacking:

> I know how it came about.
>
> They have a Street Crime unit. They go out. They were doing the type of job that my partners and I were doing, proactive policing, looking for the bad guy, the gun carrier especially, the stick-up man. Right? Because they pose imminent danger to cops and to the public as a whole. So the more guns you get off the street [the better], and that's what they're looking for, gun carrying guys.
>
> Now, the cops of the Street Crime Unit are young cops. They've flooded that unit, which does a narrow and specific job, a very difficult job, getting guns off the street. They flooded the unit with, I'm not saying these cops are rejects, but sometimes they flood them with rejects from the precincts, [guys] who didn't have the experience to be there, who didn't earn the right to be there. I really don't [exactly] remember the reason they did it. But they increased [the SCU] by two hundred cops.
>
> Now what they did was they went around to precinct commanders. They said, "I want two cops on patrol from every precinct." Okay? So what my precinct commander does? I'm a police sergeant. He takes two of the guys from my squad who are the biggest screw-ups and goes, "This is a great opportunity to get rid of these guys."
>
> So if this goes on once, this goes on thirty times. You know, maybe the majority of commanders said, "Take my two best guys and give them this opportunity." But the two best guys only had two years on the job.

And so you've got two guys who work in Central Park precinct, who've never seen a crime, basically. Okay, "I'm going to take these two guys because, they're my best summons writers, and they want to go somewhere. They haven't made arrests, but they're good guys. They're sharp guys. But they've never made an arrest, and they're good summons writers. So I'm going to give them to Street Crime, because they deserve it."

So I know from personal experience he took the two biggest screw-ups I have. The two biggest, heavy-handed, don't-know-how-to-talk-to-people screw-ups. Who I was always on, always on. So, this happened once, this happens twenty times. So they flood the unit. They flood this unit with people who don't know how to do the work. And very dangerous, very specific work.

And now you have the cowboy mentality. All right? You go out there, you're kind of reckless, or you're pushing the envelope. Hence I guess "cowboy" came to be a public term in talking about cops who run around like idiots. You know, me being one of them. So they don't have the experience to do the work, and they're out there looking and trying to make something happen.

Now, in my experience, in my partner's experience, you look for something out of the ordinary. The way I can explain it is, my ordinary is not like your ordinary. I basically live in the precinct where I work. I'm there more than I'm home, with overtime, and I'm on patrol and I'm always looking. And you know the faces and you know the names and you know the corners and you know the back alleys.

I'll give you an example. You see a guy, you know he's a drug dealer. And every day he looks at you the same way. Either he waves, he smiles, he gives you the finger, or he turns around or ignores you. Okay. You passed this guy a hundred times a day, six days a weeks. Same reaction, same reaction, same reaction.

And this one day, he looks and walks away quickly, turns his body and walks away quickly. Now, that's not out of the ordinary, is it? But it's out of *my* ordinary. It's out of what I've attuned myself to, in knowing my area and knowing what goes on.

And so I go after him. And I'm going to stop him. I'm going to say, "What's up with you?" I'm going to toss him. He didn't do something wrong here, but it's out of my ordinary.

So these cops [on the SCU] go around looking for something to happen and they don't really know what's their ordinary. You understand? Because they're young cops and they're going from precinct to precinct on different nights. So they're looking to *make* something happen.

Where we would pick our shots and say, "We got to stop this guy. We'll stop this guy," we may stop ten guys a night, they're trying to make something happen by stopping a hundred guys a night. They're just saying, "COME HERE [*in an aggressive voice*]! YOU LOOK SUSPICIOUS." And I'm not saying that they don't have a good heart. I'm just saying they don't know. And they're put in a position that they shouldn't be in. And I'm not talking about the Diallo cops yet. Now I'm just talking about Street Crime as a whole.

Kenny Boss is the most seasoned of them. And he's a good cop. They're all good cops. I'll just say that.

Sid's story had so far kept me mesmerized. As he brought it back to the specifics of the Diallo case, I asked whether he had known any of those four officers personally. "I know Kenny Boss and I know Richie Murphy," he replied. "After the fact, I've known them. I've worked with them in my present assignment." He then placed himself inside the divided courtroom John Patten had described: "The other two I met the weeks of the trial as I went up there."

Sid picked up the thread of his imagined narrative:

But they're looking for something. They're looking for anything. Now they pulled down his block and maybe this is out of their ordinary, you know, the guy standing and ducking back.

Who knows what happened, right? There's three sides to every story. There's my side, there's your side, and there's the truth. So who knows what's happened.

Whatever, they catch his eye, or for whatever reason the four of them all go in to approach this guy, and stop him, for whatever reason. They say he's the rapist or fits the description, or they just want to toss him because they think he has a gun or they think he's a burglar. Who knows?

But the conversation is quick. It's like, boom! "We're stopping this guy." They know within a split second, there's a word or a buzz word in the car, that they're going to stop this guy.

They walk up on him and whatever happens, he panics, he panics. He doesn't understand English. He turns.

The first one to fire is in a position where he shouldn't be. He shouldn't be in the point position because he . . . I don't think his persona or his experience [*pause*], umm, he should not have been in that position.

Sid explained the kind of cover the officers should, according to procedure, have taken when stopping someone they did not know to be unarmed—shielded by their car or some other object. Apparently, criticism of the officers' disposition was common in the police force. Said a police trainer:

Cops have told me they were really poor tactics, they never should have been in that close, they never should have been there, they should have been behind cars. Tactically they made errors as well. They put them in the situation where even if he had a gun and had turned around, they should have been in a tactical position where it wouldn't have mattered. So, on the inside, a lot of cops believe that.

Sid continued his story:

And once the first shot is fired, everything breaks loose, the other cops are shooting, as a response, because the ricochets are coming out, because the flashes are lighting up against the back door and it looks like he's shooting now.

[*His voice rising with emotion*] You say to yourself, "My partner is shooting! This guy's got to be shooting." So it turns into an ugly, ugly tragedy.

In the end, Sid's critical eye moved from the cops to the department. I thought of Gerry's definition of Us against Them as Sid said:

But I can't blame so much the four cops, as I can blame the police department. I have a general idea, but I'm not going to cast aspersions on their experience. Because I've been involved in eight shootings and everyone of them, I've been lucky, every one of them is different. So I'm not going to Monday-morning quarterback them, because it's been done enough.

But I can say with a clear conscience that at least a couple of them didn't deserve to be there that night, didn't deserve to be put in that situation. Just because they were inexperienced.

In common with all the others I heard from white policemen, Sid's commentary on the Diallo shooting did not include any consideration of race. Nobody speculated on how the matter might have resolved differently if the perceived rapist had been white. But if race was absent from these stories, class was often subtly implicated. Even as Sid ended with the familiar Monday-morning-quarterback disclaimer, he also suggested that the culprit in the story was organizational. Sid could not say why the SCU came to be "beefed up," but it was very clear that the decision grew very directly out of the political climate of New York at the time. Headed by Mayor Rudy Giuliani, a politician whose popularity depended greatly on his tough-on-crime position, the city leaned heavily toward defining criminality broadly and quelling it vigorously. "Proactive policing" was not simply an idea born in police quarters; it came from city hall.

In the end, the political winds shaping law enforcement strategies were what soured Gerry's romance with policing:

What turned me off on police work was like when the crack wars were going on, all right, they were more worried about corruption than the rampant drug dealing on the street.

*Beth: And who's the "they" in that sentence?*

Gerry: The brass. And they didn't want us making drug collars. Leave that for the crack units. But the crack units weren't big enough or out there enough to see the drug dealing that we were seeing. And so the drug dealers were getting a free ride. We knew who the players were. It was very easy. I'm out there every night. Here's the same guy every night at the same corner. And this guy's the bank. This guy's the steerer. This guy is the man who holds the stash. This is the guy who is the muscle, he's the guy who is holding the gun. Right?

We knew who everyone was, and we could have done narcotics arrests, but they were frowned on. Seriously frowned on. So we would just try and get the gun. So we would always be focusing more on the muscle man, the guy who had the gun.

And the dealers themselves became wise that we were just after the weapons. And then the weapons would be stored inside bodegas or stashed inside parked cars. They wouldn't be carried on any one person. There would be mules. Females would be hired; they [the supervisors] didn't want us searching females, you know, for lawsuit reasons. And they [the drug dealers] were stashing the guns on females, because they knew that we were hesitant to search females, and we didn't have enough female officers back then on the midnight [shift] to call a female all the time to search a female suspect for us.

So, there used to be a lot more guns on the street, but now . . . And that was during the Koch and the Dinkin administrations. Giuliani uncuffed us a lot. He said, Okay, we are going to make narcotics' arrests. And so on the precinct level there were drug units. And the patrol officers were no longer frowned at if they made drug collars. And then he also expanded the borough-wide and the city-wide drug units. And everybody cracked down on drugs. Then he had the Street Crime Units target for guns. And I think that's one of the reasons why crime has come down so much in New York, and it's still falling today.

*Beth: So you support the measures that Giuliani took?*

Gerry: I supported that, yeah.

But then he turned around and . . . You know, Dinkins openly did not like cops. But at least he was honest about it. You know, I could actually respect him more than Giuliani because he was honest about it.

Giuliani, he was all for us doing the job, but he would never acknowledge our productivity gains, and he never would help us with contracts. And that really soured a lot of people.

The job now has [*pause*] less and less over the years, has had less and less respect for the lower ranks. Like that's another thing that turned me off. When I was a rookie cop, you were expected to know what an arrest situation was. You didn't need to call the supervisor to every arrest situation for the boss to make a determination, Yeah, lock him up.

Now you have to call the boss. The boss has to verify every arrest, before you bring them in.

All of these swerves and shifts in policing policy reflected political stances of those in power. In the process, the ordinary cop had come to feel his authority and power corralled, steadily subordinated to the goals of the political leadership. Even when, at last, a mayor was elected on the basis of his alliance with the police, even when the more strident strategies that grew from that collaboration coincided with falling crime rates, Gerry's grievances were not allayed. He might have more permission to go after the drug dealers, but at the same time he needed more bureaucratic vetting from "the brass." His department might make the mayor shine, but the favor was not returned in the form of generosity when salaries were on the bargaining table.

If policing practices reflect individual ambitions, feelings, and beliefs; if flesh-and-blood people in uniform are also the raw material of institutions with a will to thrive; if avenues toward security for those organizations intersect political dynamics in the larger society, then in order to understand more profoundly how all that works, we must reveal and examine the under-painting; we must talk about how politics contributed to the moment when forty-one shots were fired.

# Policing and Politics

## *In City Hall*

> Giuliani got elected on the basis of the liberal vote, friends of mine, friends of yours, people who normally don't vote that way, who figured that a fascist society, a police society is better than what we had before, because it's safer.
>
> —Stuart Hanlon

> Although Mr. Giuliani was asked several times how he could answer concerns in the neighborhood about police brutality, he did not directly answer.
>
> —Elisabeth Bumiller, *New York Times*

SID O'CONNER'S ANALYSIS of the Diallo shooting is heavily grounded in politics, both of the electoral and the departmental kind. There is a profound interaction of those two factors with a third: how, under the influence of media and political rhetoric, the public thinks about crime and policing.

Everyone I spoke with about racial profiling talked about it in terms of the individual cop's perceptions and decisions. But the officers seeing people that way, making those split-second decisions, tend to be in neighborhoods that are predominantly "minority" (an increasingly inexact nomenclature as urban America becomes all-minority terrain), and that fact is based in policy, which in turn relates to political positioning, which in turn plays on popular fears of crime, which in turn are, at the very least, fanned, at the worst created by public commentary from politicians, as well as by other cultural expressions.

Crime is today, and has been often throughout the history of the United States, a politically advantageous string to pluck. The electoral success of New York Mayor Rudy Giuliani rested on his determination to control crime in his dominion. Said Stuart Hanlon, a San Francisco defense attorney who has represented many a noted progressive prisoner:

> I mean, New York is a classic example. Giuliani got elected on the basis of the liberal vote, friends of mine, friends of yours, people who normally don't vote that way, who figured that a fascist society, a police society is better than what we had before, because it's safer. I've been appalled by friends of mine in New York who basically supported Giuliani. They'll say, "We don't really like him, but. . . ." And what they're really saying is, "We're tired of all these black and Hispanic criminals, and we've got to stop them, to make this a safe place to walk and raise our kids." And I say to them, "Well, Singapore's safe; would you want to go and live there?" And they look at me like I'm nuts.
>
> So there's that aspect of it, that we've accepted the war on crime and the police are getting a mandate to go deal with that. And in New York it's gotten to the point where the mandate is to arrest juveniles and near adults who are jumping subway turnstiles and smoking pot on the street. And that's accepted these days by liberals, it's okay.

Giuliani's dedication to a policy of attacking "Quality of Life" crimes quickly earned him a part-popular, part-facetious association with the squeegee men of New York, those notorious people who used to accost the windshields of automobiles stopped at red lights, squirting and mopping away at filth over the protest of drivers who then were asked for recompense. Giuliani's theory was that if misdeeds on that level were cleared up, an environment would be created that discouraged more serious crime. The squeegee men all but vanished.

Few mayors have been more insistently supportive of the NYPD than has Giuliani, and he demonstrated that position soon after the Diallo officers were acquitted. Given the anger and mourning in communities of color, the mayor's commentary was particularly telling:

> With regards to the Diallo verdict, Giuliani said, "If police officers act in the line of duty to protect a community against violent criminals and

drug dealers, then that community should stand up and support them when police officers' lives are put in jeopardy." Although Mr. Giuliani was asked several times how he could answer concerns in the neighborhood about police brutality, he did not directly answer.[1]

The mayor commonly equated drug offenses with violent crime and emphasized the heroic nature of law enforcement's actions. So ardent was he in his partisanship that he occasionally ran afoul of minimal levels of propriety. When Patrick Dorismund, a twenty-six-year-old black man and an unarmed off-duty security guard, was killed by an undercover cop on a Manhattan street, the mayor quickly weighed in. A press report described the killing and Giuliani's response:

> An undercover officer shot Dorismond [*sic*] during a scuffle that started after plainclothes police officers approached Dorismond and asked if he would sell them drugs. Dorismond did not possess any.
>
> His death was the fourth shooting of an unarmed black man by NYPD in the past 13 months. . . .
>
> Giuliani has defended the policeman. . . .
>
> "Police officers risk their lives to protect me and my family. We can give them the benefit of the doubt," Giuliani said while campaigning upstate over the weekend.
>
> The mayor, who said Dorismond had a "propensity for violence," released details of his police record, including an arrest as a juvenile.[2]

Even supporters of the mayor balked at his release of juvenile records that were supposedly sealed and confidential, especially when it turned out that Dorismund had for years stayed clear of the law. It didn't help the mayor's case when it became widely known that Dorismund was related to a vastly popular Haitian musician.

But Giuliani's excesses demonstrate something more than a politician's ideology. Reelected in 1997, his views reflected something compelling in the consciousness of a diverse electorate. Stuart Hanlon, the left-leaning defense attorney from San Francisco, had attributed Giuliani's election to the "liberal vote," friends of his who opted for a sense of safety over their political principles. But Stuart himself then reflected on the contradictions involved:

You know, trusting cops is not so bad. I mean, I have two children, and when you're raising children and there's trouble, you call the police. That's what you do: if you have trouble you go to the cops. If I have trouble at home, I'm going to call a cop. The same cops I may try to tear apart in court, when I'm in trouble, I go to them.

So this whole black and white view that cops are bad is not fair, because you have to remember they're not all bad. We all go to them in times of trouble. It's a very complicated issue. They're just mediocre people, but they have the power of a badge and a gun, and we expect them to be close to perfect. We're hiring them to represent a society that's not perfect, and they're being trained by people who are not perfect, and we're not going to get close to perfect people in the job. And yet we're outraged when they do something terrible.

Nor are white citizens the only ones to invoke police presence. Communities of color, too, ask for protection, but with critically different consequences. Too often the latter live to regret their insistence. Cora Barnett-Simmons is an ex-probation officer and now a social worker dedicated to working on domestic violence in the Bronx. She described the dilemma of women of color who need protection from violent men folk but fear violence from the police as well. She told a story to underscore the concern:

I remember there was a situation where there was a domestic violence incident. The woman called the police. Her husband is dead now. You know, he's dead. They killed him.

Well, he was beating her up. But she didn't want him to get killed. You know, they came in there, they used excessive force. This was not what she wanted, you know.

So, in that particular area, when you work with families, the training [we give women] deals with how you can really use the system to work with you, and to help you, and to protect you. But in the meantime, don't kill your family members off. You know, that's not what she wanted. She didn't have a husband. I mean, she just wanted him to stop hitting her. But the [police] came him in and he was dead. They killed him.

That some communities must choose between being terrorized by violence on the streets or at home and being terrorized by police patrolling their neighborhoods is a very bad choice, indeed. But it is an equation people in communities of color address all the time. In addition to sitting on the Civilian Complaint Review Board, Lorraine Cortés Vázquez is also the president of the Hispanic Federation. Started in 1990 by the United Way, her organization was created to coordinate the funding of organizations in Hispanic communities around the New York City area. At the time I interviewed her, Lorraine told me her roster included sixty-six organizations to which the federation distributed close to a million dollars a year. In addition the Hispanic Federation advocated for issues affecting their membership. Among other activities, they surveyed Hispanic New Yorkers annually and published the results. One of their research areas was policing.

When Lorraine told me the story of how she'd come to sit on the CCRB, I got the impression of a less-than-smooth relationship with Mayor Giuliani. He had approved her appointment with some reluctance, after she had been chosen by the political leadership of the Bronx, where she lived.

But when I asked her about how people in her community felt about Giuliani's crime-fighting policies, what she said was far more measured than I had expected:

> You know, it's really funny because [*speaking slowly*] the way I try to balance that is to say that this city has improved over the past nine years in major ways. When the Hispanic Federation issues its annual survey of the Latino community, Latinos say that their neighborhoods are safer. Also in our survey, Latinos say they're enjoying a better economy. We have more people employed. But Latinos are also saying that they're being terrorized by the police, and that they also know that police treat Latinos very differently from others.
>
> We've seen crime go down, but the thing we can't have is a police department that's run amok. And one of the things that we have found is that during the late eighties, early nineties, we were having major crime epidemics, and there was a need for strong and aggressive street law enforcement. However, crime statistics have gone down since then. Yet some of those same police practices have not changed. So what is happening is because those tactics have not changed. And since they've not changed, more and more innocent people are being abused.

The dilemma of policing from the perspective of the citizen is clearly articulated in Lorraine's statement. On one hand, people seek protection from crime. On the other, vulnerable communities find themselves fearing the very forces they have, sometimes, invoked. Like the ever-reproducing brooms magically created by the Sorcerer's Apprentice to do his dirty work, policing dynamics take on a life of their own. Law enforcement organizations created for a particular purpose fight for life after that purpose has been accomplished, casting nets ever more deeply into community life with greater and greater blurring of lines between guilt and innocence.

How all of that works, how populace, politicians, and police officers interface in a compelling dance around the status quo, is well illustrated by the history of SWAT teams. First conceived in 1966 by Daryl Gates (at the time a detective with the Los Angeles Police Department and later an infamous chief of that organization), these Special Weapons and Tactical units, used in large cities in violent situations, gained substantial vigor in the 1990s. President Clinton had come to the White House promising new crime-fighting resources. In 1994, he delivered in the form of a crime bill providing federal funding for 100,000 new street cops throughout the nation as well as millions toward building technological capacity to aid law enforcement. Both these sources helped to build heavily armed groups of police in small and middle-sized cities across the land.

Fresno is a case in point. A city of 400,000 people, Fresno is a commercial center in the highly agriculture Central Valley of California. Its population includes large numbers of Latino people, both migratory workers and well-settled residents, and an African American community on the southwest side of the city. It is here that Fresno's SWAT team became most active after its enhancement with federal funds in 1994. Its numbers increased from 400 to 655 by 1999, and its technological apparatus achieved a place among the nation's most advanced, thanks to a federal grant of $28.4 million that bought, among other things, a computer system in patrol cars in wireless contact with electronic notepads, with the capacity to inform officers instantly of everything from outstanding arrest warrants to Department of Motor Vehicle records.

Officer Edward McMellon gives a piece of evidence back to his lawyer while testifying about the shooting of Amadou Diallo. *AP/Wide World Photos.*

This high-tech SWAT team was deployed in the southwestern ghetto with the blessings of the NAACP and local citizens. Drug activity and violence had been escalating in recent years, thanks to a combination of political and economic factors—the recession of the 1980s, rapid development of agricultural land for suburban growth, the deterioration of social services in favor of that development, and so on. A new force called the Violent Crime Suppression Unit was deployed. Heavily armed, clad in military attire, the VCSU occupied the streets, using stun grenades and other sophisticated weaponry to subdue and arrest those suspected of gang membership.

Soon, street violence did indeed diminish. By that time, the VCSU had become a force to be reckoned with. The federal grant increasing the Fresno Police Department's size ran out after three years; payroll for the additional officers took an ever larger bite out of the city budget, until by decade's end it accounted for some 45 percent.

To justify that expense, the VCSU began to redefine its purpose. Now it pursued "lifestyle" crimes, simple misdemeanors like parole violation that required little if any forceful intervention. The African American and Hispanic communities began to complain that their neighborhoods had become occupied territory, a perception mirrored in the military metaphors favored by the police force. The NAACP changed its position, demanding the withdrawal of intrusive policing from the southwestern ghetto.[3] Here indeed was a police force "run amok," in Lorraine's phrase.

Fresno is an extreme example of a phenomenon happening all across the country. Heavily armed militaristic units abet the work of undercover street units like New York's SCU. Mayor Giuliani plucked the crime chord to get elected, then reelected, and now an organizational will to live compels the continuing expansion of the SCU. "Those strategies are incongruent with the lowering crime rate," said Lorraine, "and the commissioner and the mayor are taking an incredibly long time to recognize that."

"Why do you think that is?" I asked.

> I think that the mayor has made his reputation on law enforcement, on being a strong law enforcement mayor, and that's his policy. I don't know that he's been able to, or has had strong advisors who have told him that that was effective when necessary, now we need to maybe look at new strategies. And I don't think that that has happened. I don't know if he's not getting the advice or I don't know if he's not taking the advice. Given some of his patterns, it could be either way.

Political momentum, national and local, joins an institutional will to live to redefine not just the parameters of policing, but the very definition of criminality. "More and more innocent people are getting caught up," Lorraine said. Kenneth Boss and Ed McMellon confronted Amadou Diallo because he "looked suspicious," a subjective assessment that transformed Diallo from an innocent into a suspect. But they were patrolling the Soundview neighborhood to begin with because it was believed to be a place where people walked the streets carrying concealed weapons, and it was their mission, remember, to get guns off the streets.

We return, then, to that central question left unanswered in Judge Teresi's courtroom, why the four officers were where they were. Notions of who the criminals are inform decisions by law enforcement people to be where those people live and in turn fold back on themselves in suspicions that the people they find there are armed and dangerous. Meanwhile, young men in those communities feel besieged. "My mother was a good mother in warning me to be careful, in warning me to watch out," Chris Cooper had told me. "On the one hand I wasn't to see them as the enemy but to be cautious. But on the other hand I was to see them as the enemy."

Definitions of criminality have always been debatable. However tempting it is to define a criminal as one who breaks the law, in practice nothing so simple is real. Guilt is a socially malleable quality. While criminologists contend with the question of what crime is, for the lay citizen legal rules generally resonate with moral ones. We are brought up to know right from wrong: it is wrong to take other people's property and to do violence to others. Laws against burglary, robbery, extortion, assault, rape, and murder seemingly stand beyond dispute.

But there are many flies in that too-smooth ointment, and they buzz most loudly around questions of race. A strong thread lacing together matters of race, crime, and politics is the subject of drugs. Although they did not enter directly into the Diallo case, they are very closely tied in to the creation of a popular certainty in the violent criminality of black and Hispanic men. Terence Hallinan was at the time I interviewed him the elected district attorney of San Francisco, a man of progressive politics who ran for DA, he told me, because he believed the position would allow him to impact concrete change. He and I talked about one place he hoped to have an effect, the controversy surrounding sentencing for cocaine offenses:

> In California, almost every drug with the exception of marijuana and amphetamines, is a felony. Even the smallest, tiniest amount of crack cocaine, or one rock. We had one case recently where the police got

mad at us because we didn't file a felony against a guy who had been arrested with one tenth of one gram (or three hundredths of an ounce) of crack cocaine. . . . That is to say, marijuana and amphetamines are basically white people's drugs. Everything else that minorities use are straight felonies.

Here, too, politics matters. How much cocaine in which shape constitutes a felony is a debate masking profound social questions of resource distribution, power, culture, and on and on. When people of one race are judged more harshly, for whatever reasons, than those of another, the implications spread outward, widening circles of tension between American ideals of equity and realities of social injustice.

Definitions of crime become a potent source for manipulating power, allowing politicians—mostly white politicians—to prosper by building armed forces that interact with the citizenry in brutal ways. That this dynamic happens against a background of endemic racial disparity creates a context in which crime and race become identified. I have argued that to see crime as a phenomenon of men of color is self-fulfilling.[4] As John Lamberth's studies show so clearly, we define actions by these men as criminal, expect that they will be armed, and then examine them far more closely to see whether in fact they are, forgetting that no such epidemic scrutiny of white men is taking place.[5]

Once identified, arrested, charged, men of color then undergo the dynamics of the courtroom that we saw in the trial of Diallo's killers. Race is ruled out of consideration, and law that itself embodies racial disproportion is disproportionately applied. These multiplying factors escalate once in prison, producing a population of disaffected men with few prospects for "normalized" lives once released. On the margins of society, they in turn are cited to justify the tactics of law enforcement personnel alert to "cues" about potential wrong-doing.

Given the overwhelming nature of this bundle of interacting forces, what is perhaps more surprising than the number of men of color who do turn to crime is the fact that the great majority do not. Viewed as Kevin and Matt describe, with suspicion and prejudice, American men of color in great numbers desire, though fewer than is right attain, the same comforts and securities as the rest of the population. Far more are managers and professionals than are prisoners.[6] In the 1990s, while unemployment rates for black men were more than double those for white men, nonetheless 70 percent of black men were in the labor market, compared with 77 percent of whites.[7] The stereotype on which police, judges, and politicians base their behavior applies in the sketchiest sense to a minority of men of color while the behavior is visited on all. In the eye of the culture, the foreground of criminalized men of color is visible, not the background of a peaceable community like the one I visited at Convent Avenue Baptist Church. The foreground of police action against young men of color is seen, not the background of police acquittals nor campaigns of politicians like Mayor Giuliani's that shape such jury decisions. Police departments carry out the policies established by civilian leaders; they enact profiling that may or may not be racist in and of itself but is surely a manifestation of a racially biased environment, and the politics of election and policy making are an integral part of creating that environment.

It is to that background I now turn. The question I want to address is not one of the guilt or innocence of particular police officers, but of the society in which we all participate.

# Background

# Seeking Answers Beyond Diallo

"We hold these truths to be self-evident, that all men are created
equal." Except if you're black or yellow or brown, or if you're a woman
[*laughing*]. . . . That's our beginning, and our laws are based on that.

—Janice Tudy-Jackson

FORTY-ONE BULLETS are an all-too evident, explosively visible manifestation of a social fault line. I have tried to show how differently that
line is read by different people. For most people of color, the line is a
thick racial one, a static slash across the social landscape of the nation,
longstanding and likely to remain so failing aggressive action. For many
law enforcers, however, the line is thin and shimmering; it divides good
policing from flawed policing. Serious though the problems those forty-
one shots may announce, in this second view the flaws are fixable, if only
we have good data pinpointing the trouble and a political or bureaucratic
will toward reform.

Police excess is a picture of the foreground. It describes a moment of
confrontation in a context little wider than a particular group of cops, or
at most a particular policing unit. Just behind it, shadowed by the vivid-
ness of the evident picture, lie the issues raised by Lorraine and Stuart,
issues of politics and policy.

Racial division is either a foreground perspective or a background
one, depending on your place in the racial ordering of America. For
David Grant, it is front and center: "As an African American living in
this neighborhood, I feel like law-enforcement officers are the greatest
threat to my life."

The evocative symbols of forty-one bullet holes, an ordinary door, and a dead man animate this powerful artwork, carried outside the Albany courtroom where the officers' trial took place. Long after the acquittal, Amadou Diallo's killing continues to epitomize the thick bundle of social and political forces that result in police killings of young men of color. *AP/Wide World Photos.*

"There was no sense of race in my thinking," said John Patten. John could only glimpse the centrality of race in the background, quite literally when he turned his back to the court and witnessed the division embodied in the seating pattern of the audience.

If any respite in the conflict between police and community is to be achieved, some reconciliation of such diverse perspectives is essential. I believe that such a reconciliation is only possible if we enlarge the frame under consideration. The question is not only about good and bad policing. It is about something much wider, much deeper, about the nature of our social contract, about the structures and values of our society.

I turn next, therefore, to sketch a theoretical framework for thinking about problems on that level, and to suggest some of the elements in play. In the next chapters I look at two of these elements: gender in chapter 8 and drug policy in chapter 9. Chapter 10 then considers and critiques some of the solutions most frequently proposed, and finally chapter 11 proposes a broader approach to change.

## Rights and Powers

"'We hold these truths to be self-evident, that all men are created equal.' Except if you're black or yellow or brown, or if you're a woman," Janice Tudy-Jackson said, laughing but describing a painful reality. That America is a land of social inequality is beyond dispute. But there is controversy aplenty about how and why.

A lawyer and an artist, her skills combined in a creative practice of conflict resolution, Janice lives in a comfortable high-rise apartment that is part of a complex she described as a little bit of real estate heaven improbably located in Harlem. It is a cooperative project built some thirty years earlier:

> The whole idea of co-ops was very new then, in this culture. It was a time of the flight to the suburbs. Usually people got married, stayed in the city for a couple of years. And as soon as you started to have children you moved to the suburbs.
>
> We weren't quite ready for that. But we didn't want to be renters. And so it was very attractive. It was made very attractive because the plan was to induce and entice middle-income whites to live in the community.
>
> So it was built on the perimeter of Harlem, right on the water— the Harlem River is right behind the building—with every amenity. We have an Olympic size swimming pool out there that's open in the summer months. It's the only ground level private pool that size in Manhattan. We have on-site parking. They built two schools adjoining the property. We have tennis courts on the other side of the schools. The markets, the bus terminal are there. There are two subway stops on the property. And it was rather reasonable. So we said, Sounds like a good deal.
>
> I had never lived in Harlem, and I said, I'm not moving there. But the cost was just so attractive. I said, Okay, we'll move in until we have our first child. And by the time it was built in '67 our first child was six months old. [*Laughter*] And we moved in and I said, Okay, I'll live here until she's school age. And that was thirty-three years ago.

I love it. I love it. I love living in this community. I love it. There is
such a sense of community that most people who aren't from the community don't see.

From the outside, any identifiable group of people may seem mono-
lithic; that is as true of police as it is of African Americans or Latinos or
any other "minority" group. But the fact is that each of these identities
contains within it a wide range of variations. Janice hinted at a particular
one within the black community, along class lines. To her, as to many
middle class white people, Harlem in the sixties meant something other
than an agreeable place to live. It represented both the best of African
American culture, the site of the Harlem Renaissance in decades past, of
literature and jazz and theatre. But it was also a slum, a dangerous con-
gestion of poverty-stricken black and Puerto Rican peoples. Harlem was
the essence of northern segregation, a ghetto where the race line stayed
stubbornly entrenched.

If the intention of the developers had been to attract white families
to Harlem, they did not succeed. "What's the racial composition here?" I
asked, and Janice replied:

The co-op is primarily African American, yeah.
　　Beth: From the beginning?
　　Janice: From the beginning, yes. It's a good question you're ask-
ing, because what happened was, before the developers could officially
market the apartments, the underground network had been at work.
And so people like ourselves started buying.
　　So by the time they opened the model apartment, it was already
75 percent sold.

Equality is a complex matter. In many ways, Janice, an African American woman, is herself privileged. Her reference to "people like ourselves"
referred to black middle-class families. As a result of her inclusion in
that particular "underground network," she came to own a comfortable
apartment, filled with artifacts brought home from many trips and with
artwork much of which she herself produced. It was in that welcoming
setting that we talked over a lovely, graciously served lunch. Janice enjoys
a standard of living at or above the national average. Yet when she said,

"except if you're black or yellow or brown, or if you're a woman," she spoke with emotion that was intensely personal.

I heard Janice's statement, in the context of the comforts surrounding us, as an expression of her identity as a woman of color as much as her lived experience as a relatively privileged woman of color. No doubt she could tell stories of personal disadvantage, how she had been treated badly and denied access to resources, injured in the myriad of ways, overt and subtle, that racism acts injuriously. But beyond that lived experience, she was speaking of something larger, and in that frame she was taking a position of advocacy for all people subjected to the ills of inequality. Janice spoke in a voice combining passion and thoughtfulness. I heard no hint of self-pity, only a call to constructive action.

She went on to elaborate her meaning:

We can't look at police and policing functions without looking at the total society. It's not something that's done in a vacuum. The police, as well as others but especially the police, are carrying out the norms of the society, the expectations of the society. I think why we focus so much on the police, is because it's *there*, it's there. But it is just a microcosm of our general society.

And that really talks about restructuring our society. We really have to reinvent our culture and our society. And the first thing we have to do is to be honest about what we're about, be honest without laying blame.

*Beth: What is it that we need be honest about?*

Janice: You think about the principles on which this country was founded, with the Native Americans even before we [enslaved Africans] were introduced to this country.

We're founded on violence.

Think about what's taught to children in elementary school. I know what was taught to me about American history. The benchmarks were the wars. That was the context. The periods were divided by wars. [*Raising her voice*] European history: defined by war. That becomes part of our expectation, our perspective on everything.

So one is violence. The other one is racism.

For whatever reason, we can debate back and forth the basis for it, the motivation for it. I don't think there's any one basis, and not one motivation for it. But it's an inherent part of our culture here in this country.

We push out the sides for the Civil Rights Act of 1964. Elastic pulls it right back because it goes against that basic premise of law, that we're founded on.

So we have to look at the society as a whole. And we have to be honest about that society. Because the police, their policies are just carrying out the norms and the values of society. And right now the values of our society say that the life of a person of color, especially a male, is worthless.

Police occupy the foreground, values and norms the background. Clearly, most Americans of whatever race are not walking around saying, or even thinking, that the life of a man of color is worthless. Nor does the average individual police officer believe himself entitled to slaughter anyone on the basis of race or anything else. Yet on the street that's how norms get enacted, not out of a specific value but rather as the result of an intertwined set of premises, beliefs, and attitudes, historically grounded, manifesting a structure of power within which each of us operates.

**Violence and Racism**

Violence in America is one among many examples of a clash between values and norms. Violence is a normalized part of life, even though most people hold respect for life and person to be a value. We tolerate violence, accept it as an inevitable part of the social scenery, even as we deplore it, even as we create programs go counteract it, fund institutions to control it. Paradoxically, the principle antiviolence actors, the police, are themselves violent.

"Get real," a reader may exclaim. "You can't actually expect nonviolent policing when there are guns on the street and drug dealers and gangs to use them!" The rhetorical question begs the crucial question, because violence is a vicious cycle. Unless we find a way in, a way to break the cycle, the conscience of America will continue to be clouded by Diallos.

In fact, I do not believe it is possible to understand either police or street violence without understanding the reality of policing in America in political terms. In any society, police are the frontline of social control.

A mural by Hulbert Waldroup honoring Amadou Diallo, half a block from where Diallo was killed, counterpoises images of American equality and promise to images of white racism. *Photograph by and courtesy of Cristina Gómez.*

They enforce the laws, which in turn embody codified principles of right behavior. Whose principles they are, how they come to be articulated in legislation, who decides how they are enforced, are all thick questions, rife with politics, not just in the sense of electoral procedures, but more profoundly in terms of who holds power and in what ways.

Theories of violence divide along an axis of beliefs about human nature. On one side is a view that inclinations toward aggression are inborn, a premise found both in theology and in psychology. Christian beliefs in original sin, formulations of good and evil, theologies based in notions about lower selves in need of control through spiritual practice, all somewhere devolve from an idea that, left to our own devices, we would be selfish, destructive toward others, hedonistic.

A fundamental Freudian view of human dynamics, while very different in crucial respects, shares a dualistic understanding of impulse in need of social control. Freud, child of a Victorian era, adult in an age of fascism, saw sexuality and aggression as hard-wired instincts. In and of themselves, neither was "bad"; sin was absent from Freud's vision. Indeed, one of his important contributions was to normalize sexuality, to acknowledge its existence both in children and in women. But he believed both instincts, Eros and Thanatos (what he sometimes called the death wish), were in need of sublimation or transformation through a process of socialization that took place in the nuclear family. Unbridled and in combination, they led to anarchy and violence.

There exist contrary viewpoints, my own included, that see violence as a continuum of behaviors, interrelated, generating each other, and all seated in social rather than theological or biological processes.[1] For three decades I have done psychotherapy based on the starting premise that people are essentially good, that we seek the greatest well-being we can attain given the resources and means available. The problem, in this view, is that those means are inadequate. We are taught competitiveness and individualism, not cooperation and collectivity. Most of us grow up in families suffering from a lack of labor, a scarcity of money, a failure of community, and other structural social ills. Out of our will to well-being, we construct maximizing strategies, ways of lessening the pain and increasing the good to the greatest extent we can find within the limitations of our tools and resources. But those strategies are themselves bounded by the shortcomings of our environments. Eventually, we become caught in the very methods through which we have sought escape and protection, limited in our ability to transcend them. Aggression, criminality, violence are most commonly means to an end, not simply manifestations of instinct or evil, although the ends may become lost in the momentum of the means as hope for genuine well-being fails.

I have presented very schematic statements here of all these theories of violence. I want to elaborate the elements involved, guided by the scene of Diallo's shooting but not limited to it. The first most evident fact of that confrontation is that everyone involved was male. The second is that the shooters were white; the man who in the end lay dead was black. The third is that the men who killed Diallo were performing a duty for the state.

# Coloring Manhood in Shades of Violence

Males, yeah, are always trying to prove themselves by fighting.

—Frank

I'm being slowly emasculated as a cop, handcuffed.

—Gerry

VIOLENCE IS BOTH USED AND SUFFERED by men who are at one moment victim, at another perpetrator. Although women do sometimes enact it, violence unquestionably clusters around young men: homicide is the leading cause of death for African American men between the ages of eighteen and twenty-four, and some of the most troubling of crimes in the past decade have been mass shootings by white boys in schools. But murder is not a monopoly of the young; women of all ages and races are killed by men of all ages and races, and a large proportion of deaths by gunfire are suffered by older white men killing themselves. Physical abuse of children is endemic, crossing every class and racial category. Violence, in other words, permeates society, primarily (although not exclusively, especially where children are the victims) at the hands of men, and it is in this social context that police officers, most of whom are male, are trained, whatever they are taught in the Police Academy.

The men who become cops bring with them psyches molded in the same places that have shaped us all. When men I interviewed, in and out of law enforcement, talked about violence, they expressed something more than narratives of events they had lived. Running through their stories were complex currents of emotion. It is part of men's training to understate feelings, indeed often to use extraordinarily unemotional language to convey very strong emotion. Amadou Diallo's death evoked clear feelings, rage and sorrow most obviously. But throughout my conversations with men about the Diallo case there ran another powerful emotional theme, and that is fear.

"Good cops," Chris Cooper averred, "good cops who have respect for human life . . . have courage. That doesn't mean you shouldn't feel [fear]."

Richard Murphy testified in court, "When I looked into the vestibule there was not a doubt in my mind that he had a gun. I had a sick feeling in the pit of my stomach that I was going to be shot."

Gerry told a story of capturing a man he believed to be armed inside a subway tunnel, a particularly nightmarish scenario. I asked if he was scared, and he replied laconically:

> I was feeling the adrenaline.
>
> *Beth: But you wouldn't describe it as fear?*
>
> Gerry: I was in control of my emotions. It's not out-of-control fear. But you know, you feel it. "Don't turn around. Keep walking. Keep going forward."

Quite by chance, I happened to be offered an introduction to two young men who had socialized in high school with one of the police officers involved in the Diallo shooting. Looking for a sense of the milieu in which the officer had grown to adulthood, I gratefully accepted the opportunity. I met the two friends together in a somewhat seedy hotel room in mid-town Manhattan, not my accustomed place to stay while in town but the best accommodation I had managed to secure for this particular trip. Steven arrived first, stocky and well-toned, clad in jeans and t-shirt, looking around at the setting a mite uncertainly. Frank followed a few minutes later.[1] A tall and dapper young man, he settled in without a sideways glance and waited for me to invite him into the conversation I had already begun with Steven. Both white, they described the racial diversity of the social group they had shared as teenagers with the future New York cop. We roamed over the music and culture of the time for young people coming of age in Manhattan. At length the conversation turned to that topic rarely if ever absent from the experience of teenage men in America: violence. Both men had a ready store of stories. Said Frank:

I remember going to a club one time with a bunch of friends and just walking down the street, and I passed a group of kids that were sitting on a car. And as I walked by one of the kids just punched me in the head.

I mean, that was the type of thing that would happen. Just like, boom! punched me in the head. And I turned and looked at them and it was like, I'm not going to do anything. And I just kept walking.

I asked how they had felt at these moments. At first, the two men downplayed the impact:

Steven: I just saw it as how people are, at a very young age. Why that is, I don't know.

Frank: It was more just part of the environment, I think. Looking back on it, I was definitely either jumped or near some kind of violence a bunch of times. And I never viewed it really politically, at any time. I definitely viewed it as random, being in the wrong place at the wrong time or whatever, whoever was doing the violence, and it was certainly not always black kids. . . .

Steven: No!

Frank: . . . by any stretch. It was an expression of youthful anger.

But as the conversation progressed Steven admitted how scared he had been during the violent street encounters he and Frank were describing. As he spoke it became clear that what he feared was not physical pain or injury but something else:

I was just terrified, at a lot of levels. I didn't want to be played out. I didn't want to be a punk. Also I didn't want to hurt anybody. [*Laughs*] I just was more afraid that I would lose a certain status, and I really [*pause*] I was really into testing myself how far I would go, how far I could take something.

I'm sure I acted like a tough guy, but I never ever really felt like a tough guy.

The contradiction Steven articulated between how he felt, terrified, and how he acted, tough, mirrored the statements of Richard Murphy ("I had a sick feeling in the pit of my stomach that I was going to be shot") and Sean Carroll ("My God, I'm going to die"). Steven, and perhaps in some

During his testimony, Officer Sean Carroll weeps as he recounts his horror at discovering that Diallo was unarmed. *AP/Wide World Photos.*

ways the other two men as well, had to act tough, since what he feared was being seen as "a punk," as someone weak.

In this context of social status, violence becomes something other than an individual act. It is an outgrowth of group dynamics. Interaction among men is often shaped by shared ideas of masculinity to which social status is a key attachment. Each of the four police officers at the scene of Diallo's death had to be aware of the awareness of the others. To retreat, even to pause, might have subjected a fellow cop to danger, and it might also have subjected the doer to the contempt of his fellows.

For Steven, too, consciousness of the group was central. During the scene he described, everyone knew that the rules of behavior dictated suppressing fear and acting tough. Both he and Frank readily spoke about how profoundly their behavior and their feelings were sited in their social relations. Frank articulated that aspect of their street life:

Your relationship to violence, whether you were on the receiving end, on the giving end, protected because you knew these people, it definitely had a bearing on your relationship to the larger social picture, and where you stood socially.

I mean, if you didn't have friends and you crossed the wrong people, you might get beat up. And that wasn't cool. That wasn't a cool thing to be.

"It was never cool to get beaten up," Steven agreed. "Of course, you could be just walking down the street like I was and twenty-five home boys surround you, and one punches you and you run like hell."

Being "cool" meant having "back," *not* walking down the street alone. The two young men were very clear about how that worked. Frank told a story about a classmate who transferred into their school in the sophomore year and was mercilessly harassed:

This kid was shunned, and I remember him getting beat up a couple of times. He was alone. A lot of these kids that came in the second year, they either integrated quickly into the social fabric or they kind of bounced off and didn't quite penetrate.

This phenomenon of hazing the newcomer is an institutional dynamic; it can only occur in the context of an organization that defines insider and outsider. Who belongs and who does not is clearly apparent, and it matters on the level of identity, which usually translates into a profound self-definition. To "have back" is thus to belong, to be an insider.

So too the unit to which the four Diallo cops belonged defined status and identity. The Street Crime Unit, as I have said, was an elite group. Three of the four were newcomers; perhaps they needed to do some extra proving of themselves. But it is also possible that the officers on the street that night may not have securely belonged to the precincts out of which they had so recently been transferred. I have suggested that there was a sort of bogus quality to the prestige of the SCU; more than one of the New York cops I interviewed theorized that the undesirables of more ordinary units were sent away to staff the supposedly elite corps. If true, what intensity of demand to conform to group behaviors might that contradiction have induced in McMellon, Carroll, Murphy, and Boss? It takes a good deal of self-respect, of dignity and autonomy, to resist a momentum powered by fear, to overattack a man, and a racially stigmatized man at that, who may just have shot one's partner.

For Frank and Steven, the memory lacked any comparable gravity. They went on to gossip about who their shunned peer was and who had beaten him. The name Frank mentioned in this latter category elicited a chuckle from Steven. "I'm not surprised," he said and then explained to me this fellow was a friend of theirs. Their mixture of censure, amusement, and embarrassment was richly expressive. They both disapproved and admired one peer's inhumane behavior, both regretted and accepted another peer's discomfiture.

What that subtle combination of emotions suggested to me was the way in which violence becomes normalized, for us all but especially for boys and, later, men who must deal with violence both as recipients and as perpetrators. Teasing, often in reality tormenting, more vulnerable boys is a very common part of being male. "Boys will be boys," we say, and we laugh away painful forms of cruelty. Frank and Steven told a story of status, how the standing of an individual was determined by his willingness to accept violence on both sides of the equation. I returned to the comment Steven had made about acting like a tough guy but not feeling that way. What were the "tough guy" things he'd done? I asked, and he replied:

> We would slap box. You would pretend to fight and you would slap each other in the face.
>
> I wasn't really a bully. Sometimes I would hang out with kids that were much tougher than I was. I would certainly watch them do some awful things, which I was happy I didn't partake in, especially happy about that.
>
> *Beth: What kinds of awful things were they?*
>
> Steven: Theft, robbery, bullying behavior, which I never felt good about, so I never really did it. I certainly saw a lot of kids in my neighborhood beat up or hassle gay guys, which I had no interest in. I thought it was ridiculous. But I certainly stood idly by, which never made me feel good either.

And then there were just fights in clubs and things like that, that I got involved in that I never should have and really wish I hadn't, but mostly it was because of the people I was with.

It was just tough guys doing macho stuff. But mostly it was a fear of looking like a punk and questioning myself whether I could stand up to somebody. Those were the two main questions.

*Beth: Questioning whether you could stand up to somebody was questioning what? Your courage?*

Steven: Yeah. Sure. Courage, whether you had it.

Frank: Yeah.

Steven: How much you would stand up for yourself.

Because you know, growing up in the city you get bullied all the time. There's no question. People come by you and grab your bag of potato chips and what do you do? Do you say, "No, come back," or do you just let it go. And I didn't want to be one of the people that said no. Unless I absolutely had to.

*Beth: Because saying no meant?*

Steven: Saying no meant you were a sissy. You were weak. [*Laughs*]

Frank: You were weak, yeah.

Steven: You didn't want people to take your stuff. I guess it was a question of boundaries. At the time I didn't see it that way. But at seventeen you're just terrified. You're terrified of everything. I was afraid. There was no question, it controlled me.

Physically, Steven was a formidable young man. An athlete as well as a thinker, he was muscular, stocky, handsome. For this confident and powerful person to talk so frankly about terror was impressive. He literally embodied the contradictions men face all the time. "You didn't want people to take your stuff," and by "stuff" I knew he meant far more than potato chips. He was talking about that elusive but universally understood quality called face, a quality closely akin to masculinity. He was talking about an acceptance by his peer group. But he was also talking about his relationship to himself, self-pride and self-respect. And on that level the choices he faced were painfully contradictory. He could "act tough" and hurt people, which "didn't make me feel good about myself." Or he could stand up for himself, despite his terror. Whichever choice he made, however, the very fact that he had attained membership in the group confronted him with the dilemma of complicity in others' violence, standing by uncomfortably while they "hassled gay guys."

And through it all ran the problem of acting in opposition to feelings, a task we often take for granted but which is actually very difficult to achieve. Emotion is a powerful force; controlling it, pretending to feelings we do not in fact have, is a complicated process. Like a child in a crib who learns not to cry at bedtime, we are challenged to overcome both affective and somatic impulses when we stand our ground while awash in adrenaline. In the process, we cannot help but lose some degree of access to feeling. Once suppressed, feeling is hard to regain. Along with fear, empathy also is diminished, for empathy is quite literally about "feeling with another." Clearly, none of us, male or female, perfectly suppresses emotion. Steven could quite honestly report his terror. But boys much more than girls are charged in the course of their development with controlling, and ultimately suppressing, a full range of emotion, and having done so they are more able to overcome the most powerful form of empathy: identifying with the victim of one's violence.

The elements involved in doing violence that are formative, thus, are making the decision to participate or not, finding strategies to handle fear, soliciting membership in a peer group, reconciling a positive sense of self with belonging to a group that did "awful things."

Not all individuals sharing a common identity do all of that identically. Even though the two young men inhabited the same social terrain, Frank's path was rather different:

> I was definitely very interested in where I fit into the social fabric of all that. But [*long pause*] my method of proving myself was not on the battlefield, so to speak. I mean, not too much, to a very limited degree. . . .
>
> I [encountered violence] less on an individual level, more on a group level. I think [*pause*] the way that I would more frequently engage the issue of personal physical violence was [*long thoughtful pause*] . . . the times that I was really presented with direct, physical violence in my experience, there was, at least I *felt* there was, very little opportunity for me to do anything. I was either totally outnumbered, surrounded by a million kids or . . .

Like I got mugged one time, and I was surrounded by ten kids with a knife to my throat and I was all alone. I had gone to some big party with a bunch of friends, and afterwards we were all at a Burger King or a McDonald's or something like that. And I went down this flight of stairs to leave. And the moment I was alone, I got jumped and surrounded. And it was all over. I lost my lunch money.

But most of the times that I was presented with the opportunity of conflict, it was in the context of groups. Like my group versus your group. And it was generally mostly talk. Don't do this or we're going to call these people, and get them on you, and they're going to call these people on us. It was sort of political more than really physical, for the most part. I mean you know, small things might have happened but it was not . . .

*Beth: Did you have a sense of needing to prove something about yourself?*

Frank: Yeah. Yeah.

*Beth: What was it that you needed to prove?*

Frank: For me, just that I was not soft. And I think the truth is [*slowly, thoughtfully*] I *was* soft.

*Beth: What does "soft" mean?*

Frank: Just, you know . . .

Steven: You didn't want to hurt anybody. [*Laughs*]

Frank: Someone averse to violence. Someone who would lose a fight.

Steven: Someone who *wouldn't* fight.

Frank: Yeah. I would probably say I didn't really want to engage anyone necessarily, but I just wanted to make sure that I was not *perceived* as weak.

"Soft," "weak," "sissy": these are driving words, embodying the ideas that "control" boys' behavior. Men are supposed to be hard (unfeeling?), strong (not influenced by feeling?), manly (not frightened? Not gay?). Furthermore, men are supposed to appear to be those things in the gaze of other men. We are all deeply influenced by the opinions of others, especially by those with whom we share a social sphere. For men, not being perceived as weak translates into expression as well as behavior. Courage, both Chris and Gerry told me, does not mean not feeling fear; it means not acting on it. Many men have described something similar, that they feel all sorts of things—sadness, fear, hurt—but that they dare not speak those feelings. Nor may they feel them powerfully enough that the emotion might threaten to burst through the bounds of manly behavior. Anger, on the other hand, is more permissible, because it is seen as a stronger way to be. What each of us can feel and how we can express it is very powerfully determined by the cultures we inhabit, cultures of gender to be sure, but also of race, ethnicity, community, and so on. White men are more likely to internalize John Wayne modes—silent and enduring until you reach the critical moment, when you turn suddenly on the enemy with two guns blazing—whereas black men may be more persuaded by outspokenly rageful figures, rap artists or media depictions of double-gun shooting antiheroes.

## In and Out of Control

Whatever version of these internalized gender and race dynamics might have been operating when Ed McMellon confronted Amadou Diallo, there was one level on which McMellon acted that is beyond speculation: he was doing a job. The qualities he brought to that job may have contributed to Diallo's death, but the reasons for being on Diallo's doorstep were about something else. How do those reasons relate to these themes of masculinity, status, and emotional control?

Gender is a fundamental conceptual category. How we "do" gender creates conceptual boxes very difficult to escape. What Steven and Frank described was a process by which they were socialized to a very particular set of ideas. Membership in their adolescent groups established clear lines of Us and Them, a process that shows up again and again in police discourse. The necessity of engaging brute force either as perpetrator or victim is very much an assumption of law enforcement. That the world can be divided up into dualistic categories so absolutely believed to be real that men can kill other humans is a phenomenon that populates the history of warfare as well as of policing. Indeed, gender itself is a prototypic dualism, only recently challenged and occasionally reconceptualized as a range. These absolute assumptions and clear-cut categories binding perceptions of the world easily intertwine with political interests to form lethal ways of wielding power.

It is easy to target the NYPD and its Street Crime Unit as emblems of brutal police overzealousness. Mayor Giuliani's adeptness in playing the war-on-crime game positioned him for greater criticism when Diallo and the other infamous New York cases happened. But in reality the NYPD was and is not very different from police departments in cities across the nation, and Giuliani's policies may have been more extreme in degree but not in kind.

Do an Internet search on the words "street crime unit" and Web pages for such organizations pop up in Hagerstown, Pennsylvania; Muscatine, Iowa; East Orange, New Jersey; Redwood City, California; Tampa, Florida; Charlottesville, Virginia; and on and on. It would be a mistake to assume that all of those groups are clones of New York's, but that they exist says something compelling. Some departments have lower statistical records of police killings of citizens, some higher. But there is a fundamental structural similarity across the board.

That similarity is expressed in the language of much policing. There is a "war on crime." Our cities are "besieged by drug dealers." Cops are the "blue line of defense against criminals." Perhaps it is too extreme to extend the metaphor more literally into the realm of advancing enemies threatening to conquer society. But there is a sense in the rhetoric, at the very least, of encroaching anarchy, that forces of disorder might engulf all of society if not contained by policing. Attorney General Janet Reno, a woman one would not expect to be characterologically given to military metaphor, addressed "members of the defense, intelligence, and industrial communities" in November 1993:

> So let me welcome you to the kind of war our police fight every day. And let me challenge you to turn your skills that served us so well in the Cold War to helping us with the war we're now fighting daily in the streets of our towns and cities across the Nation.[2]

Reno was not speaking entirely metaphorically. Although the Constitution mandates a strict separation of military and domestic enforcement, there is a history of sharing technology and, more subtly, strategy. Shortly after Reno's speech, the Clinton administration announced a program called "Technology Transfer from Defense: Concealed Weapon

Detection." It authorized the Department of Defense to share with the Department of Justice technology and training developed for the battlefield. Several items on the list might well have especially appealed to the Street Crimes Unit cops: night vision goggles, scanners to detect hidden weapons, and training programs that use computer simulations to hone quick-on-the-trigger responses to a suspect who appears to be drawing a gun.

How did people suspected of breaking a law become "the enemy"? The Cold War comparison is apt; some observers link secret police operations to counter radical groups in the sixties with the more warlike stance of law enforcement subsequently. Stories later surfaced about police infiltration in San Francisco as well as in New York, and lawsuits resulted in the revelation of secret files and provocations.

Simultaneously, the war on drugs was forming and gaining strength. To link antidrug policing with the control of radicalism may seem a stretch. Ideologically, however, both are at least rhetorically promoted as threats to a capitalist civil order. Conceptually both fall in a broad category, defense of a social order dualistically conceived and righteously defended by force.

To see this face of police, not as servants of the citizenry but as warriors against an internal enemy, is to highlight the social control function they perform as surely as Steven's slap boxing or his friends' bullying served to shape and control behavior within his group. This distinction between controlling crime and fighting an enemy became politically crucial after 9/11. It was no accident that the Bush administration immediately began talking about the "War on Terrorism." To frame the conflict that way gave license to acts of war against whole nations, including action to topple heads of state in Afghanistan and Iraq. Eight years earlier another attack on the World Trade Center failed to demolish the building but did kill six people and injure another thousand. A group of men were subsequently tried in criminal courts and convicted of the bombing. Terrorism, in other words, was still framed as crime. In 2001, however, calling the assault on the World Trade Center and the Pentagon an act of war handed the business of justice off from police to military. In the process, serious erosion of civil liberties took place. The administration could argue, with some contradiction, that the rules of war did not apply, defying the Geneva Convention on the treatment of prisoners, sanctioning torture and holding people without trial indefinitely at Guantanamo Bay. At the same time, lines were blurred between CIA, FBI, military, and police functions within the United States. Police were militarized while the military took on aspects of policing.

None of this is to say that police in New York and across the country do not often serve the people. Few people would quarrel with the idea that police should indeed intervene when one citizen does harm to another. The other day I passed a fight scene as I drove home from the grocery store. Two men were battering each other with fists and feet as a circle of onlookers stood by looking shocked and helpless. I called the police and was thankful that they arrived promptly and stopped the hostilities. When a burglar came through a kitchen window in the dead of night some years ago, I blessed 911; the dispatcher's calming voice kept me from hysteria as she directed me to barricade myself in a room until police arrived. I once gave shelter to a runaway teenager my sons befriended in the park. It turned out he had been severely beaten with an extension cord by his mother. A competent and compassionate policewoman came to the door with an order to return him to his home. He resisted, I told his story, she pursued the matter and, in the end, worked with us to have him placed with a father with whom the boy had lost contact and who now embraced him lovingly.

In all these cases, I welcomed police intervention. "When you're raising children and there's trouble, you call the police," said Stuart Hanlon. There are differences, however, among my three examples. In the first case, physical harm was at issue, in the second property rights, and in the third the right of a child to safety versus the parental rights of an abusive mother. Each incident suggests questions of increasing complexity. Who defines harm? Whose values defined the street fight as assault rather than a fair contest to settle a dispute? Are we promoting the worthiness of verbal battle over physical, and if so how do we reconcile military contradictions, such as a preemptive war against Iraq?

So also in the case of property crimes. Robbing my home is a crime; is it a crime when one company takes over another by hostile means? What about a business that dominates a town's labor market but "downsizes" its workforce, leaving employees with nowhere to go? We make laws that reflect a set of standards for a shared social order. Individualism suggests that workers be "free," that is to say, that employers have little or no responsibility to provide jobs. Private property suggests that a youngster on drugs who breaks into my house to steal my VCR is more criminal than the CEO who lays off thousands of workers.

To compare policies on drug control with those addressing corporate crime is to illuminate some of the values and norms underlying US policing. Diallo's death was not apparently about either drugs or big business. But it is connected. For Diallo died as a consequence of a particular way our society defines criminality, and a particular way political discourse plays on those definitions, and a particular policing is therefore constructed. There are questions that fall out of public discussion. Where does danger to society lie? Who exactly is in jeopardy, from whose hand? How might crime on the streets be different if the streets were dramatically different? What dynamics of privilege and control are perpetuated when we assume inbred criminality and tacitly or otherwise accede to its linkage with race?

By looking in some detail at the story of U.S. drug policy over the centuries, it is possible to problematize some of these assumptions and dynamics, to see that which today seems inevitable in an historic perspective. For it is only when we can see beyond the foreground of such assumptions that we can, in Janice's phrase, "reinvent our culture and our society." I agree: that is the task at hand.

# Underworld and Overworld

What drew us together was playing pool, drinking beer, smoking
pot. . . .

—Steven

IF YOU BROWSE THE STACKS of any major library looking for books
about drug control policy in the United States, you will be overwhelmed
by shelves and shelves of volumes. Now look for the section dealing
with white-collar crime: a shelf and a half will likely house everything
available.

Does that disproportion reflect the relative importance of the two
subjects? Does one arena affect the lives of citizens substantially more
than the other? Does one cost the nation more? Do more Americans die
because of one than the other?

One thing the two infractions have in common is that they are both
extremes of normal practices that are intrinsic to the functioning of
today's society. At a moment in our conversation, Steven interrupted the
flow to say:

> The other thing that was, I think, really critical to understanding that
> time and that milieu was that crack was huge. There were just wander-
> ing base heads . . . where we were going to high school. And smoking
> blunts and drinking forties, there was this whole street culture that was
> much more prevalent than it is today.

Smoking blunts and drinking forties, a blunt being a cigar laced with
drugs, usually marijuana but sometimes crack cocaine, and forties meaning very large bottles of beer, may have been more prevalent in the days

of which Steven spoke than today, but the phenomenon of boys and men bonding over intoxicating substances transcends time. "What drew us together," Steven said at another point, "was playing pool, drinking beer, smoking pot." Although blunts and beer may have a peculiarly masculine flavor, women, too, have long gathered around coffee and tea, wine and other alcoholic drinks. Modern American society is highly individualized, highly alienated. One of the most common complaints I hear from those who come to me for counseling is about the difficulties of maintaining friendships, of sustaining community. Life is too busy, connecting too bureaucratized—I find myself scheduling dates with friends weeks in advance, and the torture of trying to gather more than two people together at a time often results in abandonment of any group activities. It is far easier to collapse, exhausted, at home after a hectic day of work and errands and tortured transport around an overcrowded city. Human connection outside of work becomes focused on the family, except for that quarter of the American population (and growing!) who live alone.[1]

One of the few places where it is easy for adults to hang out in a friendly atmosphere is the neighborhood bar. Alcohol in the public space not only frames a reason to be together, but it also oils what can be cranky transitions from work time to leisure time. Alcohol helps intimate talk arise more quickly, makes confidences appear more meaningful. Meanwhile, there may be a particular other kind of intimacy offered as well, an invitation to the restroom to share a joint or a line of cocaine or a hit of crack. Teenagers hanging out, smoking pot and drinking beer, are in training for such substance-centered socializing.

That is one story about drugs and alcohol. It is a banal story of ordinary folks enjoying a bit of leisure. There is, of course, quite another story one could tell. On this terrain as much as any, the view changes according to the viewer's vantage point. Stand where the field of vision is dominated not by the sorts of occasional users I have just described but by people labeled "addict." In modern-day societies, the addict has become an apocryphal figure. He (or, less often if numbers in treatment are telling, she) is a ne'er-do-well, a progenitor of crime and debauchery. Hooked on crack cocaine, heroin, or one of the newer synthetic drugs like methamphetamine, he will go to any length to support his habit.

Down the slippery slope he slides into a cesspool of robbery and, eventually, violence. Upright citizens pass him with a shudder of moral horror as he slouches, disheveled, along the sidewalk, eyes cast down in distressed self-preoccupation. The only figure more villainous, more detestable, is the dealer who sells to him—or worse yet to children, enticing them with tabs of LSD or joints of marijuana to start them on the road to perdition. Both user and, even more typically, dealer are likely to be seen as black or Latino.

Such a version of the prototypic American drug story may be overdrawn, but it hits the essentials of the prevailing mainstream attitude: Drugs are evil (a word not infrequently used to describe them even in some scholarly literature). They do damage to users and innocent bystanders alike. They are at the heart of the criminal world, constituting a vast underground economy of greed and violence.

There is a companion to this story, the protagonist of which is the successful businessman. Playing on a global stage, he (again, much more often male than female, although with some notable women newcomers to the company) is smart and visionary, his gaze always scanning a future horizon in order to position himself and his corporation to advantage. This businessman enjoys wealth, and he deserves it. He foregoes an elaborate personal life for work, is always on the go, energetic, commanding, confident, accomplished. Everyone knows he may wheel and deal close to the margins of ethical purity, but that is all right because he brings to himself and, in the process, to society an ever-expanding pool of largesse. He is, with only the rarest exception, white.

Rarely does anything happen to contest the first story, of the drug addict. Perhaps occasionally a young entertainer for whom there is keen public sympathy dies of an overdose and a small space is created in which to humanize drug use. But the vision of drug addiction as linked (in the extreme, inevitably linked) with even minimal use and with profound debasement is widespread and seamless. The second figure, however, the corporate executive of socially positive character, has, as I write, exploded all over the pages of the daily newspaper. Periodically, these things happen. Cooked books at Enron, WorldCom, Tyco, Global Crossing, Xerox (each time I revise this chapter I add more names), perpetrated by seemingly impeccable fixtures in the world of accounting like Arthur Andersen, are shaking the confidence of investors at home and abroad in the honesty and reliability of American firms. "You only find out who is swimming naked," said Warren Buffett, the legendary investment advisor, "when the tide goes out."[2]

Yet even when the waters pull back and the extensiveness of submerged business practices in leading corporations is revealed, the consequent investigations and discussions suggest that these instances are anomalies, greedy excesses in an otherwise upright domain, attributable to individual weaknesses, not to the system at large. Drug-related crime, on the other hand, is talked about as if it is built into the nature of addiction, the chemically predictable outcome of the use of proscribed substances that is at base a product of individual weakness. It is natural, therefore, that narcotics be ruled illegal, thus creating a dominating agenda for policing.

There are some compelling inconsistencies that challenge these two versions of reality. For one thing, alcohol, a major intoxicant, clearly overused by some people at significant cost both to the individual and to society, can be lawfully purchased in most American communities. While it was briefly ruled illegal during Prohibition, from 1920 until 1933, it has for most of U.S. history not only been legal but occupied a place highly integrated into custom and social life. Tobacco, too, is proven to be injurious to those who use it. Both substances create victims: people killed by drunk drivers, for instance, and children of smokers who cannot escape the damages of second-hand smoke. One morning as I read my morning *New York Times,* I noticed a full-page ad. In its center was the smiling face of a very respectable appearing man. The bold headline read, "Gray Davis Gives Corporate Pushers the License to Kill." Gray Davis was at the time the governor of California. "He smothers successful antismoking programs while Big Tobacco pours $1 billion into California," the advertisement went on to claim.

That business at the multinational corporate level is fundamentally sound and only occasionally corrupt is a concept problematized by the story of tobacco, as one of many examples in recent times. Was it simply bad judgment by a particular cohort of men that hard data about the health hazards of smoking were suppressed for decades? Was Gray Davis an unusually unworthy politician because he accepted large donations from the very tobacco firms from which states' attorneys general were simultaneously seeking to recover huge damages?

If harm to self and society is the basis for outlawing particular substances, why do alcohol and tobacco remain legal while marijuana and cocaine are not? The task assigned cops is to exercise the state's powers of physical coercion to enforce not just written laws but the will of those who hold power. How that control is exercised is set in the context of political and organizational dynamics, all within a framework of definitions of masculinity and experiences of class, and laced throughout is the fault line of race. The essential role of police is not simply to keep order but to patrol a very particular social order.

Looking at the history of drug policy allows us to see this basic enforcement function of police in a social context.

Looking at the history of corporate crime helps us to see a differential pattern to enforcement. In other words, who is defined as a criminal, which laws are enforced and which overlooked, how laws are enforced and by whom, tell us something about the role of policing in the context of a particular social arrangement of power and values.

## Drug Policy, Policing, Politics

As I write, San Francisco is a hotbed of controversy, the topic being dogs. Our sophisticated and progressive city is divided into two camps: the on-leash folks and the off-leash folks. Each side has credible arguments. On-leash advocates cite a range of problems, from feces-polluted fields where children play sports to the hazards of dog bite from pit bulls and other fighting breeds. The emotional weight of their argument was vastly heightened when a young woman was killed by her neighbor's vicious dog (even though the dog was actually leashed at the time). On the other side of the dispute, too, there are compelling arguments: dog owners have a right to actually walk *with* their dogs, deserve not to be confined either to dog runs or to the halting, dawdling pace of an animal seeking the right spot to do its business. The dog-walking community, say off-leash advocates, should and can be required to act in a citizenly manner, picking up feces, muzzling dangerous animals, making sure dogs are trained to obedience. Certain spaces in parks over a certain size could be declared dog-free. But requiring on-leash walking at all times, this camp maintains, is an unacceptable infringement of deserved liberties. After months of vituperative campaigning, the city passed a regulation restricting most parks to on-leash dog-walking.

I walk my dogs around a charming little lake at the bottom of a hill. Two police officers patrol the area on slender shiny motorbikes. They are very formal, intimidating in their perfect gear, almost military in their bearing. One day, they paused beside a little cluster of us who are there daily, dogs romping happily off leash. "You know," one of them began, "I'm not sure why it is exactly, but we always seem to have a need to pause and rev our engines before coming down the path to the lake."

Translation: "We have no desire to enforce the new regulation. If you put your dogs on leash when you hear us coming, we'll give you fair warning."

On the other hand, when it comes to drugs, the response of police from this same department has been very different. San Francisco District Attorney Terence Hallinan complained, "We have one case recently where the police got mad at us because we didn't file a felony against a guy who had been arrested with one tenth of one gram (or three hundredths of an ounce) of crack cocaine."

When Stuart Hanlon, the defense attorney, accused cops of lying in the course of drug busts, he was doing something we might expect from a defense attorney. It is built into the system of criminal justice that cops are supposed to accuse people of wrong-doing, defense lawyers to maintain their clients' innocence. But we equally expect prosecutors to work cooperatively with law enforcement officers; that a district attorney is at odds with police is a product of the city's liberalization of drug enforcement policy. In 1995, San Francisco pioneered a different way to handle drug violations. A municipal drug court was established in which victimless drug offenders were sent to treatment and followed in a supportive fashion by the court as long as they complied, but sentenced to punishment if treatment lapsed. That police officers are less than cooperative with the court, as the district attorney suggests, points to ways in which law enforcement people both implement official law but also act autonomously. They are simultaneously "agents of the state" and a group with competing values and interests—a complex group, itself embodying internal contention about drugs and other matters, not to mention dealing with alcoholism and other substance abuse among its own ranks.

There is a history to controversy over drugs. Laced deeply into the making of America are strands of attitudinal shift and stormy difference of opinion about the use and abuse of intoxicants. Policies have changed over time, and those changes, I believe, flow from the evolving interests and goals of groups with power to influence, and on some level to make, policy decisions. From an outline of the history of drug policy decisions we might trace back a story of America's progression as a world power, as well as the choreography of changing power relations among different economic, geographic, and racial groups.

## Of Apples, Alcohol, and Opium

Take the most innocuous of substances, the apple. Popular mythology would have it that a man called Johnny Appleseed is responsible for the American love affair with apples. He traveled the land planting trees, eventually becoming a fetching Disney character loved by children everywhere. Because of Johnny Appleseed, apple pie is the essence of the national identity.

That is one story. Michael Pollan tells another. Pollan is a writer on subjects of nature and society. In a book called *The Botany of Desire* he tells us that Johnny Appleseed was a man named John Chapman. An eccentric businessman who lived around the turn of the last century, Chapman sold apple trees throughout what today is the Midwest and then was the frontier. In communities he predicted would develop into important farming and population centers, he chose wilderness tracts on which to establish nurseries. The apples that resulted were tart and unstable. The cultivation of a consistent variety of apple—Red Delicious or Granny Smith or whatever—requires grafting trees, essentially cloning them. But taste was not an issue to John Chapman's customers. Apples were cultivated, not for eating, but for fermenting to produce cider. "The reason people . . . wanted John Chapman to stay and plant a nursery was the same reason he would soon be welcome in every cabin in Ohio," wrote Pollan. "Johnny Appleseed was bringing the gift of alcohol to the frontier."[3]

While early nineteenth-century America was a land characterized by Puritanism, there were no injunctions against drinking cider. (Pollan comments that the term "hard cider" was redundant in those days; all cider was alcoholic.) Indeed, cider was readily accepted as a practical drink, easy to make, abundantly available once the orchards Chapman instigated began to bear fruit bountifully. Pressed, fermented apple juice is only mildly alcoholic. Applejack, on the other hand, a concoction brewed by distilling cider into brandy, is strong liquor. Settlers along the frontier brewed and drank "literally thousands of gallons of cider" every year, and presumably a fair amount of applejack. Lacking sanitary sources of water, frontier folk used cider as a healthier alternative. It brought comfort to a people who had little. In a land too cold to support grape cultivation, it was a milder and handier source of alcohol than grains. Besides, because of its association with the ritual of communion, wine was equated with Catholicism and regarded with a critical moral eye by the early Protestant settlers. "Cider became so indispensable to rural life that even those who railed against the evil of alcohol made an exception for cider."

It was only during Prohibition, Pollan contends, that the slogan "An apple a day keeps the doctor away" was promulgated. An example of the power of advertising, the apple's reputation was intentionally transformed by an alliance of apple growers and teetotalers through a massive advertising campaign. As sentiment in the country swung away from legal uses of alcohol, the apple became a very different item.

Substances—cider, apples—have a history, reflecting a society's changing attitudes, a progression that itself tells a story of economic and political change, and of struggles for power and control among different groups of people. In general, the story of intoxicants is one of celebration, social ritual, individual restoration, all the positive uses to which substances can be put, at war with restriction and control. Sometimes the latter forces operate through criminalization, sometimes through medicalization. How all these possibilities work out bespeaks a large story of relationships between social structures, like corporations, states, foreign powers, and value systems based in religious, and increasingly in modern times therapeutic, communities.

The first narcotic substance controlled in America was opium. Paradoxically, given San Francisco's current standing as a pioneer in addressing drug use through treatment rather than punishment, it was in San Francisco that the first anti-opium ordinance was enacted in 1875; it closed dens where opium was smoked, mostly by people of Chinese heritage. That ban was followed with federal legislation a few years later prohibiting the importation of opium by Chinese nationals.[4]

Focused though it was on how opium was used by imported Chinese workers, the attack on it emphasized morality over race while implicitly linking the two. Temperance crusaders took the lead, their thrust being to oppose all mind-altering, and presumably morally debilitating, substances. Morality rises and falls in a wider context; certainly it is better heeded in some climates than others. Before the assaults on opium took wing, drugs in general were integrated into daily life for many people. Opium was used, often without identification as an ingredient, in a wide variety of elixirs. Cocaine, too, was an unnoteworthy supplement to normalcy. Coca-Cola did in fact include cocaine as an ingredient. By the end of the century, heroin was in use as a treatment for respiratory problems. All these substances were readily available to ordinary folks. Distinctions between medically prescribed drugs and commonly available ones only began to become meaningful shortly before the Pure Food and Drug Act passed in 1906.[5]

Why did the evils of opium and other substances suddenly command policy attention only as the twentieth century dawned? "The drug issue emerged," writes Elaine Sharp, a political scientist at the University of Kansas, "at times when the nation was convulsed with anxieties about perceived threats from lower-social-class elements and racial minorities." She then cites the association of opium with Chinese immigrants and of cocaine with southern black people.[6] William McAllister, another expert on drug policy who is connected with the University of Virginia, comments that the Chinese influx to America was in part motivated by the havoc wreaked in China by opium importation. In turn, by the end of the nineteenth century, Americans were alarmed by "grossly exaggerated" (according to McAllister) anxieties that the drug's use was spreading to young white people.[7]

The opium trade has a long and global history. Two centuries before it entered into the U.S. legal record, that history had become thickly entangled with the age of colonialism, a phenomenon of British empire. Tea had a growing popularity in Great Britain at the time. The East India Company, Britain's institution for exercising imperial control in India, gained trading rights for buying tea from China. Opium was grown in India, in the region of Bengal that was by then tightly under British domination. By smuggling opium into China, England was able to secure revenues with which to pay for Chinese tea. Meanwhile, finished cotton goods manufactured by England's developing industry were shipped back to India, constituting a three-legged trading route and a balance of revenues in favor of Britain. So lucrative was it all that the British expanded opium growing into areas where it had not been grown before, including Burma, today a major supplier of the U.S. market.

In the midst of all this traffic, opium also found its way into the metropolis. Unhappy with the consequences for British productivity, the king's government banned its use at home at the same time that it promoted its widespread cultivation in South Asia and consumption in China. These contradictions reflect moral attitudes on the part of the British rulers, but also practical interests. The growth of industrial society demanded an awake working class; opium was better tolerated as an indulgence of the aristocracy than a vice of the proletariat. But in rural India or tea-producing China, the British government had no such interests.[8]

This combination of moral, economic, and political factors similarly shaped American policy toward opium. Opium was targeted, say scholars, because it was a source of pleasure and relief mainly for Chinese.[9] In the course of the century, Chinese laborers were imported in large numbers to build the railways. As the work came to an end, many turned to jobs on and around the docks of San Francisco, taking their practice of smoking opium with them. Where before these immigrant laborers had toiled away from the public view, now they became visible. They also came to be linked in the public perception with "working-class criminals."[10] At least in some cases, these "criminals" may well have been seamen and longshoremen who were beginning to campaign for the rights of labor. Until this time, opium use had very different associations. Throughout the 1800s it had grown in popularity among middle-class women, for whom it was condoned in contrast to the unfeminine practice of drinking alcohol. What once had seemed a benign adjunct to female gentility now took on more ominous hues, and by the turn of the century the idea of regulating its use had begun to be bruited.

These changes in perception and associations with opium were taking place in the context of other dynamics lying in the realm of foreign trade and shifting economic patterns. From early in the nineteenth century, American companies had been major players in the opium game, moving into the Chinese market with drugs from Turkey, where they had a virtual monopoly of supply. American ships also smuggled Indian-grown opium for English exporters. It was therefore in the interest of U.S. business to support the two Opium Wars fought by England and China between 1839 and 1858, ostensibly for the purpose of compelling the Chinese Imperial Court to accept imported opium, but also intended to open Chinese territories to Western trade in general. China maintained sovereignty, but they succumbed to the insistent pressure of the European nations for unfairly favorable trade conditions, and similarly to entry for the Americans. Drug trading thus not only benefited the economy but also increased America's strength as a world power.

But American shipping declined during the Civil War, and at the same time China began producing a significant amount of opium itself and importing less. International traders were also finding that the extent of opium use in China interfered with the creation of new markets for other kinds of more profitable imported goods. Meanwhile, the United States was asserting a military position as a world power with the Spanish-American War from 1898 to 1902, in the course acquiring control of the Philippines. Paradoxically, the Spanish had used strategies similar to England's in China, saturating the Philippines with imported opium, and the newly ascendant American rulers found themselves dealing with a serious drug problem. These various strategic and economic interests began to be opposed to opium, at the same time that religious and other moral antidrug forces within the United States were gaining voice.[11]

I have recounted this history in some detail because it clearly demonstrates something very contemporary. Drug dealing, international politics, and big business intertwined in a columbine trail of confusing thickness. Similar histories can be traced for other substances, for cocaine and marijuana especially. To see policy as an historic progression is to open space for questions that appear nonsensical in a static snapshot. Today we are immersed in a cultural assumption that drugs are so bad for people that it is natural to outlaw them. So widespread is the view it is often hard to see beyond it. But if we move to another vantage point, one suggested by the themes that emerge from histories of the apple and of opium, and look at current drug policy in the context of similar dynamics, something more complex emerges. Just as policies of the past were formed out of a mixture of personal and political forces, a convergence of values, concerns about individual lives, interests of economic organizations and of government bodies, so too drugs are today a point of intersection for a variety of similar things. I want to go on, then, to look at drugs at street level, how they work in a particular community, how drug dealing as a business compares with other forms of business in America. I then shift my perspective to consider the question of what consequences today's drug policy has, in other words at its function as described by the impact it actually has on individuals, communities, commerce, and governance.

Let me precede this discussion with a disclaimer: I am not an advocate for drug use. Neither, as you have probably gathered, am I its enemy. In many years of practicing psychotherapy, I have encountered many people who use intoxicants, alcohol and drugs, in moderation, in ways that add one kind of luster or another to life, without detectable injury. There are also many people who use those same substances in ways that are highly problematic. I ask my clients to consider three questions to assess their relationship to substances:

Does using those things hurt your body? That is, do you wake up with a hangover, do you drive unsafely, are you showing signs of liver or lung or sinus damage?

Second, are your relationships with other people negatively impacted? Does your mate pick up the pieces of what you have not done, or cover up messes you have made while high? Do you drink or smoke or snort when you are upset with others rather than working through problems? Do you turn to substances rather than to friends and family when you feel troubled, and thereby isolate yourself in ways that do you disservice and limit intimacy?

Finally, is your use of the substance in question out of your control? In other words, if you decide to use it in a clearly defined and limited way, do you find yourself unable to stop when you planned to? Do you start an evening determined to have no more than two drinks and instead finish the bottle? Any of these areas suggests a problem. But if there are no problems, then you are not a problem user.

On the other hand, more than a few of my clients do have problems with another category of drugs, ones that are dispensed by physicians. Critics have raised serious questions about the enormous growth in antidepressants, for instance. Prozac burst on the market in the late 1980s, introduced by Eli Lilly with an expectation of annual sales in the $70 million range. Instead, at its peak Prozac earned the company $3 billion a year in sales. Predictably, competitors seeking a share of that hot market followed with other drugs of the same or similar type, Paxil, Zoloft, Wellbutrin, and others. Prozac sales continued to climb for ten years, its profit curve nudged ever upward by the promotion of more and more uses for the drugs. It was prescribed by physicians not only for depression but for premenstrual distress, fibromyalgia, anxiety, bulimia, among other diagnoses. Prozac's glory was supposed to be an absence of side effects. But by 2002, the year Eli Lilly's patent ran out and Prozac sales dropped precipitously, the *New York Times* was running a front page headline that announced "Antidepressants Lift Clouds, but Lose 'Miracle Drug' Label." In a long article, the *Times* detailed ways the drug had not worked ("Millions are helped by antidepressants, with some studies indicating that 35 to 45 percent of those who take them experience complete relief from their symptoms. But millions more, 55 to 65 percent, are not helped nearly enough.")[12]

Although Prozac was not approved for use by people younger than eighteen, by 1997 the *New York Times* was reporting that there had in fact been a 47 percent increase in prescriptions for teenagers in the previous year alone, and Eli Lilly petitioned the FDA for approval. In 2000 the *Journal of the American Medical Association* published a study of the sharp rise in the prescription of psychotropic drugs for preschool age children although the go-ahead for such use had never been given. Many doctors and educators objected strongly to medicating youngsters, arguing that exuberance or sadness can easily be misinterpreted as disorder, and medication can cause serious problems later.

Compelling questions have been raised about such mammoth promotions of a variety of pharmaceuticals. These critiques stand in peculiar synergy with controversy over the war on drugs. There are good drugs and bad drugs; why is it appropriate to push some but not others? Both phenomena reflect comparable attempts: to control behaviors that can be personally painful and socially dysfunctional. It is only when the former melds into the latter, when personal behaviors become social issues, that a question of public policy arises. Depression and anxiety are frequently described in public dialogue as national calamities, affecting productivity, giving rise to troubling suicide rates. Then, too, the medications used to control it are critiqued by some as socially harmful, deadening emotion, or deflecting attention from what are matters of social organization more than individual genetics. But we neither mandate treatment for depression and anxiety, nor do we criminalize the drugs taken by millions of Americans to alter these forms of distress. We do punish those who self-prescribe cocaine and opiates, some of the time to address the very same emotional responses to similar social problems. It is in the midst of these contradictions that policing and police relations with communities, especially communities of color, take shape.

## Communities Bonded, Branded, Betrayed

Philippe Bourgois is an anthropologist at the University of California who stirred academia with a study he published under the title *In Search of Respect: Selling Crack in El Barrio*. What Bourgois searched for initially was a cheap apartment in New York City. Interested in researching underground economies, Philippe and his newly wed wife moved to East Harlem. There he began an adventure that drew him into lives dramatically unlike his own, in the course building close relationships with people with whom, he discovered, he had much in common. With compassion, horror, disapproval, and understanding, he proceeded to write the story of the drug economy surrounding his home, focused on the story of one man in particular, a dealer with the pseudonym (for purposes of the book) Primo.

The book is rich and elaborate. What stand out for me are a number of paradoxes: Selling crack emerges as a business built through entrepreneurship much like any other in the nation. In the course of that activity, bonds of identity and community are formed, a social world constructed within which individuals seek respect, and, more broadly, a sense of promise and well-being. All that takes place in the context of a relationship between the micro-world of East Harlem drug-dealing and the macro-world of mainstream America. The men and women inhabiting the streets of East Harlem have acute consciousness of a society outside their neighborhood from which they are excluded by multiple forces, some subtle, some obvious, and they feel a fluid mixture of self-loathing, resentment, fear, hope, and rage in response.

**Entrepreneurship**

Crack hit East Harlem dramatically in the late 1980s, an unintended consequence of the war on drugs. As interdiction succeeded in minimizing the flow of heroin and marijuana into the country, drug smugglers did what any good businessman might do: they sought a product that was in good supply, feasible to transport to market, and had the potential to stimulate a good demand and be adequately profitable. The product of choice was cocaine. Colombian cartels responded enthusiastically, and soon the "U.S. inner cities were flooded with high-purity cocaine at bargain prices".[13]

Crack is a simple mixture of powder cocaine and baking soda. The result is a crystallized form that allows the release of the mind-altering component when smoked (as opposed to snorted or injected). It is an inexpensive drug that gives a short, intense high and creates a strong desire for more—in short, an ideal consumer product, for it constantly re-creates demand even as it is used up.

In East Harlem, a mid-thirty-year-old man called Ray in Philippe Bourgois's book saw the opportunity and established himself as a competent supplier of the drug. Newly released from a prison term for armed robbery, he acquired two storefronts, one of them a video arcade called the Game Room where crack dealing had been initiated by a less-successful entrepreneur and where Primo worked occasionally as a seller. Ray soon promoted Primo to manage the crack house.

Primo was himself addicted to crack, a habit he had formed while working in a legal, low-end job. Over the first year of managing the Game Room, though, he switched his consumption to occasional lines of cocaine and more frequent alcohol. Ray lowered prices for his wares and increased their quality; business boomed and Primo began to sub-contract, hiring friends to act as guards and companions, and to share in the selling and rewards. As the organization grew, "Ray proved himself to be a brilliant labor relations manager," Bourgois comments. According special marks of status to Primo (buying a better brand of beer for him than for others hanging around the Game Room, for example), Ray also used kinship ties, inviting Primo to be godfather to his son, to construct a relationship of trust. But over time, Ray milked ever greater profit margins for himself, diminishing the rate-per-vial at which he paid Primo and undercutting his autonomy and authority by limiting the days he worked.

While dynamics like these parallel those in legitimate business dealings, Ray also traded on fear of violence. Stories circulated about his dangerous youth. Caesar, Primo's friend and employee, described Ray as "Real crazy. Yeah! Ray's a fuckin' pig; Ray's a wild motherfucker. He's got juice. You understand Felipe? Juice! . . . On the street that means respect."[14] Primo went on to describe, in nuanced and personal terms, the place of violence in their street culture:

> It's not good to be too sweet sometimes to people, man, because they're just gonna take advantage of you. You could be a nice and sweet person in real life but you gotta have a little meanness in you and play street. . . .

In language that reminded me of Steven's description of youth culture way downtown, Caesar went on to sketch the goal—being cool without being overly injurious:

You can't be allowing people to push you around, then people think
that you're a punk and shit like that. And that's the whole point: making people think you're cool so that nobody bothers you.

You don't really want to be a bully or violent or nothing. . . . And
there's a way of not having really big fights or nothing, but having the
rep—like "That dude's cool; don't mess with him"—without even having to hit nobody.

And then there's the other way of just total violence.[15]

The calculations Ray and Primo made about how to conduct their
business with maximum profitability, their strategy of building a coterie
of committed employees and instilling in their organization a clear hierarchy buttressed by symbols of status and power, these and other pieces
of applied wisdom run very parallel to the approaches used by most
successful corporations. When Enron, the huge energy conglomerate
based in Houston, Texas, collapsed in 2001, people displaced by the
cataclysm wrote letters to the Houston Chronicle about their feelings.
"I was part of the greatest team I have ever seen or heard of," wrote one
ex-Enron employee:

Now it's over. . . . I made some good friends at Enron, but I know I
won't see many of them again. Enron took those friendships, Enron
took my 401(k), they took my stock options, they took away the day-
old pastries that were always on the desk outside my office, they took
the free sodas and the big screen TVs and the foosball table. . . . They
took away the admin who always teased me because I ate like a pig and
never gained weight. . . . They took away my boss and my co-workers,
whom I considered a family. I loved my job, and in the end they took
that, too.[16]

### Identity and Community

Teasing and bonding, perks and a strong sense of participation in something special: these are qualities common to both underworld and over-
world. The wish to belong to something special is strong in both stories:

Primo: I was the first one of the regular crew to start working with this
guy [Ray]. . . . And I used to hang out with Ray. At that time, he didn't

have no cars yet. He use to be on foot. And I use to stay with him, hanging around every night.[17]

Former Enron contractor: Enron was what I thought epitomized a global "American Dream" of sorts. . . . By far my best days in my career were as a consultant for Enron.

Enron ex-employee: I loved my job and my co-workers. We worked hard to make Enron what it was. We all believed that we were a part of something special.[18]

Ray gave Primo a better beer and a generous cut of the profit; Enron gave employees foosball, giant televisions, and contributions to a 401(k) retirement account. Both created conditions that fostered bonds of friendship with fellow workers, in a context of loyalty to the bosses, as well as fear.

As keen as the desire to belong is a sense of regret, indeed of betrayal, as things change. "I fully intended to retire after 10 or 12 more years. Now, there is nothing," said an Enron employee. Reflecting similar betrayal, at the end of a shift after Ray had moved the Game Room operation upstairs to a vacant office, Caesar and Primo bemoaned the poor return:

Caesar: [*speaking slowly*] Tonight was slow, we only made twenty-two dollars and fuckin' fifty cents. . . . Ray's gonna lose a lotta business with no light up there. And no one wants to walk up those stairs.

Primo: No, it's not the place of the business. It's just that we're selling two-dollar bottles for five bucks.[19]

Similarly, an old-timer marked the point of irreversible change in the culture at Enron:

Anonymous ex-employee: I went to work for Enron in September 1989. I was laid off in August 2001. For the most part, I enjoyed my time here—until about two years ago—when Jeff Skilling [ex-CEO who was convicted in 2006 of multiple felonies] took over. . . . We grew so fast that they started hiring a lot of people from other companies who did not have what I call the "old" Enron ethic—teamwork. People just wanted to get ahead, no matter what. . . . [20]

In both cases, what people are registering is, at bottom, an assessment of their control over the conditions of work. That Primo strutted the street with Ray in the beginning of their relationship was not simply about reflected glory; it was also about access to power. So, too, when the Enron employees write about teamwork, they are expressing something about their capacity for effectiveness, a strengthened ability to contribute to the success of the company that flowed from collaboration and was lost in the new atmosphere of dog-eat-dog individual competitiveness.

Seen in these terms, the stories told on the street and in the office bear a striking resemblance to the narratives of New York police officers. Gerry's complaints about the brass, the protest of Sid, the officer indicted for "dropping" a prisoner, are also about the betrayal of an implicit pact with their organizational higher-ups. That dynamic and the goal of well-being that lies behind it are common across institutional domains; what is very different is the means by which to accomplish effectiveness.

Violence is one of those means. Primo and Caesar, lower in the organizational hierarchy of the crack industry, created a strategic aura of invulnerability, built on what was part illusion, part reality of their willingness to use violence. Ray traded on a much more dire popular profile of ruthlessness. Lacking legal means to enforce his ownership rights to the business, operating in a shadow world in which routes of supply may dodge and shift in response to pressures from the law, without access to predictable capital inflows or structured deal making, dealers in Ray's position keep order in their organizations through the raw exercise of physical force. They take the threats and positional excursions through which masculinity was formed in Steven and Frank's world to their outside extreme.

The use of coercion, of course, is not confined to the streets of the barrio. Legal companies tend to use other forms, the threat of job termination, for instance, or the loss of promotion. But above-ground businesses need not resort to violence because they have recourse to law. Corporations have highly protected legal status, considered in law to be individuals entitled to all the protections of due process accorded citizens.[21] In contests with true individuals, however, they bring to bear powers and influence most citizens do not have: deep pockets from which lawyers are paid, political influence flowing from extravagant contributions combined with informal networks of association, standing in society as institutional actors, and so on. Legal regulations have been enacted to protect individuals as well. Consumer rights are legally enforceable, as are employee rights. The right to organize unions was hard-won; only once that protection was in place did the element of violence diminish virtually (but not entirely) to a disappearing point in contests of labor rights.

In general, an organization living within the circle of the law has little need to exert raw force; it can afford a more subtle approach to coercion. It can do so, in part at least, because the boundary of law is maintained by a proxy organization, law enforcement, authorized to use violence if needed. To be sure, we no longer see anything as blatant as police forces called out by industrialists to beat the heads and break the organizational backs of strikers. But like a photographic print lying in the developer bath just beginning to form an identifiable image, there is a hazy, hard to delineate connection between police weapons on the streets of East Harlem and the degree of protection afforded today's industrialists. The critical focal point in developing that image is the criminal, the person defined as the object of police action.

## Setting Police to Control What?

A few statistics tell a dramatic story. Reagan's war on drugs was launched in 1982. At that time, about 6 percent of state prisoners and a quarter of those in federal prison were convicted of drug offenses. By 1996, the proportions had grown to almost a quarter of state prisoners and a dramatic 60 percent of federal prisoners. Not only had the numbers of prisoners grown some eleven- or twelve-fold (from almost 5,000 to just over 55,000 in federal prison, from 19,000 to almost 238,000 in state prisons) but the length of sentences had also increased. Mandatory minimum sentences (five years, for instance, for possession of five grams of crack cocaine), three strikes laws, and a general climate of severity kept more people in jail for longer times.[22]

Some tough policing lies behind these figures. Decade by decade, the numbers kept increasing. By 2007, there were 2.2 million in state and federal prison, a 500 percent increase over thirty years. To capture and convict all these people police forces required added manpower, more intensive street coverage, and more violent methods. In chapter 5, I wrote about the growth of heavily armed intervention teams, like the SWAT unit in Fresno, California. New York's SCU also reflects a trend toward more specialized policing, as Gerry, the cop prohibited from arresting dealers, complained. Police officers are mandated to get guns and drug offenders off the streets and into jail and, simultaneously, are warned to avoid compromising their superiors or their superiors' superiors, who are political office holders.

How great police officers' temptation must be to round the corners of official policy and make things work, as they find themselves facing these contradictory and demeaning instructions. Stuart's description of cops who routinely lie to justify searches without sufficient cause corresponds with the perceptions of Joseph D. McNamara. At one time a New York City policeman, later chief of police in Kansas City and San Jose, McNamara is currently a fellow of the Hoover Institution at Stanford University. In an article entitled "Has the Drug War Created an Officer Liars' Club?" McNamara answers his own question in the affirmative. "These are not cops who take bribes or commit other crimes," he writes. "Other than routinely lying, they are law-abiding and dedicated. They don't feel lying under oath is wrong because politicians tell them they are engaged in a 'holy war' fighting evil."[23] While most officers may be law-abiding, there is also a steady stream of police corruption scandals involving cops who are outright dishonest. Police corruption has existed throughout the history of American policing (and has dotted the history of British law enforcement as it has that of most nations). As the twentieth century came to a close, newspapers were reporting serious infringements in Los Angeles and other large cities. Encouragement to lie about one thing, we might imagine, creates a climate of tolerance for other misbehaviors, a moral weakening in general that may also spring from the sort of demoralization Gerry described to me.

In this atmosphere of slippery rules and galloping momentum toward more and more arrests, race has become a greater and greater factor. "Then, too," McNamara goes on to write, "the 'enemy' these mostly white cops are testifying against are poor blacks and Latinos."

Here are some more statistics that profile the dimensions of the racial inequalities in incarceration:

• For context, in the early 2000s the United States was the third most prosperous among affluent countries in the world, had the second highest concentration of wealth owned by the richest 10 percent of the population, paid the second lowest amount in taxes, spent next to least for social programs, and had the highest poverty rate.[24]

• In 2006, the United States imprisoned far more adults than any other country: 737 per 100,000 population compared with 611 in Russia.[25] Among affluent countries, New Zealand ranked second with 132; Germany's rate was 65, Japan's 39.[26]

• In 2007, 41 percent of U.S. prison inmates were black and 20 percent were Hispanic. Fewer than 10 percent of non-Hispanic whites were incarcerated.[27]

• By 2001, one in six black men had been incarcerated.[28]

• of 2007, black males had a 32 percent chance of serving time in prison at some point in their lives, Hispanic males a 17 percent chance, and white males a 6 percent chance.[29]

• By 1999, 57 percent of inmates in federal prisons were convicted of drug related crimes. Seventy percent of those sentenced to state prisons in 1998 were convicted of nonviolent crimes, including 31 percent for drug offenses, and 26 percent for property offenses.[30]

Several pieces of differential sentencing practices contribute to the racial disproportions reflected in these figures. "In California, almost every drug with the exception of marijuana and amphetamines, is a felony," Terence Hallinan said. "That is to say, marijuana and amphetamines are basically white people's drugs. Everything else that minorities use are straight felonies." A good deal has been written and said about the unfairness of cocaine-related sentencing. For many years, if you were caught with 500 grams of powder cocaine that you intended to sell, you were subject to a five-year sentence. Possession with intent to sell only 5 grams of crack cocaine netted the same length of time behind bars. In fact, simple possession of 5 grams of crack mandated a five-year prison term, while holding most other drugs in comparable quantities generally resulted in probation at most. About two-thirds of crack users are white or Hispanic, but most crack convictions go to African Americans. Over half the people convicted of possessing powder cocaine, on the other hand, were white.[31] This differential sentencing practice was struck down by the Supreme Court in 2007.

That there was something with social significance embodied by this profound focus on crack convictions, disproportionately aimed at African American men, is made even clearer when compared with the leniency with which drunk driving tends to be treated. Far more white men are apprehended drunk behind the wheel, and they most commonly get off with a misdemeanor charge, fines, license suspension, community service, but no jail time. Yet deaths and injuries from drunk driving occur in much greater numbers than deaths attributable to crack-associated crime. According to Mothers Against Drunk Driving, an advocacy group campaigning for stricter enforcement of laws, 16,653 people were killed in 2000 in accidents where alcohol was involved, about 40 percent of all traffic fatalities.[32] In 1999, 13,243 Americans died from homicide[33]; even if 60 percent of these were drug related (the proportion of prison inmates who say they were under the influence of alcohol or drugs when they committed the crime for which they were convicted, probably a high estimate of murders associated with crack), we'd be talking about fewer than half as many violent deaths as from alcohol-related driving accidents.

The case for sternly punitive control of drugs is that they are costly to society, causing damage to the health of those who use them and crime, property loss, and violence afflicting those who do not. Yet that argument implicates alcohol and probably tobacco as well, especially if we were to include a number of less-than-honest business practices by the alcohol and tobacco industries as criminal. If we accept that policy decisions about substances do not come about solely as a function of moral attitudes, then the question becomes, Why are these particular drugs banned? One answer suggested by the statistics on racial discrepancies is, Because that ban is a means to exercise control over certain populations, most recently especially black and Hispanic men, but at other moments in history other groups.

Who exactly is asserting that control, and why? Let us unpack that question a bit more. Government, the ultimate decision-making body about policy matters, is itself an amorphous thing. Federal policy is made by presidents and congressmen and senators. It is interpreted and challenged and re-crafted by several levels of courts. All these people's decisions are influenced by staff members and clerks and lobbyists, by contributors and spouses and voters. Who "the government" is changes frequently; that is to say, the individuals composing government are not the same from one period of time to another. To be sure, policy changes also, but the war on drugs, with some differences of emphasis and strategy, has withstood seven presidents, fifteen Congresses, and the terms of many different senators. Throughout, the numbers of people of color affected has risen steadily, disproportionate to the increase in the overall number of prisoners, which also by 2001 had become high enough to place the United States ahead of Russia as the nation with the highest rate of incarceration in the world.[34]

We do also have the highest crime rate of the industrialized world. Yet aggressive policing and extensive imprisonment does not follow naturally from that fact. Putting people in prisons may help to lower crime rates simply by virtue of keeping large numbers of potential criminals off the streets. But it does not necessarily make the nation a safer place. A study of recidivism in 2002 showed that rates had actually increased during the period of massive prison building. Imprisonment was not a deterrent to a life of crime.[35] The researchers speculated that the reason may lie in reduced funding for rehabilitation programs, including substance abuse treatment, job training, and so on. Those funds had gone instead to building more prisons, staffing them, paying the massive bill for housing almost two million convicts.

Interestingly, murder rates in the United States have fallen significantly, from a fifty-year high of 10.2 in 1980 to 5.6 in 2005.[36] Almost half of both perpetrators and victims were black, although African Americans comprise only about 12 percent of the population. That statistic suggests that a great deal of murder is black-on-black. A murderer is far more likely to be executed, however, whatever his or her race, if the victim is white, a measure of compounding dynamics of racial bias in the criminal justice system. Meanwhile, over those same twenty years adult arrests for drug offenses rose from about 350,000 to almost 1.5 million, 62 percent of whom, as I have said, were people of color.

How has the United States come to be in this seemingly endless cycle of crime and punishment and renewed crime? For it is in this context that reforming police practices run afoul. We cannot expect law enforcement officers to change their behaviors substantially if their assignment continues to be so suggestive of the very actions we seek to reform. Slogans about protecting and serving the public mask more severe purposes at the same time that they express something about how we wish our society to be: benign, respectful of individual rights, egalitarian. But the truth is we live with a troubling contradiction.

"'We hold these truths to be self-evident,'" Janice quoted, "'that all men are created equal.' Except if you're black or yellow or brown . . .'" Nowhere does that reality show up more clearly than in the story of law enforcement and criminal justice.

# Remedies and Realism

A person is a person through other persons.

        —Desmund Tutu

I think why we focus so much on the police, is because it's *there,* it's there. But it is just a microcosm of our general society. And that really talks about restructuring our society.

        —Janice Tudy-Jackson

THE FAILURES OF POLICING are symptom as well as cause of a greater social malaise. In this frame, policing is a foreground phenomenon, inequality and discrimination background. Drug policy tells us something about the political nature of definitions of criminality, their embodiment in law and in enforcement—about who holds power (which is, after all, fairly evident). Excesses of policing tell us something about how power is exercised.

When Ed McMellon pulled the trigger on Amadou Diallo, the tragedy he initiated was both personal and political. Just as Diallo was at that instant transformed from man to symbol, so also were McMellon and his colleagues. Each instant in their confrontation was both a matter of irreversible change in all their lives, and also a moment representing all the social tensions I've been describing.

That the officers were "there," as Janice called it, flowed from decisions and actions on the parts of four young New Yorkers, and also on the parts of mayors, police commissioners, congressional representatives, voters: all these enactors of history and cultural production and political process stood in the shadows surrounding the five young men present in the flesh.

The four officers were "there" because of conceptions and decisions that altered their individual lives but involved little of their individual will or agency. It was the mayor's office that decided to increase the size of the SCU at the critical moment; it was a precinct commander who chose the men to be sent there. It was a long series of presidents who promoted policies on crime fighting, circling around but not confined to the war on drugs, that created a climate for local politicians to tie their campaigns to the issue and stimulated federal funding for expanded police forces. It was media that produced film after film, television show after television show, headline after headline, dramatizing crime and policing that intensified public fear in such a way as to create a climate of opinion favorable to the politicization of policing. It was the many, many ways that race is integrated into each of these processes that resulted in the four police officers' patrolling a community of color that night.

At the heart of all these dynamics lie definitions of crime that embody very particular ideologies giving rise to retributive forms of criminal justice. I once visited Iceland, a small society with attitudes toward criminality very much in contrast with those in the United States. Even the most onerous of crimes, murder, nets small sentences. Property crimes are often met with rehabilitative services rather than punishment. Underlying these actions lies the premise that the individual who breaks a law is expressing a problem. Furthermore, the community at large accepts a significant degree of responsibility, reflected in the act of providing rehabilitative services. Once released from prison, the offender is welcomed back into the community with little stigma attached to his character. Because the person is not defined as an "ex-con," because the motivation to offend has been addressed through the training and other services received in jail, people have little or no expectation that there will be new offenses committed. Forgiveness, trust, acceptance all flow accordingly.

In the United States, in contrast, the person expressing a social problem through a criminal act is seen as being the problem. Criminality is commonly viewed as a character defect, something so entrenched in the individual's persona and identity that it might be controlled but cannot be altered. Feature stories are written about the reformed convict, lauding him as a sort of hero, identifying him as exceptional.

This individualized conception of criminality is right in keeping with the profound emphasis on individualism in the capitalist West. Conceptions of human nature tend to track the needs of society for particular kinds of people. Consider, for example, farming societies where land use is structured around relatively small parcels, where pooled labor is a necessity and the needs of the agricultural process vary greatly from one season to the next. Family units are well suited to meet those needs. Isolated on farms, children are raised to a sense of responsibility to others and a loyalty to the land. A spirit of collectivity in the community, an additional asset to the work of farming, is encouraged by the stability of landed relationships.

For urban workers, in contrast, dependent on jobs that may migrate from one place to another, independence is a higher virtue. Children are raised to be self-reliant, and families expect youths to leave home and support themselves autonomously. Notions of personal responsibility importantly bolster conceptions of personhood. Explaining why post-apartheid South Africa opted for a Truth and Reconciliation process rather than criminal prosecutions of those who inflicted the most brutal of devastation on so many people, Archbishop Desmond Tutu tried to render into English the African concept of *ubuntu*. "'A person is a person through other persons,'" he wrote. "It is not, 'I think therefore I am.' It says rather: 'I am human because I belong. I participate, I share.'"[1]

There is a strong sense in which, despite ourselves, we Americans also live in a paradigm of *ubuntu*. Steven and Frank's need to belong, the social honor flowing among Primo's crack dealers, the phenomenon of the thin blue line that runs so fiercely through police culture: all are manifestations of our need for group membership. Yet this urge to belong is in keen tension in Western industrialized societies with values and ideology of individualism. "Group" becomes detached from "humanity." I am because I am one of Us, in contrast to Them. In the act of belonging, I am also separating. Through a bounded collectivity, I am finding individuality. Other societies, of course, construct group boundaries as well: ethnicity, tribe, religion, class, and so on. But they are more often experienced by an individual to place her or him within a network of relationships rather than to define a separate sense of self.

This experience of one's humanness lying in a web of relationships is sharply opposed to the idea that I am responsible only to myself and only for myself, the essence of individualism. The latter belief has a function, as I have suggested. A social order that relies on competitiveness grounded in materialism is undermined by a communitarian consciousness. For our purposes here, its importance lies in the way criminality is defined and therefore law enforcement policy is designed, and in this case its importance lies in the result that Amadou Diallo lay dead that night in the entranceway to his home.

Thus, when Ed McMellon pulled the trigger he was and was not acting as a culpable individual. The fact that he was where he was in a largely black and Hispanic neighborhood, that there was a weapon in his hand, that the weapon was a semiautomatic, that he and his companions were new to their assignment, that their assignment (to seek a rape suspect) was laced with euphemism, that they came of age in a time and a world defined by issues of race, that they brought with them definitions of manhood laced with issues of violence: all those social factors were implicated in the muscle contraction that pulled the trigger and began a barrage of forty-one bullets.

So many seemingly immutable factors went into the act that redress may seem impossible. Indeed, one of the most startling findings of my many interviews about the Diallo killing is the narrow uniformity of solutions people proposed. Across the political spectrum, from mainstream politicians to radical leftists, from churches in Harlem to prosecutors' offices in San Francisco, the most dramatic reform anyone mentioned was community policing. But community policing has a history; it has been implemented and eroded many, many times over past decades. It helps. Incidents of lethal force diminish—somewhat. When I asked those same people how much confidence they had that even the most soundly based programs of community policing would solve the problems they were describing, most said, "Very little hope."

So is it hopeless? I do not think so. But I do echo Janice in believing solutions must be sought at layers much deeper than the most obvious ones of departmental policy, or even political maneuvering. I believe that a serious effort to address law enforcement injustices takes us into the heart of social justice, to an examination of what a just society might look like and what we would have to do to construct it.

Am I guilty of unseemly idealism? Yes, of course. But I believe idealism is, ultimately, far more practical than short-term pragmatism. Realism suggests that we need be willing to accept a certain level of tragedy as the cost of protection. Arguments about the needs of security at odds with the needs of justice have been around for a long time, and they are particularly poignant in the period after 9/11. That attack raised the issues involved to a high pitch; the Bush administration's preemptive strike policy cast them on an international plane. The furor aroused by the destruction of the World Trade Towers and the repeated statements that Saddam Hussein hid weapons of mass destruction inside Iraq prime the public to accept war and Patriot Acts without substantial consideration of alternatives. Once launched, armed attacks abroad and quiet constriction of civil liberties at home create whole new sets of problems, giving us greater polarization, lessened protection, and, at the end of the day, far greater insecurity than we began with.

A pragmatic argument for security runs something like this: There are wrong-doers out there in the world, in the streets: criminals who want to murder and rob others, terrorists who want to massacre as many of us as they can. Humankind will always need some manner of effective protection.

Maybe. For the moment, I will not quarrel with the premise underlying this argument; at root it is that aggression and violence lie in some innate zone within the human condition. But even if I accept that hypothesis (and I do not), I must ask other questions: Protection by what means and for whom?

Many of the people I interviewed spoke eloquently about the dangers posed to their communities by police officers placed there supposedly for their protection. Cora Barnett-Simmons, the Bronx social worker, talked about African American and Hispanic men killed by cops called in by their wives to intervene in domestic violence. Lorraine Cortés Vázquez of the Hispanic Federation spoke of dismay in communities that requested additional police presence to control violence on their streets, only to find themselves the target of disrespectful and too often violent police actions. David Grant decried his own sense of vulnerability at the hands of officers who regularly stopped and questioned him as he went about his daily business.

Police departments may speak of their mission being to protect and serve, but communities of color generally feel themselves to be neither well protected nor well served. Doug Muzzio, the professor consulting with the NYPD to develop new antibias training approaches, articulated the problem:

> I think the Giuliani approach [of lifestyle policing and other assertive strategies] was very positive. Now, clearly it had downsides. They dramatically expanded the Street Crime Unit, didn't train them, leads to Diallo. They didn't monitor enough the numbers of stop-and-frisks that are going, particularly in minority communities.
>
> So there was excess in the implementation of the strategy, which has both life and death consequences for some people, and some civil liberties consequences for others. I think that I would have to say that in the main the strategy is a good one, but it needs to be modified. It needs to recognize these other variables that need to be measured, and clearly it has to be more sympathetic to civil rights. But it worked. New York, it's a palpably different place to live in now than it was eight years ago.
>
> It's just safer. People feel safer, in fact *are* safer. There's more walking around in the streets. In various neighborhoods during the day and at night, people feel safer. If you read the polling numbers, people [say they] feel safer. Blacks feel safer, Hispanics feel safer, whites feel safer.
>
> And even though minority communities feel the brunt of the negative impacts of this, they're really of two minds. They do feel safer. They want to feel safer. They want more cops on the streets. But at the same time, they say that the NYPD doesn't treat all groups equally, and they don't treat all groups fairly. And blacks and Hispanics are the groups that they don't treat fairly, but at the same time, they want more cops, want their streets safe, because they were the victims of the statistics before.

That communities housing people of color face such a dilemma puts security at odds not just with justice, but with simple fairness. For white people that reality charges us with enduring the knowledge that our security is paid for by danger in other people's lives. Whether we are willing to live with such a daily challenge to our own ethical integrity, many people in New York's communities of color told me clearly that those trade-offs are not in fact acceptable to them. Moreover, ultimately they do not work, not for citizens of any race or ethnicity. Injustice breeds more injustice, and with it somewhere down the line more violence and disunity. New York is in no way unusual in this respect; all over America people struggle with these same dilemmas, with more or less intensity.

Doug Muzzio called for reforms to moderate what he saw as excesses. The four most common proposals for curtailing excessive police force I heard are training, recruitment of "minority" cadets, citizens' oversight, and community policing. Each has something to be said for it; none, either singly or in combination, has proven able to solve the problem.

## Training

Doug and his team were engaged by the NYPD to create tools for training officers for non-discriminatory policing. By producing training tapes and antibias courses in the Police Academy, they believed they could counteract on-the-street tendencies toward racially oppressive behaviors. A belief in the power of education can hardly be misguided. The more any of us knows about other people's cultures, the better, in terms of both understanding and enrichment.

But my inquiries suggest that the results of cultural sensitivity curricula for police cadets have not been great. Officers told me that whatever they were taught in the Academy counted for little when they reached the precincts. Old-timers quickly initiate rookies into a policing culture that prioritizes "street smarts," and *those* strategies little resemble the ones taught in the manuals. That is not to say that some people may not retain a measure of understanding and compassion. But from my own work in education, psychotherapy, and mediation, I have come to believe that concepts of cultural sensitivity embody the problem they seek to address. The notion that individuals of one identity need to learn sensitivity to the cultural practices of another group recognizes differences among communities, but it also obscures very central issues of power. The "sensitivity" proposed is supposed to stream from those in authority to those who are subordinate, but in real life the direction is more often exactly the opposite. When Chris Cooper's mother told him how to behave to cops, she was doing what he regarded as responsible sensitivity training. Only we do not call it that when it flows in the direction of the vulnerable to the powerful. We call it life preserving, or at least strategically protective. Both Chris and his mother were strongly motivated to learn and to teach the necessary sensitivities, because Chris's life was at stake. While police officers also sometimes feel in danger of their lives, that is not their prevailing experience. If it were, no doubt they would not last long on the force. More often, they feel very much in control. Said Gerry, "I was in control of my emotions. It's not out-of-control fear." While Kevin Davenport might say something similar, it would have a different connotation. Stopped by the traffic officer, Kevin knew how he must manage the encounter—hands visible, ask permission to get out of the car, be polite. He did not ask for the experience, was in fact surprised at its banal outcome. On the other hand, while Gerry sometimes experiences himself as a "target," he is more often enjoying the adrenaline, doing a job he chooses to do, legally armed with a dangerous weapon, identified and protected by the blue he wears. The difference is not simply meaningful; it is critical.

No amount of training in the police academy can overcome the momentum of Us and Them. However excellent the videos and manuals to which cadets are exposed, once they hit the streets these newly minted cops are subject to the overwhelmingly prevailing currents and tides. Adding to the momentum is the fact that these men and women carry within them, as we all do, invisible assumptions and attitudes defining identity and social inequities. Communicating across cultural divides is an extraordinarily tough task in modern America, in all the ways I described in the beginning of this book. The barriers for police are especially formidable because they resonate so strongly with other prevailing social forces, such as the gender dynamics I have discussed. In their precincts, the rookies take their place in a community, the blue, that tends to operate on rules rather than sensitivity, force rather than empathy—the very same proclivities that define Western masculinity. The new cops are set out on streets where they are vulnerable but professionally and culturally enjoined to be "in control of their emotions," to be unafraid. They live and work in an environment that equates, with more or less subtlety, dark skin with criminality. They belong to organizations that replicate racial inequity in their composition and hierarchy, thereby communicating a racial value system on a daily lived level. They are subject to political pressures to perform to a set of expectations that is biased along both racial and class lines. They are initiated into a mindset that casts them as entitled to dominance on the streets, while they simultaneously must tolerate subordination in their positions within law enforcement organizations.

Against the mix of all those forces, sensitivity training is at best a weak tool.

## Enhanced Diversity

To be better able to meet the needs of policing a diverse population, many people contend, a diverse police force is needed. Recruiting "minorities" to departments, once a hot-button challenge to the hegemony of white ethnic solidarity, has long since become accepted practice. Most urban departments across the country have programs for affirmative action hiring in one form or another. The demographic profiles of many departments have indeed changed. Officers who "look like us" lend a degree of reassurance and access to residents in communities of color. Especially in neighborhoods where language is an issue, cops who can communicate easily are a clear benefit. So too are African American patrol officers who may better understand the streets they oversee with more cultural sophistication than can possibly be imparted, given the subtle and profound chasm between racial groups, by academy trainers.

But there are problems here, too. Even at its best, focused hiring practices rarely lead to departments whose demography mirrors that of the cities served. In New York, for instance, the first half of the 1990s saw no appreciable change in the proportion of white to minority officers; 43.2 percent percent of the city's population but more than 74 percent percent of cops were white.[2] By the 2000 census the latter proportion had dropped to 65.3 percent.[3] But the white population of New York City had fallen to 35 percent, meaning that the disparity in representation in the police force remained significant.[4]

Over the decade of the nineties Chicago's police department tackled reform with exceptional vigor. Increases in numbers of officers of color were atypically high. Most of that change reflected a doubling in the proportion of Latino personnel. As in New York, however, the police force barely kept pace with changes in the city's demography. Over the decade of the nineties white Chicagoans diminished from 66 to 58 percent of the population, while Hispanic communities grew 68 percent, from a share of the city's population of 11.4 percent to 17.1 percent. That ratio compared with 12.7 percent of the police force, an improvement over earlier decades but still significantly less than parity. Possibly reflecting a concentration of patrolling in African American neighborhoods, black Chicago police officers outstripped the African American share of city population: 25.9 percent to 19 percent.[5]

In terms of tackling diversity, most police departments differ little from other American institutions confronting racial inequities. Even when the faces in the ranks change, hierarchy does not. A third of the NYPD may be composed of officers of color, but nine-tenths of supervisors—sergeants, lieutenants, and captains—are white.[6] Promotions to positions of authority have typically been far slower to reflect diversity than hiring in general.

Movements toward racial parity are slow and uneven. Even where they do result in more officers of color working in racially or ethnically like communities, their mere presence does not necessarily ameliorate systemic tendencies toward harsh policing. As I have argued throughout this book, the problem of excessive force grows in very large measure not from the personal characteristics of individual officers but from the politics and dynamics of policy and organization. Rev. Al Sharpton contends that racial profiling has nothing to do with the race of the officer, but solely with the race of the victim. I might imagine that some instances of more compassionate policing occur as a result of greater racial diversity (as Chris Cooper exemplifies), and some because of a larger number of women officers (although that, too, is debated by some scholars and trainers). Nonetheless, the heart of the problem remains to be solved.

## Citizens' Oversight

If cultural synergy, whether through training or demography, does not sufficiently meet the need for change, what other options exist? In my discussions, two other approaches came up: citizens' oversight of police departments and community policing. The first looks toward control of problematic behaviors, the second toward structural change in the disposition and approaches of personnel.

Citizens' review organizations grew out of protest against the failure of internal police oversight structures to address complaints by people of color about police misconduct. In 1981 a Police Foundation study reported that in a group of cities 42.3 percent of complaints were filed by African Americans (who at that time represented 21.3 percent of the populations of the cities included in the study). Yet only 27.3 percent of complaints sustained upon investigation were those brought by black citizens. Latinos failed to bring complaints in any significant numbers at all.[7] Creating entities independent of the departments to which accused officers belonged made a great deal of sense.

But Lorraine Cortés Vázquez's comments on the limitations of citizen review boards in chapter 5 reflected a widespread experience. Over the past twenty years many cities have organized such groups. Very few of them, however, are truly independent. Police personnel sit on a number of them and others have complex interconnections with the departments under review. Like Lorraine's group, these citizen agencies have authority to investigate but often not to punish. At most, they can recommend action to the involved departments. Political appointment of members, questions of funding, interlocking relationships with police authorities all add to dynamics that undercut their ability to take meaningful action.

In the 1990s a number of oversight groups began using mediation to address citizens' complaints. Grounded in the growing conflict resolution field, the approach brings a complainant and an involved police officer face-to-face for a clear-the-air conversation facilitated by a trained mediator. The objective is to resolve such "conflicts" through emotional expression and increased understanding. Most programs are careful to inform citizens bringing complaints that the mediation process stops the investigation, because an officer who is still in jeopardy of punitive action may not, in his or her own self-interest, be able or willing to engage in a frank and honest exchange with the person bringing charges. Similarly, officers have the option of taking part or continuing to be investigated. New York's review board, the CCRB, began offering mediation as an option in 1997. By the mid-2000s, they were mediating something over a hundred cases a year, out of about 7000 complaints reviewed.[8]

The choice to mediate carries a case into a realm called restorative justice. Eschewing punishment, or retributive justice, mediation seeks to restore a human relationship between individuals, theoretically involving insight and changed behaviors that lead to forgiveness and improvement. In its origins, restorative justice draws on traditions operating mostly in small societies where people have face-to-face relationships with each other, or at least are connected by webs of acquaintanceship. "Restoration" is seen as a community affair. It is a means to reconnect an individual with a community that has been injured by some offending action by that person. I saw examples of such processes when I worked in Bangladesh many years ago. One instance involved a man who beat his wife; the elders of the nongovernmental organization with which I worked saw that behavior as unacceptable to the community and called forth a process by which the husband could be persuaded to better behavior while the wife was consoled with apologies by the elders for the failure of the community to protect her.

Three decades later I was asked to train volunteers to mediate police-citizen conflicts in a California city. The program had been in effect for three years, during which time exactly three cases had been mediated. Police in this community were not happy with the approach. They were invited to take part in the training as a way to provide a deeper understanding of the process, and also in order to bring a realistic view of the police experience to the prospective mediators. Several officers accepted the sponsoring organization's invitation, but when the day came only one showed up. He, it turned out, was ready for retirement and interested in exploring a second career as a mediator. (I found him a thoughtful and vibrant person whom I would recommend as a mediator anytime!)

Officers in this community especially bridled at the notion that they might be called on to apologize for their actions. If they participated at all, they said, they would be there in their occupational role as officers, and it was in that role that they had acted during whatever engagement had led to the complaint. Therefore, they could not in all honesty apologize for something they did according to the rules and regulations of their official position.

That distinction seems to me to be meaningful, because it taps into the difference between a process that addresses individual actions resulting in injuries to other individuals, versus one that seeks to alter fundamental organizational and social problems as manifested by particular human-to-human dramas. Here, too, we are in the realm of a foreground-background problem. The foreground is a facilitated session between two people involved in an altercation. The background is a web of thick dynamics of the sort revealed by the Diallo killing. The latter realm of reality tends to disappear from mediation processes, unless the facilitator has a high degree of awareness of how it is in fact present. The definition of "mediator" is often given as "a third-party neutral who facilitates the process not the content of a dispute." But the very notion of neutrality—in any mediation, I would say, but certainly in one involving an agent of the state and a private individual—can prohibit the facilitator from doing exactly those sorts of interventions that address inequalities between or among participants. Mediation presupposes a certain equality among participants. If a person believes herself to be vulnerable to serious consequences as a result of something she says in the process, then why would she speak honestly? The only tool of mediation is the spoken word; honesty is a prerequisite to success. A police officer is acting within the parameters of a job, and as an employee is entitled to certain protections against a threat to his or her livelihood. But at the same time, the job at issue involves carrying firearms and implementing the coercive power of a state. In this view of the matter, power is very unequal. How to "level the table" is a real problem—not impossible in a few exceptional circumstances, but a limiting factor of significant proportions.

To be sure, anything that helps to heal the human heart and advances understanding even in a few instances is a useful thing, but it can also be a misleading thing, guiding us away from the political realm where problems actually lie to the individual one where little meaningful change can ultimately take place. It is one more indicator of limitations on the power of lay review organizations to bring about fundamental change.

Nonetheless, the scrutiny of an outside group of respected citizens does create at least some avenue for exercising moral if not legal influence over the behavior of police officers. Expanding their effectiveness, like their creation in the first place, requires ongoing political struggle. But even at best, outside oversight is far from solving the serious problems that lead to deaths like Diallo's.

## Community Policing

Community policing, as I have mentioned, is the one forward-looking proposal almost everyone I interviewed made. There is an obvious appeal to the idea of cops who are known to people on the street, who in turn know who is who and what a significant departure from normal looks like. In some ways, community policing evokes nostalgia for a kind of community of the past, neighborhoods where people in general knew each other, looked out for each other's kids, maintained a moral order about which there was wide consensus.

In fact, the policeman as an integral part of community disappeared for many of the same reasons that community itself vanished. That history is intertwined with the story of the automobile, which in turn represents a steady restructuring of the relationship between work and residence. Starting in the western United States in the 1920s, policemen began to be taken off foot patrol and put in cars. By the 1950s radio patrol cars were universal across the continent, as were freeways and commuter systems carrying workers from suburban homes to urban workplaces. Those left in the inner cities were largely poor people, often people of color. Patrol cars increasingly took on the aspect of military occupation, cops coming to represent first the abandonment of these neighborhoods by government and then domination by those same authorities. This growing alienation substantially altered the service aspect of policing, transforming it into the troubled relationship we too often see today.

The contrast between then and now was made vivid to me by Nick Covino, a retired police officer I interviewed in his home in a suburb of Boston. Up there in years and hard of hearing, Nick hollered at me on the sun porch of his home as he regaled me with stories of his career. Speaking of how he got started in 1947, he said:

> We went on a job, and we had one week training by an officer, a lieutenant, who was probably on the job for about fifteen or twenty years. He gave us a week schooling of how to patrol, how long it should take to answer calls. He took us out and showed us how to ring the boxes. In those days, you had a call box to ring. It happened pretty much all over the state. Boston was also ringing call boxes. That was not too pleasant in those days.
>
> *Beth: What made it not too pleasant?*
>
> Nick: Well, if you arrested a prisoner, you'd have to wrestle him up to that call box to get assistance. You didn't have radios. People didn't have telephones in their homes. If they saw you struggling, they didn't run in the house and call the station to get you some help. The fact of the matter is you're probably wrestling with a neighbor, whom they were more commiserating with than you. And therefore, you didn't get too much assistance.

Different from today, yes, but not especially rosy. Nick was dispelling some romanticization of the foot-patrolling community officer: less a hero to the neighborhood, more an outsider, even though he too was a neighbor. He went on to elaborate pluses and minuses of the call box system:

> We'd have walking routes. That's where the call boxes came into effect. You had to ring a call box every three-quarters of an hour. When you open the call box door, you pull the lever and you have to wait for two minutes. That two minutes was if they wanted you to go see Mrs. Brown close by, because she had a problem in the area, they would send you, instead of bothering the cruiser.
>
> Because they only had two cruisers, one on each side of the city. So you had to wait there two minutes. And sometimes they would test

you, but not often. Two minutes seem an awful long time when you're waiting, especially in the winter time or if it was rainy. And you could not hit the same box twice in a row. You had to go hit somewhere else. Then you could come back.

"Hitting" different boxes allowed the brass to ensure that a foot patrol officer was in fact patrolling. One of the problems of the system was the difficulty of supervising cops who knew all the byways of their communities and could easily lose themselves by choice. Indeed, the temptation to do so was fairly strong:

> The routes were numbered one to twelve. The policeman was supposed to get around his route. And, the routes were relatively long. Probably, to be conservative, by the time you walked around your route, you were probably doing about five miles, in the course of a shift. But anyway, I didn't ever read about policemen freezing to death. So we had plenty of places to go rest.

Forbidding as the streets might be, they were not wholly cold:

> You made friends. And you had to make friends on the route, because if you wanted some help, you knew where you would get the help. So, I think that was a good way to meet people.

Meeting people and making friends was, of course, the point of the exercise. But it, too, held perils. Dangers ranged from collusion to corruption. The closer officers were to the people they policed the more opportunities there were for independent entrepreneurial action. Close supervision was therefore a built-in necessity, therefore the call box routine.

But all that changed, both the means for supervisors to exercise scrutiny and the relationship of cop to community, as cars and radios came to be widely used:

> As time progressed, there were no walking routes. There are no call boxes now, because, for one thing, we have radios. And the call boxes were difficult to maintain, where today, each policeman has a radio. Radios became cheaper. Now it's almost like Dick Tracy with a wristwatch. And it's for the better.

Nick bemoaned the losses as well as applauding the progress. In addition to officers' being under greater management scrutiny, relationships with the folks on the street suffered:

> The loss is the closeness. Now the policeman comes by in the car and he says to the group of young kids, "Hey, come on! Get off the corner." He doesn't even get out of the car.

Many people who wished to see community policing instituted used exactly this image to describe its advantages: cop and kid relating personally, officer modeling socially appropriate adult male behavior for adolescents teetering on the edge of misbehavior. To Nick such a relationship depended not so much on working in a particular community but on living there:

> I think a policeman residing in the community treats the people in the community better than he would as a stranger, if he only has to come in and put his work day in and leave. Then he goes home and he doesn't care about the community. Where if you reside in the community, I think you'd take a better interest because if you're raising children, your children are going to go into high school. And if they meet them in the lower grades, they're going to meet them in the high school. And the word's going to get out, "Your father is a policeman and he's a lousy one." Or "He did this to me," or "He did that." Usually, they ask for it, but they don't explain that part where they're talking to your children.

Nick speaks to a different sort of citizen's oversight, operating informally through the web of community relationships. He is constrained to "treat people . . . better than he would as a stranger" because he does not wish his children to suffer the consequences of his bad behavior—even though he slips in some justification for such behavior: "Usually, they ask for it, but they don't explain that part. . . ." There are subtle but distinct flavors to Nick's story of his insider/outsider status. His, too, is a narrative of Us and Them, of a blue line, pale blue in this case perhaps, dividing him not only from the people he polices but from the community in which he lives.

What of the prospects for resurrecting old-style community policing? There are two questions contained within that one: First, how effective has it been in places it has been tried? Second, what are the prospects for its widespread implementation?

New York is one case in point. In 1990 the city's first African American police commissioner, Dr. Lee Patrick Brown, launched an ambitious and thoughtfully constructed program of community policing. David Dinkins, New York's first black mayor, had just been elected, propelled into power by uproar over the killing of a young black man, Yusuf Hawkins, by a crowd of young white men living in the Bensonhurst section of Brooklyn. Hawkins had journeyed to the neighborhood with friends to buy a used car; his group was attacked and Hawkins, fleeing across a busy road, was hit by a car and killed. The resulting sensation paved the way for an experiment with a different form of policing.

The previous commissioner had already instituted a small pilot project. Brown and Dinkins built on that beginning, aided by something close to panic in the city as economic downturn and an explosive crack epidemic heightened crime rates. Called Safe Streets, the program added five thousand officers to the force and funded new programs for drug treatment, education, job counseling, and other remedial actions.

There were some well-publicized successes: a block-watch program in Manhattan, an alliance with citizens to expose drug dealing in their local park in Brooklyn, systems for anonymous reporting of illicit activity in neighborhoods. But there was also stiff resistance within the police department. It was still a very small minority of officers assigned to community policing; most cops knew little about it, and many held it in considerable contempt. The pilot version of the program was called Community Patrol Officer Program, or CPOP. Nonenrolled officers often called their community-oriented brethren "See-Moms" instead of "C-POPs." The program met an untimely demise when riots occurred in Crown Heights after a car accompanying a limousine transporting an orthodox rabbi spun out of control and hit two small African American children, injuring one and killing the other. Believing the Jewish entourage had been protected by police and the stricken children neglected, the community took to the streets. The next day, a young rabbinic student from Australia was stabbed and killed in the neighborhood. The NYPD came in for heavy criticism on both sides of the schism, and the administration of Mayor Dinkins was badly damaged. The mayor was accused of weakness and indecision, and whatever will there had been for humane policing fell away.

Had it not been Crown Heights, something else might well have interfered with the successful implementation of community policing. Across the nation other forces were compelling change in an entirely other direction. I have mentioned a meeting between Attorney General Janet Reno and military leaders; the relationship she was nurturing there reflects a growing trend toward the militarization of domestic policing (and, as we were soon to see in places like Iraq, the use of military for policing abroad.) War rhetoric is more than symbolic. Soon after Reno's meeting, a Memorandum of Understanding was signed between the Department of Justice and the Department of Defense for a five-year arrangement described by some as a partnership to develop shared technology, by others as a transfer of technology and training from military to police departments. Never before had it been permissible for the U.S. armed forces to equip civilian organizations. Suddenly, one-stop shopping was available for gizmos such as night goggles, devices to detect hidden weapons, "smart guns" able to be fired only by authorized users, and quick-response training through the use of computer programs. This latter technology was promoted by its manufacturer through a story that echoed eerily of the Diallo shooting scene:

> You've got him in your sights. Drawing a gun, he turns, you fire. A life and death situation? Not if it's a simulation system from Firearms Training Systems (FATS).[9]

The momentum to buy these technologies was fueled by the steadily increasing budgets of police departments all over the country. Subsidized by federal grants and initiatives, commanding ever-greater shares of local and state budgets, high-tech equipment purchases interacted with bolstered SWAT teams and street crime units to propel aggressive policing. Those actions in turn created demand for more cultural production of support, television programs showing terrifying police actions (both reality and made-for-television shows), screaming headlines and week-after-week reporting of sensational crimes. Images like these bolstered anxiety many Americans felt about existing in a society where insecurity was common, economic uncertainty interacting with an anticipation of violence that occasionally proved true but more often was apocryphal. In turn, as Stuart Hanlon suggested, voters leaned toward hard-on-crime politicians. In the mix, community policing appeared to be unacceptably weak.

And, indeed, I believe it is. To put cops on foot in neighborhoods beset by poverty and decay is to burden them with social problems that far outweigh their resources. Like teachers in underfunded, overenrolled public schools, the patrolman is left to deal with a range of distressed behaviors, from madness to property crime to domestic violence to substance abuse, all of which I view as symptoms of a distressed social order much more than cause.

Chicago's program, called CAPS for Chicago Alternative Policing Strategy, is a prime example. Started in 1993, the community policing experiment was looked to as a prototype for the nation. In December 2002 an evaluation was done by a team headed by Professor Wesley Skogan of Northwestern University. The first contrast with New York suggested by this report is Chicago's consistency. Over a decade, the political will to reform policing seems not to have diminished. From the training of rookies to a community policing orientation, to the building of neighborhood committees and skills in joint police-citizen problem solving, CAPS steadily penetrated Chicago's department.

While the Skogan evaluation details programs and success stories, it focuses on crime rates:

> Since 1991, crime has declined in almost all areas of the city, but it has declined most dramatically in African-American communities. Crime rates generally declined the least in predominately white areas, where they were not very high at the outset. By the beginning of the 21st century, Chicago was a substantially safer place than it was 11 years before, and residents of African-American neighborhoods have seen much of the improvement. Compared to 1991, 2001 saw almost 300 fewer people murdered in African-American areas of the city, and 1,100 fewer raped. Gun crimes there dropped by 17,400 incidents, and 17,675 fewer people were robbed in predominately African-American beats in 2001.

The exception to all of this good news is the murder rate. Chicago's homicide rate declined more slowly than it did for the nation as a whole: the local murder rate dropped by 31 percent, while the national rate dropped by 41 percent. The year 2001 also saw an actual increase in the city's murder total, from 631 cases to 666 cases. Over time, the ability of the Chicago police to solve the murders that do occur has declined as well.[10]

Can all these changes, for better and worse, be attributed to CAPS? On a crude statistical level, there is some doubt. Robbery, which the authors consider "a bellwether urban crime, combining theft, risk to life and limb (a gun is often involved), and premeditation and predatory intent," did decrease more than the national average: 58 percent compared with about 44 percent. But, as the authors note, murder declined less than the average. Accounting for changes in crime statistics is a tricky business. Aside from complexities in how crime is counted, there are fundamental questions of cause and effect. Other changes had been afoot in largely black neighborhoods in Chicago over those years. Simultaneous with the CAPS initiative the Chicago department underwent a major change in demography, under pressure of complaints by the few black officers hired in the seventies and eighties. By the early 2000s, some 40 percent of the force was African American. There was also a requirement that police live in the city. Generalized economic improvement also played a role. One of the better established linkages is between a rising economy and a decline in crime rates. That Chicago enjoyed progress in this sphere was evidenced by a drive down the avenues surrounding downtown. Once seriously blighted and virtually exclusively the domain of poor black Chicagoans, the streets became lined with new housing projects and renovated brownstones.

But however one interprets the reasons for a decline in crime rates, there is reason to question such figures as a fit measure of the success of community policing. Chris Cooper challenged assumptions reflected in evaluating the CAPS program in such terms:

> I don't think community policing exists to reduce crime as much as it exists as a way to keep people behaving in a way that's manageable for law enforcement.

*Beth: What does that mean exactly?*

Chris: Well, it's the police finding a way to keep social order, to try to reduce the number of altercations on the street, arguments, noise complaints, animus toward the police. A way to get help from members of the community for the police.

Yeah, I think it's a farce if a police administrator believes, and he or she argues, that community policing is a way to reduce crime. I mean, it's really a way to just control people. I'm not saying it's a bad idea. If it works, go ahead and do it.

Chris did not so much disapprove of policies that constructed more respectful relationships between citizens and officers as he critiqued mystification of the motivation. "I think that what's unfortunate is that there are very seldom admissions by police administrators as to the real purpose of a community policing initiative." That purpose, he argued, was racial in essence:

It's finding a way to control black people, Puerto Rican people, Mexican people. You can do that through community policing initiatives. Because you'll send out some officers with a smiling face, and you'll gain the trust of the people, and you'll make the people think that things are going to change. Meanwhile, the vast majority of police officers who see these people as animals, they'll continue to behave as they always have.

Wesley Skogan's evaluation included surveying community residents about how they felt about the police. As Chris suggested, respondents did indeed feel friendlier than in the past—by a small measure, about 10 percent. But most measures of the relationships still fell below a 50 percent rating for African Americans and Hispanics. Only "police demeanor"—Chris's "smiling face"—received higher approval.

By 2003, Chicago was beset by a controversy about the disposition of police forces in different parts of the city. Once again, the mayor's office responded to complaints about rising crime rates by ordering that mobile units of special forces be organized and deployed to high crime areas. In 2007, after a string of scandals involving police, civil rights advocates sought to make public a list of more than six hundred cops who had

ten or more citizens' complaints against them in a five-year period. The
department fought ardently to keep the list private. Nonetheless, the *New
York Times* obtained a copy and found that four of those officers had fifty
or more complaints, resulting in nothing but a fifteen-day suspension for
one and reprimands for two.[11]

### What's to Be Done?

Each of the reforms I have discussed—cultural sensitivity training,
enhanced diversity, citizens' oversight, and community policing—makes
matters some measure better, at least temporarily. Neither separately nor
together, however, do they solve the problem. As I write, Amadou Diallo's
counterparts are still being shot and killed; police forces still appear in
communities of color as occupying forces. Crime and law enforcement
continue to be as much about political postures as they have always been.

I do not believe that the failure to address Diallo's challenge is entirely,
or even essentially, a moral one. Americans of all races continue to be horrified by such killings. We do not come to grips with the essence of the
challenge for much more complex reasons. To face honestly what is at issue
is to critique very fundamental characteristics of our society. Training,
diversity, oversight, and community policing all are foreground revisions.
It is in the background, muted, only dimly visible, yet essential to the context of the tragedy in the foreground, that causes and solutions lie.

# Diallo's Challenge

## *Making the Just Society*

We can have democracy in this country, or we can have great wealth concentrated in the hands of a few, but we can't have both.
— Supreme Court Justice Louis Brandeis

The most important political office is that of the private citizen.
— Justice Brandeis

Men feared witches and burnt women. It is the function of [free] speech to free men from the bondage of irrational fears.
— Justice Brandeis

IN THE END I return to Janice Tudy-Jackson's words:

> We can't look at police and policing functions without looking at the total society. . . . I think why we focus so much on the police, is because it's *there,* it's there. But it is just a microcosm of our general society.
>
> And that really talks about restructuring our society. We really have to reinvent our culture and our society.

The need to restructure our society is nowhere made clearer than by a death like Amadou Diallo's. The means for reinventing our culture are not. How do we go about a project that large? To start with the obvious, start with belief that change is possible and that we are its instruments.

Janice spoke about the foundations of our country lying in violence and racism. That Diallo's death was violent is obvious. That it was racist seemed equally obvious to all the people of color I interviewed, stoutly denied by many of the white people. Moreover, the nature of the violent act that killed Diallo is equally controversial. The jury judged the shooting to be self-defense, implying that violence originated in the street, not with the police. But David Grant spoke for many black and Hispanic people when he suggested police officers are for him the source of danger. There is a point at which those two stories converge: some streets *are* dangerous, if only a minority of them, and beyond the actual numbers, there *is* an environment of violence prevailing throughout the country. If, as the officers claimed, the shooting were a reaction to that environment, then we must ask how such a collective sensibility has been constituted. Even more, how has a sense of danger come to be so intricately associated with race? We might give the individual cops the benefit of the doubt, but even if they personally were not racist (as attorney John Patten suggested), they operated inside a frame and against a background that is. I have tried to demonstrate, as have many other observers, how race enters into assumptions about violence and about criminality, even though, taken as a broad category, violence is in reality easily demonstrated to be far more strongly correlated with gender than with race. I have argued that police carry the burden of our society's confounding of race with crime. The New York Police Department, like most comparable organizations across the country, comes in for a great deal of criticism from citizens and scholars alike. Some of it is deserved; tendencies to in-growth, for instance, the blue line phenomenon, encase institutions in hard-to-penetrate shells of denial and stagnation, locking the organization into actions that become the genesis of violence rather than its remedy.

But some of the criticism is misguided. Critics too often expect particular social institutions—public schools, welfare agencies, police departments—to solve problems lying well beyond their means, much closer to the core of the social contract. Police departments operate out of broad concepts of the relationship between law and citizenry. Some of these visions essentialize criminality, seeing it as an inevitable stream in society calling for coercive force. Control is the issue and policing therefore should be akin to the military. That was Rudy Giuliani's approach in New York, and in taking that direction he was clearly not alone. I remind you of Janet Reno's speech identifying the enemy within, and of the

After the police officers indicted for killing Amadou Diallo were acquitted, protests against police brutality continued. Women in the forefront of a march down Broadway toward New York's City Hall on April 5, 2000, linked Diallo's death to police shootings of other young men of color. *AP/Wide World Photos.*

Clinton administration's funding of programs to share military technology with law enforcement departments.

Other visions, such as programs for reform urged by the NAACP[1] and Amnesty International, turn in the opposite direction. They want more humanized policing, to draw the police more into cooperative relationship with the citizenry, to construct partnerships with those people they believe to be law-abiding and community-interested. But, as Chris Cooper pointed out in his comments about Chicago's community policing program, the objective even of these departments is still social control. And however seemingly race-neutral the laws being enforced may be, so many indicators suggest that law enforcement in essence is a discriminatory practice, not because individual police wish it to be so, not because (or not only because) particular departments are corrupt or misguided, but because the society to which these organizations answer is laced with dangerously discriminatory dynamics. "The law follows culture," wrote Bernard Lefkowitz in a perceptive book about the lenient sentences of a group of affluent white boys who gang raped a developmentally disabled girl, yet, with the support of their community, escaped punishment.[2]

Change, therefore, is needed at a level deeper than law enforcement policy. Here is the paradox: in the service of effectively altering the dangerous nature of policing, we must simultaneously focus on police excesses and look beyond them. We must both be horrified by the dual drama of our streets—violent crime and violent policing—and we must refuse to be distracted by those dramas from the social needs underlying them. I do not mean by that statement to discount the anguish victims may well feel. To be the target of criminal activity can be a terrible thing. But while our current criminal justice system may sometimes solace and reassure both victims and onlookers, it does not solve the problem of crime. Indeed one might argue that prevailing notions of justice are themselves complicit in the genesis of crime. I believe they are especially culpable in the perpetuation of violence in the many spheres we see it afflicting victims. The idea of controlling behavior either by force or by punishment alone engages the agent of control in a cycle of violence that adds layers and layers of obfuscation to the root causes of the behavior in question.

## Social Control and the Anxiety Epidemic

Systems of control through reward and punishment characterize much of American life. They permeate child-rearing, whether in the form of beatings, spankings, or "consequences." School systems put teachers in overcrowded rooms, control their creativity by enforcing standardized testing (often state imposed and funding related), charge them with containing consequent classroom disruptions, and thereby turn educators into wardens. Inner city schools vividly reflect the failure of such an approach; kids, resisting containment, escalate the conflict, and schools end up miniature battle grounds. Meanwhile, at home another kind of battle often rages; violence infects the heart of intimacy as spouses try to reshape each other across breaches opened by shifting gender and family patterns, as parents try to force offspring into social roles that youngsters resist with all their might. I could go on and on, listing the many aspects of life based on assumptions about the efficacy of harsh confrontation and punishment, the same principles on which the criminal justice system rests.

No wonder anxiety has come to be recognized as a national affliction. There are so many places in life where hazards threaten security, places that should provide comfort and community instead. Anxiety is an amalgam of feelings of fear and ideas about one's powerlessness. Politically, that combination is fertile. How appealing is a mayor who identifies the source of fear as crime, and at the same time promises that he can control it. But in reality most people are not touched by criminality. They are neither criminals nor victims. Then what is there genuinely to fear, what actual vulnerability lies unnamed under the surface? "Really, there are so many evils in our society that crime is just one aspect of," Stuart Hanlon said, "housing, education, food shortages, you can go on and on. And yet we talk about crime, and the police are given [a mandate to make war against it]." Insofar as most Americans experience violence, the chances are good it is at home, at the hands of someone who supposedly loves them. "According a National Violence Against Women Survey, 22 percent of women are physically assaulted by a partner or date during their lifetime."[3] About 11 percent of murder victims were killed by someone with whom they shared an intimate relationship, and most of those were women, about twice as many white as black.[4] How much easier it is to believe the problems of life reside over there, in someone else's ghetto. How tempting to assign responsibility to the most vulnerable sector of society, easily identified as Other by the stigmata we have tacitly agree to attribute to race. Soon after Diallo died when the World Trade Towers crashed, the definition shifted slightly, from black and Hispanic men to Muslim terrorists. But the finger of blame still points in the direction of a racially identified enemy.

Fear is an emotion that neatly embodies the biological and the social. Its chemical aspect is adrenaline driven. Our animal selves feel fear when faced with a danger. That process is positive, life preserving. Adrenaline signals the need for response: fight or flight, tend and befriend. But socialization also has a profound effect on the experience of fear, transforming simple stimulus-response into something more complex. How danger is perceived and defined is importantly influenced by ideas about the world and about oneself in it. Does this person facing me fall into a category of people I believe to be safe or scary? Is that gesture one I have been taught to see as threatening or nurturing? Recognition of danger, in short, is to a large degree socially constructed. So, too, is a sense of what a given individual can do about it. Am I strong enough to hold my own in a fight? Can I talk my way out of this situation? One piece of the calculation of how effective a response we can mount lies in a reckoning of the resources we bring to the moment. Some of those resources lie within the domain of the body—physical strength, adeptness of speech, and other forms of personal power. But there are sources of power that also lie in social realms: Who has my back? How good a shield is my badge? How harshly or gently am I likely to be treated by the criminal justice system? At that level of interaction, power implicates social identity as well as role. Will the person confronting me take me seriously? Will I be heard? Believed? Seen as sufficiently powerful to hold my own? Underlying all these questions is the key one: How can I be safe?

This combination of inward and outward reckoning is shaped both by lived experience and by social training. Chris Cooper is a strong young man, in superb physical condition, trained to the physical arts. Nonetheless his mother's cautions about white cops remain with him as a field against which to judge the actions of particular cops. In this way, each of us early in life constructs what elsewhere I have called internalized ideology, a mapping of the world with our own location well pinpointed.[5] These templates for consciousness can and do change over time. But they also have elements of continuity, themes and attitudes that are anchored in identity and are therefore resistant to challenge. The theme most common in an individualized society like ours concerns powerless. Beliefs in the impossibility of resistance or change are widespread, promoted by the systems of coercion I have described just above. No individual's internalized ideology is an individual affair. We all are shaped by similar social forces, especially by a relationship to privilege. Our experience of advantage or its denial, the many tacit ways we live effectiveness in the world, along with silent agreements and collusions within our virtual or real communities, bolster and protect our beliefs about external reality.

To trace out the genealogies and dynamics of internalized ideologies is to map the construction of such social categories as gender and race. Even in matters as primeval as fear, these identities matter. I have said that one's perception of danger is formed in the larger context I am describing, and that one's options for responding are as well. Shelley Taylor has demonstrated the gendered nature of fear responses in her important work *The Tending Instinct* (2002).[6] Women, she claims, as often react to danger with an impulse to tend and befriend, to join with others for protection and response. How much this difference is socialized, how much biological, is, of course, subject to debate. But it is a fair guess that the answer involves some interaction of the two. What is undeniably socially contrived is the fact that "tend and befriend" comes as a surprise; we assume "fight or flight" to be the natural response to danger because the behaviors of those who enjoy privileged social identities, in this case masculinity, define the norm.

Systems of control and of privilege and disadvantage are thus reproduced and then anchored in the psyches of individuals. Politicians could not convince the citizens of New York, or any place else, of their need for draconian protections if those citizens were not already existing in a state of indeterminate anxiety, saturated with assumptions about the necessity of punishment and its effectiveness. But I would argue that punishment is neither inevitable nor effective. There are better means of rehabilitation, other more constructive protections than punitive incarceration: citizens' watches, well-lighted streets, encouragement of community street life, unarmed and well-acquainted police officers on foot patrol, and above all investment in communities so that they enjoy economic security and well-being. Statistically, as I have mentioned elsewhere, in an average lifetime the average citizen is far more liable to face some other form of mayhem than violence from an unknown assailant, dangers like automobile accidents, cirrhosis of the liver, cancer bred of environmental depredations, domestic violence, and so on. But the confluence of a politician's ambitions with a citizenry's conviction that crime is a clear and immediate threat gives rise to an unsolvable sense of anxiety and the criminal justice system as we know it. Meanwhile, the more anxious we become the more we try to control all behavior we fear might be threatening, whether at home or in the streets or in our most familiar institutions.

All these dynamics were enormously heightened by 9/11. The Bush administration capitalized on an already exaggerated fear of terrorism, using it to promote both domestic and international agendas. We can debate how much cynicism was involved. But what is beyond controversy is that terrorism became a towering addition to the monsters inhabiting Americans' closets. Did wars abroad and civil liberties incursions at home make us safer? I suspect the actions taken by Washington increased that familiarly helpless sense of anxiety for more people than they reassured. Meanwhile, frozen in our moral outrage at the hideous exactions of terrorism, we failed to explore with depth and realism the causes underlying such horrors.

Perhaps that is the point: the more we try to imprison, bomb, or shoot our way to safety, the more hazardous the world becomes and the more distracted we are from that reality. While dramas of crime and terrorism compel out attention, we focus less and less on problems that really do threaten us. We are left with distress without a name. We manifest that distress in a myriad of forms—"acting out" by children; drugs and alcohol by teens and adults; violence by men (mostly).

In an earlier chapter, I tried to "read" the gestures of the five men who met at a doorway in the Bronx that February night, to garner meaning from their actions. Similarly, if we were not intent on controlling behaviors throughout our society, we could find meaning in them, lessons in where our social world is inadequate, where it needs to change. The energy focused on controlling the inner cities (and, as I write, on preemptively attacking other countries) could be turned to solving the problems now discordantly expressed. Consider, as an example, interpreting the gestures of a child whose behavior displeases adults. I deeply believe if we listen rather than punish, what we will hear is something credible—a need, a desire in conflict with the needs or capacities of others, a fear, a confusion, a creative impulse for which the child has inadequate expression. Too often, the attending adults cannot meet the need, resolve the conflict, protect from the fear, provide the means for creativity. That lack is not willful; it is not individual failure. The adult may have neither time nor patience remaining after a day's travail. The fault lies with the priorities of a society that allocates resources elsewhere—to profit making by a very few, to armed forces tasked with controlling disaffection, to enormous bailouts of ailing financial institutions. Can you see the cycle swirling here? An economy operating through a vastly imbalanced distribution of resources gives rise to inadequate means in the hands of ordinary people. The lack of resources results in thwarted needs and wants, which give rise to disaffected behavior, which threatens those in control of resources, who commit more resources to controlling such behavior. Perhaps we could close the loop by speculating that the privileged few who benefit from the portion of those resources that go into profit justify their wealth by believing themselves to be morally superior and therefore worthy of their unequal benefit. No doubt this schema is too simple; the dynamics operate on many levels, from the physical to the psychological, from the cultural to the material. But the function of simplicity is to clarify causes and suggest strategies for change.

Given this analysis, change begins with a set of social premises the opposite of those that currently operate. Instead of a profit-oriented society, we must imagine a people-oriented one. Instead of criminalizing certain behaviors, we must assume meaning in those behaviors. Instead of condemning people, we must trust that the problems they express are real, and moreover that they concern us all. Indeed, this people-oriented approach flies in the face of a premise of individualism, assuming instead something much closer to Bishop Tutu's definition of *ubuntu:* I am because we are. It calls for a nation based not on violence and racism but on meaning and justice.

I realize it is a big leap from four officers shooting Amadou Diallo in the Bronx at midnight to a social vision so fundamentally altered. But I make that leap because I truly believe nothing less has any real hope of stopping the killing. Moreover, in my decades-long dialogue with clients in counseling and mediation, I have been privileged to witness how strong a desire people have to live more in community, to be more forgiving and generous and gentle, to receive such treatment from those around them. To say we should not think about profound solutions because they are impractical is to say we are indeed powerless to do anything but apply

Band-aids to a gushing wound. Either we are powerless, or we are not. If we do not look seriously at causation, if we do not imagine serious solutions, then we are certainly powerless. We may doubt we can achieve such profound change in our lifetimes, but we *know* we cannot achieve it ever if we do not try. Many changemakers have gone before us; we build on their foundations even when we are only vaguely aware of what they have done. Likewise, if we act responsibly in *our* moment of history, we leave to our children a stronger foundation on which they can progress, however evident or ephemeral those structures might be.

## Steps Toward Change

So what does trying look like? What can you and I do? I have written a story in this book of many kinds of causalities, all interacting, together leading to Amadou Diallo's death, from political grandstanding to the shaping of masculinity, for example; from the persistence of racism to the susceptibility of an insecure population to sensationalized reporting of crime. Just as the making of disaster is a complex process, so too is progress. Change one element and something, however minor, changes in the whole system.

For me, change requires two things, both simple, both difficult: hope and engagement. Two things, but very much connected. Hope is about effectiveness, and effectiveness is about engagement, and the worst loss we can suffer is to hope so little that we cease to act. This book has been a painful one to write because it is about human tragedy at its most raw. But I wrote it because it was one thing I *could* do to address something I found intolerable. I invite you, urge you, to find the things you can do. Here are some proposals that lie close to my heart. The first set are things I firmly believe each of us *can* do, for they are changes within the realm of the mind and heart.

### Resist Political Appeals to Fear

Manipulation of fear for political ends is a hazard to the lives of individuals and the well-being of the nation (not to mention the lives and well-being of those elsewhere in the world). To submit is to consent to sleight of hand. While you are watching those dazzling danger alerts, you are not noticing more immediate and more real threats to your own interests.

Crime and terrorism *are* real. Any one of us could be injured by them at any moment. But statistically, as I have said, the chances of that happening to any one American are slight. They are greater if you are black or Hispanic and live in the inner city. They are less if you are white or you live in an economically comfortable community, the World Trade Center notwithstanding. I do not suggest we should not be trying to contain and ameliorate the hazards of crime or terrorism. But I suggest that while we do that we are better served if we are also attending to their root causes. Moreover, there is a convergence of issues that give rise to the dissatisfactions of violent actors and to the more banal grievances of ordinary citizens. Just as the Muslim world protests American injustice (even while only a very small minority of Muslims become terrorists), so also people in this country sometimes react to injustice by turning to crime. If in fact a larger proportion are people of color, that is a reflection of the greater measure of injustice they suffer. I wrote "if" advisedly. Although basic statistics say that disproportion is true, the criminal justice system is so infected with racially discriminatory dynamics that we cannot know with confidence what comparisons by race might show under genuinely equitable conditions. Even given the circumstances that exist today, let us not lose sight of the fact that close to half the prison population is white. The human distortions induced by injustice, disaffection, anger, and despair are nondiscriminatory phenomena. Not only does crime cross racial lines but, as occasional rashes of corporate scandal suggest, it crosses class lines as well. Distortions of thinking flow upward as well as downward when injustice characterizes society. I think about greedy fraud among the wealthy as a fit juxtaposition to violent rage among the poor.

At the same time, one truth obscured in the background eclipsed by the drama of crime is that, despite abundant media depictions to the contrary, the problem of criminal behavior is smaller than our society makes it out to be. Most people living in the Bronx or in Harlem, as in most places, are law-abiding. They are the Davids and Coras and Kevins of the world, the Amadou Diallos, not violent criminals. When mainstream culture first associates—falsely—race and violence and then enacts violence, both at the hands of police and at the hands of people of color who *do* do violence for reasons deeply entwined with the prescriptive association to begin with, it becomes our responsibility to disbelieve those associations, not to accept them on face value. In the process, we have a greater possibility of recognizing and taking seriously the parts of our own lives that conflict with well-being, and of finding issues in common with those who react through illegality. The greatest source of powerlessness we all experience is disunity. When we accept the idea that the interests of one group of ordinary people is fundamentally at odds with those of other groups, we lose potential allies and are far less powerful in our ability to take care of ourselves. Racial divisions pit us against one another, interfering with awareness of those basic ills we experience in common and therefore with effective action.

### Pay Attention to Anxiety

Pay attention to anxiety, your own and others', and critically seek to understand its true sources. One route to recognizing what it is that ails each of us is to treat anxiety as a source of information. Assume such feelings point to something real. It is a politically retroactive mythology that anxiety is pathological, and that psychological symptoms are genetically caused. I write in a time when there are vast pharmaceutical industries dedicated to the proposition that emotions such as anxiety and depression are both irrational and biological. How neatly that theory fits with the political dynamics I am suggesting. If distress is wholly an individual experience deriving from individual genetic makeup, then not only do the pharmaceutical folks profit grandly but also the political leadership has a well-plowed field to seed with fear of enemies.

In whatever ways your biology may contribute, it is well worth acting on the assumption that if you feel it, there is good reason. At worst, you will fail to find the reason and have to change your assumption. But if you assume anxiety is wholly irrational, you will not begin the quest to find its source and therefore you are guaranteed not to find any.

This action suggests a need for basic emotional literacy.[7] A second benefit of being able to discern and to act effectively on what you feel is the capacity to build better relationships. The line connecting social wrongs and personal feelings is actually a vicious circle. Having been reared to take a place in a competitive world, we learn all kinds of strategies for individuating and maintaining relational distance. We learn correspondingly few skills for working through difficulties in relationships. It is not surprising that a common complaint therapists hear is about isolation. The same dynamics that interfere with making strong couple relationships also get in the way of building community or acting to reshape the social environment with the strength of unity. Many a political group I have seen has undercut their own agenda by competing with potential allies while indulging quarrels internally to no good end, losing members along the way to alienation and a renewed sense of helplessness.

It is therefore a political act to respect your feelings and the feelings of others. In my discussion of fear and anxiety, I tried to describe the intermixing of biologically based feelings and socially constructed ideas. Raw emotion is valuable; indeed, I would argue, it is a necessary part of being politically competent. But it is not sufficient. It is equally necessary to sort emotion from ideology, to counteract those beliefs and attitudes that distort feeling and often undercut both effective action and effective relationship.

The English language confuses thoughts and feelings. We say, "I feel that (fill in the blank: the world is a dangerous place/that person is out to get me/you are an irresponsible slob)." None of the words that conclude the sentence is in fact a feeling; they are all ideas. It would be more accurate to say, "I feel afraid, angry, hurt, etc., because I think the world is dangerous, etc." The thought involved is actually a complex one. It embodies a perception of some behaviors (perhaps today's headlines about a sensational crime), an interpretation of that behavior (perhaps that similar crimes are very common), and a conclusion (therefore I am in constant danger). Taking apart the thoughts and feelings gives one the ability to question each part: perception, interpretation, and conclusion. Developing analytic abilities like these is, once again, both personally and politically useful, because it gives us the ability to both protect and console ourselves (and others) and at the same time to identify real issues we can strategize to address.

On the front of the building on Wheeler Ave. in the Bronx, where Amadou Diallo lived and was killed, a sign appeals to documentary filmmaker Michael Moore to help uncover evidence in the case. *Photograph by and courtesy of Cristina Gómez.*

## *Work to Change Detrimental Conditions*

Having translated anxiety into fear and fear into problems-in-need-of-solution, we need to learn about and challenge the conditions that give rise to those problems with imagination and energy. Some actions can be taken individually—speaking up about injustice where you see it for example, or voting for candidates and issues that reflect your values. Many other actions require collective effort, finding neighbors or Web sites or organizations with whom to act in concert. Crafting the list of changes that most engage you is a crucial part of the process. Here are a few issues on my list. However generalized they may be, they actually reflect the very specific dynamics acted out on Diallo's doorstep.

RECOGNIZE AND CHALLENGE THE MANIFOLD FORMS THAT RACISM TAKES IN THE MODERN WORLD. Racism lay at the heart of the Diallo matter. Whether the particular cops were influenced by their victim's skin color or not we may never know with certainty. For one thing, the primary inquiry into the matter happened in a court of law from which the issue of race was ruled out. But the very fact that race was the controversy stimulated by Diallo's death speaks to how deeply implicated the reality of American racism was.

I speak in terms of "racism" but I think more broadly about all sorts of discriminatory experiences. To understand how one "ism" works is to gain insight into the phenomenon itself, wherever it occurs. One benefit to doing this work is that most of us fit into some identity group that is at some point in life disadvantaged: age, gender, sexual orientation, physical ability, class—the list is long and comprehensive. Moreover, even if one were never a target of inequity oneself, there is a substantial, and largely unrecognized, advantage to acting on behalf of justice for others. I deeply believe that human beings, through whatever processes, have a strong sense of justice. We know at an early age what is fair and when we are being treated unfairly. We are unselfconscious as small children in demanding that our needs be attended to—needs in the broadest definition, for smiles as well as shelter, for cuddling as well as food. But over time we become socialized to accept deprivation, imposed not by the ill-will of deficient adults but by the limitations of our caregivers' resources, and we lose our sense of outrage at mistreatment. To suppress outrage requires the suppression of many other internal experiences. We become deadened; we lose a spark of humanity to which we are profoundly entitled. We come to regard our now-useless emotions as symptoms of pathology.

So if you are a member of a dominant group, to take on racism is not (only) an act of righteousness. It benefits you as well. Nowhere is that idea more evident than when it comes to the tragedies that result from police shootings. Whether you and I are personally vulnerable to that particular danger, we all suffer the consequences in the many ways I have been describing, because every loss by police bullet of a young life is a loss of hope, of justice.

Many fine writers on the subject define racism as a systemic phenomenon, something that is embedded in the functioning of institutions and operates independently of the intentions of particular individuals. Beverly Daniel Tatum explains the relationship between individual and institutional racism through an image of people on a moving sidewalk. If the sidewalk is racism, then some people may walk determinedly in the direction in which it moves: active and intentional racism. Others may stand still and simply be carried along. Daniels describes this stance as a collusion with racism. In order to counter racism, she claims, one needs to walk determinedly in the opposite direction, in other words to take distinct action.[8]

That is an uncomfortable, and sometimes a risky, thing to do. I wrote this chapter in a cabin in the country north of San Francisco. A cold winter-time storm blew outside. Shivering while my wood-pellet heating stove worked away as hard as it could, I decided it was time to replace the large single-paned windows lining the walls with double-paned ones. An estimator came and made a persuasive pitch. I was sold, all ready to sign the contract. He began to laud the skills of his installers. "No need to worry," he assured me. "They're all white." I gasped; I had a sudden disorienting sensation of being rushed along on the moving sidewalk. Seeing my expression he said, "What I mean is that they're not immigrants."

"What's wrong with immigrants?" I choked out.

Sensing I had something positive going for immigrants, he said, "Well, some of them are immigrants, but they're Russian."

Finally, I started walking against the motion of the sidewalk. "You're losing a sale," I said, and then explained precisely why.

"I'm not racist," he protested. "I can't be; I'm Christian."

I handed back the contract, unsigned. In the end, the estimator thanked me for making him aware—of what, I was not entirely sure: How to make a better sales pitch? How to recognize and counteract racism he did not know he believed? But shaken as I was, I felt immeasurably better for having spoken than I would have had I just quietly taken my business elsewhere.

This example is actually a good deal more overt than many I believe we encounter every day. The cultural domination of mainstream-centered values is invisible to most white people, painfully experienced (with or without consciousness) by people marginalized by society. Gay people listen silently to banter about marriage and weddings, feeling on the outside of a joyful (and deeply prescriptive) celebration of heterosexuality. Jewish people decide how to deal with Christmas, adopting strategies ranging from leaving the country, to decorating a tree with the least religious objects they can find. Or maybe just try to ignore the whole thing. Whatever the choice, the very fact of having to deal with a holiday assumed by the Christian mainstream to be universal is alienating. People of color are often reared in cultures of time-reckoning at odds with dominant values. Working with colleagues of color, for instance, I learned how oppressive it was to them when I insisted on adhering to a strict time line. They got the needed business done, but through a rhythm of work quite different from mine. As a matter of fact, once I learned to trust their less linear, more relational way of making decisions and accomplishing tasks, I experienced a great relief from the other side of that particular coin: white women are often the ones responsible for driving the accomplishment of tasks, and in the process we suffer tons of anxiety, not to mention a lot of bi-directional resentment that is oppressive to ourselves and our co-workers.

A colleague and I facilitated a meeting of a university faculty beset by internal conflict. In the course of the day, one of the only two women faculty of color described to her colleagues the moment years before when she had decided to stop talking in meetings. She had made a suggestion about the matter at hand, and the men (they were all men at that time, and all white) had listened politely and then gone on as if she had not spoken. They were considering something about which she had a great deal of experience and, she thought, a unique point of view, so she tried again. Again, the flow of conversation paused briefly, then resumed with no reference to what she'd said. A third try finished her. From that moment on, for years, she had said as little as she could manage.

Listening to her, the men of the faculty were aghast. They were men of good conscience, trying hard to be respectful and inclusive. But they had had no idea, had not, in fact, noticed her silence. One colleague, an older fellow with a warm heart and particularly fond feelings toward this woman, cried out. "I'm so sorry! But why didn't you ever tell us?!"

"Well, I didn't think you'd listen."

"How could you think that! I don't understand why you didn't speak up."

"I was hurt and pretty angry. And after that meeting I was discouraged."

"Yes, but why didn't you say anything."

At this point, I intervened. "I think you're doing the same thing now you inadvertently did then," I said. "You're not listening to her. She's told you several times now why she didn't speak, and yet you continue to ask the question. In the process, you've turned the tables. You've made her the problem. If you can stop and hear her, and reflect on what you could have done differently then, you'll be doing it differently now."

Like my window estimator, this man had no awareness of the racial and gender implications of his assumptions and behavior. More assuredly than the estimator, he was truly grateful to learn.

Whenever we are in a dominant position, that is all we can do—and that is a lot: we can listen well, we can believe what we hear, we can take it to heart, and, without guilt (which instigates another kind of oppressive dynamic and retards understanding), take responsibility for our unawareness by learning. My colleague Roberto Chené often says that living in a multicultural society means learning on the job.[9] None of us really knows how to do it. We are not responsible for what we do not know, but we are responsible for knowing that we do not know it and being open to finding out.

Meanwhile, dynamics of inequality, especially racism, operate in arenas well beyond the interpersonal. They are imbedded in the policies, cultures, and histories of organizations. The notion of "diversity" is often approached by majority-white groups as a matter of inviting people with a different complexion or lifestyle to join "us." The expectation may be that nothing will change except the faces at the table. But that is a recipe for conflict and eventual failure. People with different backgrounds and different life experiences bring with them different ways of doing things, perhaps even different objectives. In my work with organizations dealing with intercultural conflict, I have learned that "diversifying" requires a willingness to start over in genuine collaboration with everyone involved. That means being open to rethink values, goals, policies, strategies for doing things—in short the purposes and cultures of the organization. It is possible, although by no means guaranteed, that the process of openness will travel around to goals similar to the original. But perhaps not. Old-timers need be ready to let their vision expand in the promise that something new and valuable will result. The very process of real collaboration, of real equality, is itself rewarding, very different from an invitation to "them" to join "our" group.

Most of us have some degree of ongoing experience in diverse groups, whether at work, in the neighborhood, at the grocery store, in our children's schools. To bring to those encounters a will and a consciousness such as that I have suggested here is to initiate change that has a connection, however roundabout, with Diallo's death.

CAMPAIGN TO DECRIMINALIZE DRUGS. There was nothing explicitly about illicit substances involved in Diallo's death. Nonetheless the intersection of law enforcement and racism is crowded with the consequences of the war on drugs.

The debate about maintaining the illegal status of recreational drugs tends to focus on whether drug abuse will be encouraged or diminished by legalization. It seems to me that question is a red herring. Few people I know who use banned drugs have much difficulty accessing them. Drug dealing is endemic in major metropolitan areas and suburbs, and increasingly in smaller cities and rural areas. Nor does cost do much to discourage use; those who want drugs manage to afford some version of them, sometimes through illegal activities like robbery or prostitution. Indeed, people concerned with treatment often argue that substance abusers who fear prosecution are less likely to seek help stopping their drug use. The resources that go into the war on drugs could provide greatly expanded, and ideally improved, chemical dependency treatment. In the few places it has been tried (like my hometown, San Francisco), treatment on demand has proven its worth.

Rather than engage the debate about what might lead to more or less drug use, I want to make a different (although not unrelated) case for decriminalization. As I have suggested earlier, the war on drugs is a vehicle for legalizing highly discriminatory and too often lethal behaviors on the part of the criminal justice system. If we ask a question not focused on addiction but instead on racism, I believe the argument for decriminalization is strong. In chapter 9 I outlined the dynamic interrelatedness of drug policy and racism. The war on drugs is based on two fundamental assumptions: that the use of certain drugs is so dangerous they need to be banned, and that drug dealing is primarily a ghetto enterprise. A corollary is the belief that guns go along with drugs and that they too are concentrated in communities of color. I address the weapons question in a moment, but for now I want to reiterate the consequences of those assumptions in an environment rife with discrimination. Police forces are concentrated in communities of color. Men of color are arrested in large number. Laws governing the drugs most commonly used in those communities dictate disproportionately severe sentences. The criminal justice system—police, prosecutors, and judges—enforce those laws. Each step compounds the effects of the others, and we end up with a prison population top-heavy with "minority" convicts. Among the many other consequences of incarceration, many of these prisoners once released are disenfranchised, and insofar as voters constitute a more potent political constituency than nonvoters, the power of people of color to give effective voice to their interests is undermined. At the same time, assumptions about the correspondence of race, drugs, and criminality are reinscribed in both popular and legislative consciousness. The laws become unchallengeable, either by proposals to adjust the racially infected disproportionate sentencing laws or to decriminalize drugs altogether. The potential for political exploitation grows ever stronger, and we end up with popular support for militarized police forces conducting a war, not only against drugs, but against vulnerable communities. So much energy is occupied by all this within those communities that their ability to focus on their many urgent problems—housing, unemployment, inadequate educational facilities, and so on—is undermined. Hardships such as these, combined with a sense of constant hostility and neglect by the mainstream, encourage resort to mind-altering drugs.

This cycle is very vicious indeed. Racism far predated the war on drugs and the abuse of intoxicants has happened throughout time. But substance abuse policy has come to be centrally implicated in racism today. To interrupt a major process in the circle, the criminalization of drugs, would be a dramatic—perhaps even an essential—step in reversing intractable dynamics of institutional racism in this country.

SUPPORT EFFECTIVE GUN CONTROL. As successful as efforts have been to rule street drugs illegal, that is how unsuccessful the nation has been at constructing legal controls on guns. Meanwhile, not surprisingly, having criminalized large segments of the black and Hispanic communities through the implementation of drug policy, we then assume that those are the places where illegal guns will be found. The SCU officers would not otherwise have been patrolling the particular street where Amadou Diallo lived at the moment when he stood at his front door. Nor would they have been armed with such impulse-encouraging weapons.

Remember the police argument for controlling inner city neighborhoods when searching for guns, the ostensible purpose of the SCU. John Patten put it this way:

> If we stopped a hundred people who were actually charged with possessing guns on the street, how many of those hundred would be minority, black, Hispanic, and how many would be white? And I think the police argue there would be eighty percent or more black or Hispanic.

In fact, that argument is flawed. In 1994, the National Institute of Justice conducted a country-wide survey of gun ownership. They found a glaring racial imbalance: 27 percent of whites owned guns, but only 16 percent of blacks and 11 percent of Hispanics. Many of those weapons were "long guns," rifles and shotguns. But 17 percent of whites owned handguns compared with 13 percent of blacks and 7 percent of Hispanics.[10] By this reckoning, chances are greater (given a majority white population) that patrolling among white people will net more guns than patrolling among people of color. The only clear distinction is gender based. It would do little good to be stopping women to search for guns. Forty-two percent of men versus only 9 percent of women own them.

Once again, I am not so much focusing on issues intrinsic to the possession of guns as I am concerned with how weapons policy grows out of and in turn promotes racism and contributes to the likelihood of Diallo-type confrontations. There have been plenty of experiences in the United States that demonstrate the unintended consequences of ruling things illegal, from alcohol during Prohibition to abortion before Roe v. Wade. Controlling guns is a matter to be addressed at its roots. Not an expert myself in these matters, I nonetheless understand how important they are. I include the topic as one to be researched, understood, and taken on in depth.

LOBBY FOR CAPS ON EXECUTIVE SALARIES AND PROFITS. As an immigrant in a poor neighborhood of a wealthy metropolitan center, Amadou Diallo was a living example of profound economic inequities. And those economic facts of American life reflect values that clash severely with the stated principles of American polity. Not the least of their consequence is a profound inequality in vulnerability to violence, both from peers and from police.

The U.S. ratio of CEO-to-employee salaries has grown steadily greater over the recent decades:

> According to *Business Week,* the ratio of CEO pay to factory worker pay at the biggest 365 U.S. companies was 326 to 1 in 1997, up from 44 to 1 in 1965. In Japan in 1995, the equivalent ratio was 16 to 1, and in Germany, 21 to 1. Some of the biggest CEO pay raises have been awarded right after huge layoffs, leading to criticism that top executives are being rewarded for eliminating American jobs.[11]

While this ratio was increasing eight-fold, the proportionate contribution of corporations to the federal budget was decreasing. In the 1930s individual and corporate income taxes were about equal. By 1965, individuals were paying almost double what corporations paid. In 2002, individuals contributed almost six dollars to every one from corporations.[12]

To campaign for a readjustment of the tax code is a starting place. But there is fertile territory in this arena for creative intervention. United for a Fair Economy is one of the premier organizations working toward greater equity through excellent research and advocacy. They often alert citizens to impending legislation that would help or hurt the situation. Look for groups on a local level as well seeking means to readjust the distribution of resources in a variety of forms.

LOBBY TO REDIRECT PUBLIC RESOURCES INTO PROGRAMS FOR WELL-BEING. Economic justice is not a matter of principle alone; it needs to be reflected in the most direct allocation of resources, starting with support for changing conditions in depressed communities like the Bronx and going on to fund a long list of programs that enrich life in working- and middle-class communities as well.

How often do we hear that one program or another for the betterment of ordinary people's quality of life must be cut because of budgetary realities. Art in the schools: out. Reduced elementary school classroom size: sacrificed. Affordable housing subsidies: reduced. Support for medically indigent children: struggling. Welfare: transformed into welfare-to-work (thereby eliminating an important source of free childcare for welfare recipient's friends and relatives who are working.)

It is not really true that funds for these kinds of supports are unavailable. What is true is that they are allocated elsewhere. If the almost $20 billion currently spent annually on controlling drugs[13] were redirected, if the many loopholes that allow the country's richest individuals and corporations to pay lesser shares of tax revenue were closed, if subsidies to agro-industry and other business sectors were reassessed and the issues they supposedly address rethought, even without challenging the military budget which today is just shy of $400 billion (and I *do* challenge it), there would be funding aplenty available for advances like the following.

*Local development zones:* A program creating enterprise zones does currently exist. Designed to train resources on disadvantaged neighborhoods, it is supposed to support local entrepreneurship and increase local employment. Harlem is one such zone. The subject came up in my conversations at Convent Avenue Church; Matt Meacham, a young accountant, critiqued the program:

> They've designated this area Upper Manhattan Enterprise Zone. It started off with over three hundred million dollars earmarked for this,

and matching funds from private, federal, and state agencies. But then it's not really benefiting the residential or business people in Harlem. We found that Sony, which is a national company, or Magic Johnson's Theatre, Old Navy come into 125th Street, what they did actually they displaced small proprietors and brought these national companies in.

*Beth: Are they using those funds to bring in these national companies?*

Matt: Absolutely. Those funds qualify for enterprise money. Of that $300 million, I think some thirteen million dollars, which is a fraction of it, was actually given to small businesses, and I would call it a co-payment, it was shared.

[The national corporations are] perfectly entitled to the money. It's just because a small business a lot of time isn't presenting a business plan, or they don't have the initial seed money to go and qualify for that money. So the system calls for it and it devolves to national corporations.

I have worked with communities receiving generous funds from private funders for the purpose of supporting economic development. At the end of the grant period, the foundation concluded the program had failed. Without significant help to learn skills like making business plans, work through competition that inevitably arises when a community with unlimited needs receives generous but still limited funds, handle conflicts reflecting ethnic and other identity-based differences compassionately and constructively, and so on, money, however fundamental, is still not enough.

But there is a great deal known, much of it from "failed" experiments like this one. We are still learning how to handle the problems that arise, but the possibilities of creating truly effective community development approaches are real and increasing.

*Affordable housing:* The neighborhood where I live, Bernal Heights in San Francisco, has a long tradition of building and nurturing affordable housing within its boundaries. "Nurturing" is a major part of the deal. Affordable housing is more than bricks and mortar; it is support to manage projects in ways that involve residents from the very beginning and leave the power of decision-making in their hands. As with economic development experiences, we know that grass-roots democracy is not an easy thing. People need to learn how to do it. But there are many examples in my own back yard of how feasible that is, indeed how very exciting it can be.

What has made these projects possible in Bernal Heights is a local community center with a focus on the issue of housing. For many years, volunteer boards and a small paid staff has learned to utilize federal Housing and Urban Development funds, as well as to work with city level redevelopment programs. They have researched experiments in other communities, worked closely and collaboratively with residents in what used to be some of the worst low-income housing projects to create new visions and designs for intentional communities. Those older projects are now gone, replaced with a variety of new styles.

There are many ways to be involved in housing programs. It takes a group of concerned citizens including current and potential residents. Another approach is organized by Habitat for Humanity, a group started by Jimmy and Rosalind Carter to renovate and build homes for poor people. Other more local organizations in some places buy decaying buildings, renovate them using unemployed community members, and make them available at minimal cost.

*Food programs:* Harvesting food that would otherwise go to waste and making it available to homeless and other poor people is a low cost approach to ameliorating hunger in this country. America's Second Harvest is a network of charities who participate in getting surplus food to those who need it. Estimating the rising number of hungry Americans to stand at about 33.6 million people in 2001, they reported 23.3 million of them used their services.[14]

In a land as prolific as this one, how is it that so many people can be insufficiently fed? Now ask that question in the context of massive agricultural subsidies, many of which go toward supporting farmers *not* to grow food. Michael Pollan writes about the politics of food; his articles often appear in the *New York Times Sunday Magazine.* He brilliantly unravels the connections between industry, government, nature, and you and me. Pollan has me convinced that there is little in the modern American diet that is not saturated with politics. Here is a prime candidate for a people-focused policy rather than a profit-focused one. Places to engage the process are not hard to find, or to create. In San Francisco a group called Food Not Bombs distributes surplus food culled from restaurants and grocery stores to homeless people in the parks. The program is the essence of simplicity—and highly controversial.

*Workers' and immigrants' rights:* Lobby against repressive laws and for legislation that protects the rights of immigrants. It should not be necessary for people seeking refuge in the United States to contrive stories of egregious wrongs in their homelands, as Diallo may have done. Few people would choose to make the life-wrenching change that is emigration had they no compelling reasons. Immigrant-bashing is a form of sleight-of-hand, deflecting protest from the failure of the United States to construct meaningful support for employment by wrongly blaming immigrants for taking "American jobs." In fact, immigrant workers rarely take jobs that would otherwise be filled by citizens. They form a needed pool of migrant and seasonal workers in rural America, and they staff major retail industries at below-minimum wages enabling consumers to delight in hugely discounted bargain goods. In the process, of course, wage levels for all workers are deteriorated. To oppose workers from other countries, however, is to succumb to divide and rule tactics that undermine shared interests. Fair employment practices have never been a gift from on high. They were won through struggle by the American labor movement. Today, a job-poor economy has taken structural form. If workers in this country are to win and protect reasonable hours, job security, and living wages, unity across all sectors is vital.

Educate yourself about the labor history of this country and about present conditions and movements. Support union activity if it exists where you work. If not, and if organizing is not a possibility, look for or help create alliances, such as the Neighbor-Labor Alliance in my city, a collaboration between unions and citizens dealing with issues in their home communities.

*Art and beauty:* The un-funding of creativity in daily life is a serious matter, up there with all the other deficiencies I have been detailing. During the depression of the 1930s a program called Works Project Administration hired writers and artists to teach in communities, paint murals on public buildings, compile volumes of poetry, and so on. Not only were individual artists able to earn a living, but the life of the community as a whole was also immeasurably enriched.

Except for individuals who define themselves as artists, the creative process is today allowed primarily to children and the elderly. We permit children to draw with crayons, use finger paints, act in home-grown performances, take dancing lessons. On the other end of the generational spectrum, retirees populate art classes in community colleges and perhaps take workshops on memoir writing or poetry. But for the main sector of the adult population, art is seen as frivolous, a luxury ill afforded when the important business of earning a living takes precedence.

I deeply believe that the impoverishment of the spirit that results from the embargo on art is complicit in the disengagement of ordinary people from processes of civic responsibility. Creativity is an experience of accomplishment. It taps into the productivity of imagination, the effectiveness of construction, the richness of human experience without which hope diminishes. We know how much better children learn when teaching incorporates creativity (and in most schools, given budget constraints and overfilled classrooms, it rarely does). What we know less well is how poorly adults thrive when creativity is restricted from their daily experience.

▼  ▼  ▼

More subtly but just as surely, to accept the notion that we all have a right to beauty and creativity is to establish a right to a richly humane quality of life. For middle-class Americans (and that designation covers a lot of class territory since so many Americans see themselves as middle class), distress is caused by relatively intangible things: a sense of meaninglessness, isolation, too little camaraderie, too much work. A steady job (and there are few enough of those around these days) and a functional marriage (and divorce rates attest to the tenuousness of those these days) are not enough to constitute a satisfying life. We turn to religion to find meaning and solace in life, and church can be a rich source of comfort and community. But we deserve to have those qualities translated into daily-ness, to spend not just Saturdays or Sunday mornings or Friday nights but most of our time engaged with people doing activities that are rewarding.

The high rate of anxiety disorders among people whose lives might seem to be functioning well is evidence of the contradiction I am describing. Beyond insecurity, beyond the one-paycheck-away-from-poverty syndrome so prevalent in the United States, beyond the phenomenon of the working poor, there lies another vista of possibility: genuine satisfaction. We deserve no less. I would like to imagine that it was some such quest that motivated Amadou Diallo to heed "Born in America" and follow its call to New York. No less, I heard from the police officers I interviewed, were they drawn to police work for similar reasons. White, black, Hispanic, Asian; gay, straight; young, old: people of all identities and descriptions have in common a right to such a life. Yet lacking serious social change it is for most people highly unattainable.

There are many ways to be engaged in shaping civic life: reflect on your own talents and proclivities and choose accordingly. I do things ranging from writing this book to joining a neighborhood committee to walking the streets on election nights "getting out the vote." Voting is an activity available to all citizens over eighteen but actually done by a minority of those eligible. Voiced most often in terms of cynicism about politicians, disaffection with the electoral process is another manifestation of alienation born from the coupling of money and power. It takes so much money to run an effective campaign, and laws about campaign financing have so little accomplished a divorce between big business and government, that many, many potential voters simply assume they will lose at the polls and stay home. Electoral alienation is especially strong for people of color. In a gubernatorial recall and election in California, now a state with no ethnic majority, it was nonetheless a white electorate that unseated the governor and elected a popular muscle-bound actor. Only 13 percent of registered African Americans and 7 percent of registered Hispanics voted. Given the choices it was understandable they stayed home. Engagement in the electoral process must start much earlier than election day itself. It involves identifying, even grooming, candidates of substance, backing them with hard work, maintaining active dialogue with them once in office, and, no doubt, much more participation than I have so far articulated. Reforming the electoral system is an urgent need about which few people seriously speak. And that is not surprising: those in office have an interest in continuing things the way they are; those not in office feel discouraged about making a difference.

I have sketched a few suggestions simply to prime the pump. Look around you and notice all the many places where life could be improved for you and for others with an eye sharpened by optimism, with a heart quickened by creativity. You and I did not create the problems we encounter, but we can create the means to take them on.

## Diallo's Challenge

At the end of the day, what would all this activism accomplish to ward off the kinds of police brutality manifested in Diallo's killing? At the simplest level, engagement in the daily life of our own communities emboldens us to engage those official institutions that so impact our lives: schools, medical facilities, and the police. In the communities most affected by killings like Diallo's, organizing to confront police misdeeds is relatively common. Citizens groups, clustered around churches or other community institutions, may remonstrate with law enforcement officials when tragedies happen. Occasionally, community-police dialogue is established. At their best, such proceedings result in more understanding of the issues each group faces, more cooperation, more compassion, less killing. Rarely, however, are the results sufficiently lasting. They touch the foreground issues, perhaps ameliorate them, but do not profoundly revise the background.

In the 1950s my father, a private citizen in a mid-sized city in Texas, watched the evening news with horror as film was shown of policemen shooting and killing an enraged black man on the front lawn of his mother's house. There happened to have been a cameraman for a network news organization passing by as the action came down. It turned out the victim had just been released from a psychiatric hospital. Under intense criticism, the local police chief seemed in jeopardy of losing his job. My dad telephoned him and suggested a way out: he offered to organize a course for police officers on handling psychiatric crises, including a dialogue with members of the local African American community. The chief gratefully accepted. In the end, the entire police force met with citizens who told them what it was like to be confronted by cops for

The plain coffin in which the body of Amadou Diallo traveled from the Islamic Center of New York to the village of his birth in Guinea, a week after his death, speaks to the simplicity of his life and the injustice of his killing. Thousands filled the Manhattan mosque and many more stood outside, paying tribute to the young man. *AP/Wide World Photos.*

no apparent reason, to be addressed with racist language, to hear the "n-word" describing them on police radio bands, and more. For a time, relations were much eased. The course, created with the help of the Anti-Defamation League of Texas, was codified and adopted by many police departments across the nation. Over time, some of the positive effects eroded; clearly, something more structural, more on-going was needed. Nonetheless, the lesson was helpful: one person who uses imagination and initiative can at least start something useful.

Even more, my father demonstrated a drastically missing piece to efforts to reform police relations with minority communities: the will of the majority. Every time a young man of color dies as Diallo did, it tells us we must all engage all the many reasons for that lethal moment. Too often white citizens exclaim in horror and then return to business as usual, and that normalcy does not include daily, active engagement with the business of building a just society. As a white woman, I may not be personally responsible for the four white cops who shot Diallo, but I do share responsibility for putting them in that spot, armed and suspicious, jumpy and confrontational. We are collectively responsible for all the laws that criminalize people of color, and for much of the violence that constructs masculinity. And we are most responsible when we are guilty of inaction, of disengagement from the life of the community. I want to add quickly that, as with most questions of guilt and responsibility, there are many reasons, eminently understandable reasons, why we disengage. But those reasons lead straight to the heart of our common plight, our shared need.

We do not engage because life is consumed by work, because we are demoralized by small experiences of powerlessness throughout the day, because we are discouraged by our occasional attempts. We do not engage because we cannot figure out how to connect with others, because we are beset by individualistic values enjoining us to go it alone, because we are exhausted by the struggles inside our families and friendships. All those problems that shape disengagement are common to people of all races; they perfectly describe what it means to be denied quality lives. We all deserve warm communities, families that shelter and comfort, work that stimulates creativity, lively prospects for our children, secure futures for ourselves. How few of us can say we enjoy lives like that?

Acting to change the most egregious of wrongs requires acting to cure the most banal of wrongs. The line from security to happiness is a direct one. The line connecting Diallo lying dead in that foyer in the Bronx to each of our daily struggles is hard to see, hard to follow, but real and imperative.

Engagement and hope: let us not demonize men and women in blue, but see them as actors in a drama bigger than themselves, a play in which we too figure large. Let us not look away in despair but rather look beyond the moment so that we may confront wrong treatment constructively, with lasting effect.

Notes

Bibliography

Index

# Notes

### 1. Introduction: The Tragedy of Amadou Diallo

1. W. N. Grigg, "NYPD Tragedy," *New American* 15, no. 10 (May 10), 1999.

2. Winnie Hu, "The Diallo Case: The Deliberations; When Case Was Weighed, Prosecution Was Wanting, Juror Says." *New York Times*, Feb. 28, 2000.

### 2. Defining the Question: In the Courtroom

The epigraph quoting Judge Joseph Teresi is from the *Transcript of Proceedings, People of the State of New York against Kenneth Boss, Sean Carroll, Edward McMellon and Richard Murphy*, Feb. 23, 2000, morning session, 15. Hereafter referred to as "Transcript."

1. Amy Waldman, "The Diallo Verdict: The Deliberations; The Crucial Defense Element: The Judge's Instructions," *New York Times*, Feb. 26, 2000.

2. Transcript, 15–16.

3. Somini Sengupta, "The Diallo Case: The Jurors; 2 Jurors Defend Diallo Acquittal." *New York Times*, Feb. 27, 2000.

4. Transcript, 17.

5. Ibid., 33–35.

6. Ibid., 42–44.

7. Ibid., 178.

### 3. Defining the Question: In the Street

The first epigraph is from "Remaining Defendants in Diallo Shooting Say They Thought Victim Pointed Gun at Them," *Court TV Online*, Feb. 15, 2000. http://www .courttv.com/archive/national/diallo/021500_ctv.html. The second epigraph is from "Tearful Carroll Says He Fired at Diallo Because He Thought His Partner's Life Was in Danger," *Court TV Online*, Feb. 14, 2000. http://www.courttv.com/archive/national/ diallo/021400_am_ctv.html.

1. Kadiatou Diallo and Craig Wolff, *My Heart Will Cross This Ocean: My Story, My Son, Amadou* (New York: One World/Ballantine, 2004).

2. "Guinea," *The World Factbook* (Washington, D.C.: Central Intelligence Agency, 2008). http://www.bartleby.com/151/gv.html.

3. Diallo and Wolff, 193. After Amadou was killed, Springsteen wrote a song called "American Skin." It was wildly controversial, especially when he performed it at Madison Square Garden in New York with the Diallo parents in the front row.

4. All police officers I interviewed are identified by pseudonyms, for the officers' professional protection.

## 4. Defining the Question: In the Community

In the epigraph, Saikou Diallo is quoted by Tom Hays, "Jury Selection Begins in New York City Shooting Case," *Associated Press*, Jan. 31, 2000.

1. Getting accurate figures on gun ownership is, for obvious reasons, difficult. But the Department of Justice reports that 27 percent of white Americans own guns, compared with 16 percent of blacks and 11 percent of Hispanics. The distribution of gun owners is skewed: more rural whites own them, more urban blacks. See U.S. Department of Justice, National Institute of Justice, "Guns in America: National Survey on Private Ownership and Use of Firearms," May 1997.

2. David Kocieniewski, "New Jersey Troopers Avoid Jail in Case that Highlighted Profiling," *New York Times*, Jan. 15, 2002.

3. David Cole and John Lamberth, "The Fallacy of Racial Profiling," *New York Times*, May 13, 2001.

4. Eliot Spitzer, *The New York City Police Department's "Stop and Frisk" Practices: A Report to the People of the State of New York from the Office of the Attorney General*, New York: Civil Rights Bureau, Dec. 1, 1999.

5. Ibid.

## 5. Policing the Boundaries: In the Precinct House

1. W. E. B. DuBois, *The Souls of Black Folk* (New York: New American Library, 1969).

2. Alex Cukan, "Officer Says Diallo Was in Combat Stance," *APB News*, Feb. 15, 2000.

3. Lou Cannon, "One Bad Cop," *New York Times Magazine*, Oct. 22, 2000.

4. James Lardner and Thomas Reppetto, *NYPD: A City and Its Police* (New York: Henry Holt, 2000), 253–58.

5. *The NYPD: Blueprint for Reform*, presented by Peter F. Vallone, Speaker, New York City Council, May 12, 1999, 9–10.

6. Alison Gendar, "NYPD Management Still a Whiter Shade of Male: Study," *New York Daily News*, May 9, 2008.

7. *The NYPD: Blueprint for Reform*, 332.

## 6. Policing and Politics: In City Hall

1. Elisabeth Bumiller, "Giuliani Backs Police in Bronx Killing and Urges Restraint." *New York Times,* Mar. 3, 2000.

2. Phil Hirschkorn, "Latest Police Shooting of Unarmed Man Fuels New York Senate Race Debate," CNN.com. March 22, 2000. http://www.cnn.com/2000/ALL POLITICS/stories/03/22/clinton.giuliani/.

3. Christian Parenti, *Lockdown America: Police and Prisons in the Age of Crisis* (New York: Verso, 1999), 111–27.

4. See especially my paper "Stick Figure Against a Background of Color: Racial Profiling and the Case of Amadou Diallo," *Journal of Intergroup Relations* 38, no. 3 (Fall 2001), 17–32.

5. Wesley G. Lamberth, "Driving While Black: A Statistician Proves That Prejudice Still Rules the Road," *Washington Post,* Aug. 16, 1998. In 2000, Lamberth formed Lamberth Consulting, which has worked with a number of police departments across the country tracking racial dynamics. See for instance, Lamberth Consulting, "Racial Profiling Data Analysis Study: Final Report for the San Antonio Police Department," Dec. 2003; Lamberth Consulting, "Data Collection and Benchmarking of the Bias Policing Project: Final Report for the Metropolitan Police Department in the District of Columbia," Sept. 2006.

6. U.S. Bureau of the Census, *Statistical Abstract of the United States: 1994,* ed. 114 (Washington, D.C.: Government Printing Office), 1994, table 637. Jason Ziedenberg and Vincent Schiraldi, "The Punishing Decade: Prison and Jail Estimates at the Millenium," *Justice Policy Institute,* Dec. 2000.

7. William P. O'Hare et al., "African Americans in the 1990s," *Population Bulletin* 46, no. 1 (July 1991): 22.

## 7. Seeking Answers Beyond Diallo

1. Mariah Breeding, "The Shirt on My Back: The Daily Continuum of Violence" in *Re-Centering Culture and Knowledge in Conflict Resolution Practice* (Syracuse: Syracuse Univ. Press, 2008); Breeding, *Violence and Domination in Sibling Relationships: An Ethnography of the Unacknowledged "Business As Usual" of Childhood* (unpublished dissertation, Univ. of California, Berkeley, Fall 2008); Phillipe Bourgois, *In Search of Respect: Selling Crack in El Barrio* (Cambridge: Cambridge Univ. Press, 1995).

## 8. Coloring Manhood in Shades of Violence

1. "Steven" and "Frank" are pseudonyms.

2. "Technology Transfer From Defense: Concealed Weapon Detection," *National Institute of Justice Journal,* no. 229, Aug. 1995 http://ncjrs.org/txtfiles/nijj_229.txt.

## 9. Underworld and Overworld

1. "Households by Age of Householder and Size of Household," U.S. Census 2000. http://www.allcountries.org/uscensus/61_households_by_age_of_householder_and .html.

2. David T. Cook, "Crisis in the Corner Office," *Christian Science Monitor,* July 2, 2002, 1.

3. Michael Pollan, *The Botany of Desire* (New York: Random House, 2001), 9.

4. Leif Rosenberger, *America's Drug War Debacle* (Brookfield, Vt.: Avebury Press, 1996), 17.

5. M. Bentham, *The Global Politics of Drug Control* (Basingstoke, UK: Palgrave Macmillan, 1998); Rosenberger.

6. Elaine Sharp, *The Dilemma of Drug Policy in the United States* (New York: Harper Collins, 1994), 23.

7. William McAllister, *Drug Diplomacy in the Twentieth Century: An International History* (New York: Routledge, 1999), 18.

8. See David C. Jordan, *Drug Politics: Dirty Money and Democracies* (Norman: Univ. of Oklahoma Press, 1999), 57–65.

9. Rosenberger, 17.

10. Bentham, 65–75; David T. Courtwright, *Dark Paradise: A History of Opiate Addiction in America* (Cambridge: Harvard Univ. Press, 2001).

11. McAllister; Bentham.

12. Erica Goode, "Antidepressants Lift Clouds, but Lose 'Miracle Drug' Label," *New York Times,* June 30, 2002.

13. Phillipe Bourgois, *In Search of Respect: Selling Crack in El Barrio* (Cambridge: Cambridge Univ. Press, 1995), 75.

14. Ibid., 24.

15. Ibid., 25.

16. HoustonChronicle.com, Dec. 4, 2001. http://www.chron.com/cs/CDA/print story.hts/side/1160419.

17. Bourgois, 83.

18. HoustonChronicle.com, Dec. 4, 2001.

19. Bourgois, 102.

20. HoustonChronicle.com, Dec. 4, 2001.

21. That corporations are included under provisions intended to extend due process to individual citizens is an unintended consequence of the Fourteenth Amendment granting citizenship to freed slaves. The legal status of corporations was hotly contested during the early years of nationhood. In 1886 the U.S. Supreme Court handed down a counterintuitive ruling that private corporations were "natural persons" under the precepts of the Fourteenth Amendment requiring due process in criminal prosecutions.

Corporations used the ruling to buttress their right to a wide variety of activities intended to further their interests, to greater control over employees and more successful pursuit of profit. (see Richard L. Grossman and Frank T. Adams, *Taking Care of Business,* 1993. http://www.ratical.org/corporations/TCoB.html#p7.

22. "Drug Policy and the Criminal Justice System," Sentencing Project, 2001. http://www.sentencingproject.org/brief/5047/htm.

23. Joseph D. McNamara, "Has the Drug War Created an Officer Liars' Club?" *Los Angeles Times,* Feb. 11, 1996. See http://www.druglibrary.org/schaffer/DEBATE/mcn/mcn6.htm.

24. Peter Dreier, "The United States in Comparative Perspective," *Contexts* 6, no. 3 (Summer 2007): 38–43.

25. Ben Kage, "United States mprisons More People than China, Russia or Any Other Nation, Experts Say," *News Target,* Dec. 13, 2006. http://www.newstarget.com/021290.html.

26. Dreier, 45.

27. Marc Mauer and Ryan S. King, "Uneven Justice: State Rates of Incarceration by Race and Ethnicity," *Sentencing Project* (July 2007), 1–2. http://www.sentencingproject.org/Admin/Documents/publications/rd_stateratesofincbyraceandethnicity.pdf.

28. Mauer and King, 3.

29. "Facts About Prisons and Prisoners," *Sentencing Project,* June 2007. http://www.sentencingproject.org/Admin%5CDocuments%5Cpublications%5Cinc_facts aboutprisons.pdf.

30. "Drug Policy and the Criminal Justice System," 3.

31. "Crack Cocaine Sentencing Policy: Unjustified and Unreasonable," *Sentencing Project.* http://www.sentencingproject.org/brief/pub1003.htm.

32. MADD Web site. http://www.madd.org/stats/0,1056,1112,00.html.

33. National Center for Injury Prevention and Control, Center for Disease Control. http://webapp.cdc.gov/cgi-bin/broker.exe.

34. The rate is 690 per 100,000 population in the United States compared with 675 in Russia, 400 in South Africa, 125 in United Kingdom, and 40 in Japan. "U.S. Surpasses Russia as World Leader in Rate of Incarceration," *Sentencing Project* http://www.sentencingproject.org/brief/usvsrus.pdf.

35. Eric P. Baumer, Richard Wright, Kristrun Kristindottir, and Helgi Gunnlaugsson, "Crime, Shame, and Recidivism," *British Journal of Criminology* 42, no. 1 (Winter 2002), 40–59.

36. "Murder Rates 1995–2005," Death Penalty Information Center (Sept. 2006). http://www.deathpenaltyinfo.org/article.php?did=169 .

## 10. Remedies and Realism

1. Desmond Tutu, *No Future Without Forgiveness* (New York: Doubleday, 1999), 31.

2. "Police Brutality and Excessive Force in the NYPD," Amnesty USA, www. amnestyusa.org/rightsforall/police/nypd/nypd-02.html.

3. Brian A. Reaves and Matthew J. Hickman, "Police Departments in Large Cities, 1990–2000," Bureau of Justice Statistics, http://www.ojp.usdoj.gov/bjs/pub/pdf/pdlc00.pdf.

4. New York City Department of City Planning, http://www.ci.nyc.ny.us/html/dcp/html/census/popdiv.html.

5. Nancy McArdle, "Race, Place, and Opportunity: Racial Change and Segregation in the Chicago Metropolitan Area 1990–2000," Civil Rights Project at Harvard Univ. http://www.civilrightsproject.harvard.edu/research/metro/Final%20Chicago%20Paper%20Part%201.pdf.

6. "The NYPD: Blueprint for Reform," presented by Peter F. Vallone, Speaker, New York City Council, May 12, 1999, http://www.council.nyc.ny.us/loi/blueprint.htm.

7. Samuel Walker and Betsy Wright Kreisel, "Varieties of Citizen Review: The Implications of Organizational Features of Complaint Review Procedures for Accountability of the Police," *American Journal of Police* 15, no. 3 (1996): 66.

8. "CCRB Performance," New York City Civilian Complaint Review Board. http://www.nyc.gov/html/ccrb/html/about.html#7.

9. Report of Firearms Training Systems, Inc., Suwanee, Georgia, quoted in Frank Morales, "The Militarization of the Police," *Covert Action Quarterly* 67 (Spring-Summer 1999).

10. Wesley G. Skogan et al., *Community Policing in Chicago, Years Eight and Nine: An Evaluation of Chicago's Alternative Policing Strategy and Information Technology Initiative,* Institute for Police Research, Northwestern Univ., Chicago, Dec. 2002, i.

11. Libby Sander, "Chicago Revamps Investigation of Police Abuse, but Privacy Fight Continues," *New York Times,* July 20, 2007.

## 11. Diallo's Challenge: Making the Just Society

The first epigraph is from P. Strum, ed., *Brandeis on Democracy* (Lawrence: Univ. Press of Kansas, 1995). The second is often quoted but the source is unknown. The third is from *Whitney v. California,* No. 3, Supreme Court of the United States, 274 U.S. 357. Argued Oct. 6, 1925, decided May 16, 1927. http://www.bc.edu/bc_org/avp/cas/comm/free_speech/whitney.html.

1. Mary Prosser, Abbe Smith, William Talley, Charles J. Ogletree, Jr., Harvard Law School Criminal Justice Institute, and National Association for the Advancement of Colored People, *Beyond the Rodney King Story* (Boston: Northeastern Univ. Press, 1995) reports on extensive hearings about police practices conducted by NAACP. For Amnesty's case against racial profiling and the death penalty, see http://www.amnestyusa.org/.

2. Bernard Lefkowitz, *Our Guys* (New York: Vintage Books, 1998), 494.

3. "Let's Talk Facts About Domestic Violence." http://healthyminds.org/factsheets/LTF-DomesticViolence.pdf.

4. "Homicide Trends in the U.S., Intimate Homicide," U.S. Department of Justice, Bureau of Justice Statistics. http://www.ojp.gov/bjs/homicide/intimates.htm.

5. Beth Roy, *Bitters in the Honey: Tales of Hope and Disappointment Across Divides of Race and Time* (Fayetteville: Univ. of Arkansas Press, 1999).

6. Shelley Taylor, *The Tending Instinct: Women, Men, and the Biology of Relationships* (New York: Holt Paperbacks, 2003).

7. A term coined by my colleague, Claude Steiner. See *Emotional Literacy: Intelligence with a Heart* (Fawnskin, Calif.: Personhood Books, 2003).

8. Beverly Daniel Tatum, *Why Are All the Black Kids Sitting Together in the Cafeteria?* (New York: Basic Books, 1999).

9. Roberto M. Chené, "Beyond Mediation—Reconciling an Intercultural World: A New Role for Conflict Resolution" in *Re-Centering Culture and Knowledge in Conflict Resolution Practice* (Syracuse: Syracuse Univ. Press, 2008), 32–36.

10. National Institute of Justice, U.S. Department of Justice, "Guns in America: National Survey on Private Ownership and Use of Firearms," May 1997.

11. "Shareholders Spotlight CEO-Worker Wage Gap at 8 Companies," *Responsible Wealth.* http://www.responsiblewealth.org/press/1999/shareholder_pr.html.

12. "Historical Amount of Tax Revenue by Source," Tax Policy Center, Urban Institute and Brookings Institute. http://taxpolicycenter.org/TaxFacts/TFDB/TFTemplate.cfm?Docid=203.

13. Ernest Drucker, "Drug Prohibition and Public Health," *Public Health Reports* 114 (Jan./Feb. 1998).

14. America's Second Harvest fact sheet. http://www.secondharvest.org/site_content.asp?s=59.

# Bibliography

America's Second Harvest fact sheet. http://www.secondharvest.org/site_content
.asp?s=59.

Baumer, Eric P., Richard Wright, Kristrun Kristindottir, and Helgi Gunnlaugsson. "Crime, Shame, and Recidivism." *British Journal of Criminology* 42,
no. 1 (Winter 2002), 40–59.

Benson, Bruce L., and David W. Rasmussen. *Illicit Drugs and Crime.* Oakland,
Calif.: Independent Institute, 1996.

Bentham, M. *The Global Politics of Drug Control.* Basingstoke, UK: Palgrave
Macmillan, 1998.

Bourgois, Phillipe. *In Search of Respect: Selling Crack in El Barrio.* Cambridge:
Cambridge Univ. Press, 1995.

Breeding, Mariah. "The Shirt on My Back: The Daily Continuum of Violence"
in *Re-Centering Culture and Knowledge in Conflict Resolution Practice.*
Syracuse: Syracuse Univ. Press, 2008.

———. *Violence and Domination in Sibling Relationships: An Ethnography of the
Unacknowledged "Business As Usual" of Childhood.* Unpublished dissertation, Univ. of California, Berkeley, Fall 2008.

Bumiller, Elisabeth. "Giuliani Backs Police in Bronx Killing and Urges
Restraint." *New York Times,* Mar. 3, 2000.

Cannon, Lou. "One Bad Cop." *New York Times Magazine,* Oct. 22, 2000.

"CCRB Performance." New York City Civilian Complaint Review Board Web
site. http://www.nyc.gov/html/ccrb/html/about.html#7.

Chené, Roberto M. "Beyond Mediation—Reconciling an Intercultural World:
A New Role for Conflict Resolution" in *Re-Centering Culture and Knowledge in Conflict Resolution Practice.* Syracuse: Syracuse Univ. Press, 2008.

Cole, David, and John Lamberth. "The Fallacy of Racial Profiling." *New York
Times,* May 13, 2001.

Cook, David T. "Crisis in the Corner Office." *Christian Science Monitor,* July 2, 2002.

Courtwright, David T. *Dark Paradise: A History of Opiate Addiction in America.* Cambridge: Harvard Univ. Press, 2001.

"Crack Cocaine Sentencing Policy: Unjustified and Unreasonable." Sentencing Project. http://www.sentencingproject.org/brief/pub1003.htm.

Cukan, Alex. "Office Says Diallo Was in Combat Stance." *APB News,* Feb. 15, 2000.

Diallo, Kadiatou, and Craig Wolff. *My Heart Will Cross This Ocean: My Story, My Son, Amadou.* New York: One World/Ballantine, 2004.

Dreier, Peter. "The United States in Comparative Perspective." *Contexts* 6, no. 3 (Summer 2007): 38–43.

"Driving While Black: A Statistician Proves That Prejudice Still Rules the Road," *Washington Post,* Aug. 16, 1998.

Drucker, Ernest. "Drug Prohibition and Public Health." *Public Health Reports* 114 (Jan./Feb. 1998).

"Drug Policy and the Criminal Justice System." Sentencing Project, 2001. http://www.sentencingproject.org/Admin%5CDocuments%5Cpublications %5Cdp_drugpolicy_cjsystem.pdf.

DuBois, W. E. B. *The Souls of Black Folk* (New York: New American Library, 1969).

"Enron Letters." *Houston Chronicle* Dec. 4, 2001. http://www.chron.com/cs/ CDA/printstory.hts/side/1160419.

"Facts about Prisons and Prisoners." Sentencing Project, June 2007. http:// www.sentencingproject.org/Admin%5CDocuments%5Cpublications%5Ci nc_factsaboutprisons.pdf.

Gendar, Alison. "NYPD Management Still a Whiter Shade of Male: Study." *New York Daily News,* May 9, 2008.

George, Tara. "Cops Tell Their Story." *Daily News,* Feb. 15, 2000. http://www .nycpba.org/archive/nydn/00/nydn-000215-diallo.html.

Goode, Erica. "Antidepressants Lift Clouds, but Lose 'Miracle Drug' Label." *New York Times,* June 30, 2002.

Grigg, W. N. "NYPD Tragedy." *New American* 15, no. 10 (May 10), 1999.

Grossman, Richard L., and Frank T. Adams. *Taking Care of Business.* 1993. http://www.ratical.org/corporations/TCoB.html#p7.

"Guinea." *The World Factbook.* Washington, D.C.: Central Intelligence Agency, 2008. http://www.bartleby.com/151/gv.html.

"Guns in America: National Survey on Private Ownership and Use of Firearms." National Institute of Justice, U.S. Department of Justice. May 1997.

Hirschkorn, Phil. "Latest Police Shooting of Unarmed Man Fuels New York Senate Race Debate." CNN.com. Mar. 22, 2000. http://www.cnn.com/2000/ALLPOLITICS/stories/03/22/clinton.giuliani/.

"Historical Amount of Tax Revenue by Source." Tax Policy Center, Urban Institute and Brookings Institute. http://taxpolicycenter.org/TaxFacts/TFDB/TFTemplate.cfm?Docid=203.

"Homicide Trends in the U.S., Intimate Homicide." U.S. Department of Justice, Bureau of Justice Statistics. http://www.ojp.gov/bjs/homicide/intimates.htm.

"Households by Age of Householder and Size of Household." *U.S. Census 2000.* http://www.allcountries.org/uscensus/61_households_by_age_of_householder_and.html.

Hu, Winnie. "The Diallo Case: The Deliberations; When Case was Weighed, Prosecution Was Wanting, Juror Says." *New York Times,* Feb. 28, 2000.

Jordan, David C. *Drug Politics: Dirty Money and Democracies.* Norman: Univ. of Oklahoma Press, 1999.

Kage, Ben. "United States Imprisons More People than China, Russia or Any Other Nation, Experts Say." *News Target* Dec. 13, 2006. http://www.newstarget.com/021290.html.

Kocieniewski, David. "New Jersey Troopers Avoid Jail in Case that Highlighted Profiling," *New York Times,* Jan. 15, 2002.

Lamberth, Wesley G. "Driving While Black: A Statistician Proves That Prejudice Still Rules the Road." *Washington Post,* Aug. 16, 1998.

Lamberth Consulting. "Data Collection and Benchmarking of the Bias Policing Project: Final Report for the Metropolitan Police Department in the District of Columbia." Sept. 2006.

———. "Racial Profiling Data Analysis Study: Final Report for the San Antonio Police Department." Dec. 2003.

Lardner, James, and Thomas Reppetto. *NYPD: A City and Its Police.* New York: Henry Holt, 2000.

Lefkowitz, Bernard. *Our Guys.* New York: Vintage Books, 1998.

"Let's Talk Facts About Domestic Violence." American Psychiatric Association. http://healthyminds.org/factsheets/LTF-DomesticViolence.pdf.

Mauer, Marc, and Ryan S. King. "Uneven Justice: State Rates of Incarceration by Race and Ethnicity." Sentencing Project, July 2007. http://www.sentencing

project.org/Admin/Documents/publications/rd_stateratesofincbyraceand
ethnicity.pdf.

McAllister, William. *Drug Diplomacy in the Twentieth Century: An International History.* New York: Routledge, 1999.

McArdle, Nancy. "Race, Place, and Opportunity: Racial Change and Segregation in the Chicago Metropolitan Area 1990–2000." Civil Rights Project, Harvard Univ., May 2002.

McNamara, Joseph D. "Has the Drug War Created an Officer Liars' Club?" *Los Angeles Times* Feb. 11, 1996. http://www.druglibrary.org/schaffer/DEBATE/mcn/mcn6.htm.

Morales, Frank. "The Militarization of the Police." *Covert Action Quarterly* 67 (Spring-Summer 1999). http://www.covertaction.org/content/view/95/75.

"Murder Rates 1995–2005." Death Penalty Information Center, Sept. 2006. http://www.deathpenaltyinfo.org/article.php?did=169.

New York City Department of City Planning. http://www.ci.nyc.ny.us/html/dcp/html/census/popdiv.html.

O'Hare, William P., et al. "African Americans in the 1990s." *Population Bulletin* 46, no 1. (July 1991).

Parenti, Christian. *Lockdown America: Police and Prisons in the Age of Crisis.* New York: Verso, 1999.

Pollan, Michael. *The Botany of Desire.* New York: Random House, 2001.

Prosser, Mary, Abbe Smith, William Talley, Charles J. Ogletree, Jr., Harvard Law School Criminal Justice Institute, and National Association for the Advancement of Colored People. *Beyond the Rodney King Story.* Boston: Northeastern Univ. Press, 1995.

Reaves, Brian A., and Matthew J. Hickman. "Police Departments in Large Cities, 1990–2000." Bureau of Justice Statistics. http://www.ojp.usdoj.gov/bjs/pub/pdf/pdlc00.pdf.

Rosenberger, Leif. *America's Drug War Debacle.* Brookfield, Vt.: Avebury Press, 1996.

Roy, Beth. *Bitters in the Honey: Tales of Hope and Disappointment Across Divides of Race and Time.* Fayetteville: Univ. of Arkansas Press, 1999.

———. "Stick Figure Against a Background of Color: Racial Profiling and the Case of Amadou Diallo." *Journal of Intergroup Relations* 38, no. 3 (Fall 2001), 17–32.

Sander, Libby. "Chicago Revamps Investigation of Police Abuse, but Privacy Fight Continues." *New York Times,* July 20, 2007.

Sengupta, Somni. "The Diallo Case: The Jurors; 2 Jurors Defend Diallo Acquittal." *New York Times,* Feb. 27, 2000.

"Shareholders Spotlight CEO-Worker Wage Gap at 8 Companies." *Responsible Wealth.* Press release. http://www.responsiblewealth.org/press/1999/shareholder_pr.html.

Sharp, Elaine. *The Dilemma of Drug Policy in the United States.* New York: Harper Collins, 1994.

Skogan, Wesley G., et al. *Community Policing in Chicago, Years Eight and Nine: An Evaluation of Chicago's Alternative Policing Strategy and Information Technology Initiative.* Chicago. Institute for Policy Research, Northwestern Univ., 2002.

Spitzer, Eliot. *The New York City Police Department's "Stop and Frisk" Practices: A Report to the People of the State of New York from the Office of the Attorney General.* New York: Civil Rights Bureau, Dec. 1, 1999.

Steiner, Claude. *Emotional Literacy: Intelligence with a Heart.* Fawnskin, Calif.: Personhood Books, 2003.

Strum, P., ed. *Brandeis on Democracy.* Lawrence: Univ. Press of Kansas, 1995.

Tatum, Beverly Daniel. *Why Are All the Black Kids Sitting Together in the Cafeteria?* New York: Basic Books, 1999.

Taylor, Shelley. *The Tending Instinct: Women, Men, and the Biology of Relationships.* New York: Holt Paperbacks, 2003.

"Technology Transfer from Defense: Concealed Weapon Detection." *National Institute of Justice Journal* 229 (Aug. 1995). http://ncjrs.org/txtfiles/nijj_229.txt.

Transcript of Proceedings, *People of the State of New York against Kenneth Boss, Sean Carroll, Edward McMellon and Richard Murphy.* Feb. 23, 2000, morning session.

Tutu, Desmond. *No Future without Forgiveness.* New York: Doubleday, 1999.

U.S. Department of Justice, National Institute of Justice, "Guns in America: National Survey on Private Ownership and Use of Firearms," May 1997.

"U.S. Surpasses Russia as World Leader in Rate of Incarceration." Sentencing Project. http://www.sentencingproject.org/brief/usvsrus.pdf.

Vallone, Peter F. *The NYPD: Blueprint for Reform.* New York City Council, May 12, 1999. http://www.nyccouncil.info/html/pdf_files/reports/nypd blueprint.pdf.

Waldman, Amy. "The Diallo Verdict: The Deliberations; The Crucial Defense Element: The Judge's Instructions." *New York Times,* Feb. 26, 2000.

Walker, Samuel, and Betsy Wright Kreisel. "Varieties of Citizen Review: The Implications of Organizational Features of Complaint Review Procedures for Accountability of the Police." *American Journal of Police* 15, no. 3 (1996): 65–88.

*Whitney v. California.* No. 3, Supreme Court of the United States, 274 U.S. 357. Argued Oct. 6, 1925; decided May 16, 1927. http://www.bc.edu/bc_org/avp/cas/comm/free_speech/whitney.html.

Ziedenberg, Jason, and Vincent Schiraldi. "The Punishing Decade: Prison and Jail Estimates at the Millenium." *Justice Policy Institute.* Dec. 2000.

# Index